THE THEATRE IN ASIA

THE HISTORY OF THE THEATRE

General Editor: Martin Esslin

A. C. SCOTT

THE THEATRE
IN ASIA

WEIDENFELD AND NICOLSON
5 Winsley Street London W1

ISBN O 297 99474 3 cased

ISBN O 297 99586 3 paperback

Printed in Great Britain by
Willmer Brothers Limited, Birkenhead

TO
MY MANY FRIENDS OF
THE ASIAN THEATRE WORLD

CONTENTS

ILLUSTRATIONS

PREFACE

Asia does not lend itself readily to those orderly chronological classifications of period styles which aid the western student of the theatre. The time span involved is too gigantic, our knowledge of the way people lived in the past inadequate. There is an old Indonesian proverb which says that the search for truth is like looking for the footsteps of a flying bird. It is an apt saying to remember when unravelling the facts about Asian theatre history.

The history of the Asian theatre has been stamped by a complex blending of cultures due to the spread of the four major religious doctrines of Hinduism, Buddhism, Confucianism and Islam. Great movements of population arising from trade expansion and territorial aggression, as well as religious proselytization, the impermanent nature of theatrical art itself and the restless life of the stage performer, have all compounded the patterns of Asian cultural growth in labyrinthine ways.

On the basis of these factors alone any attempt to treat collectively the many lands and people involved must plainly be regarded with reserve. When it is considered, to take but a single example, that India recognizes fourteen major languages and scores of different regional forms of theatrical expression, the magnitude of the scope becomes apparent. The wealth of dramatic-sociological detail and its diversity adds a proportionate difficulty in reducing it to a reasonably ordered narrative which will not confuse the ordinary reader for whom this book is in the first place intended.

Western historians in general follow the plan of distinguishing three major spheres of cultural development in Asia, consisting of east Asia, south Asia and the middle east, dominated by the Chinese, Indian and Islamic civilizations respectively. In this book Japan has been treated as a fourth major area, not with any intention of isolating her culture as unique from the rest, but because the importance of her contribution to theatre demands it in a work of this kind.

It could be argued on these grounds that if Japan, having a cultural affinity with Chinese civilization, has been treated separately, then those countries having their roots in Indian civilization require equal emphasis. Unfortunately, in a book as condensed as this one has to be the question of what must be left out is no less pressing than what may be put in. The minimal reference to so many forms of Asian theatre and the total omission of others has been dictated by expediency and not from any wish to minimize their existence or importance.

This is a book about the social circumstances surrounding theatre as much as theatre itself, but the sociologist will discover no answer to his questions, for this survey does not ask them. The formulae and statistics which are the professional tools for assessing the realities of human behaviour belong to a different kind of study from mine. All the reader will find here is an unashamedly descriptive narrative having its justification in empirical knowledge. The account of theatre as a social activity has been treated in an unavoidably broad way, but with the hope that at least the main outline will not be lost.

I am grateful to Messrs John Constable and Co. Ltd for permission to use the quotation from Arthur Waley's poem on p. 11 and to the Sangeet Natak Akademi, New Delhi for allowing me to use the passage from Tagore on p. 45. I am also grateful to the American Society for Eastern Arts, San Francisco; Mr Torao Saito, Tokyo; and Mr Kwok On, Hong Kong for the use of the photographs credited under their names. My wife prepared the bibliography as well as patiently assisting with the checking of the manuscript.

The terms Asia and Asians have been used to denote the area and its people in a general sense, including those of the Islamic world, for the sake of consistency.

A.C.S.

I

THE FRAMEWORK
OF ASIAN THEATRE

Theatre is an elusive art, no more easily labelled in Asian society than it is in the west, so much depends on what is regarded as theatre. One could generalize by saying that in Asia the high purpose of theatre has been to induce a personal communication, an immediate experience, a mood raised through the combination of dance, music and poetry drawing a response beyond the limits of empirical time and place in the onlooker's mind. This amounts to a statement of ancient Hindu theory, and it will be seen that stage practice in Asia owes a great deal to India as an ancestral source. Indian influence on dance and theatre, which are one and the same thing in Asia, was like some great subterranean river following a spreading course and forming new streams on the way.

This definition of dramatic function represents the great tradition, the classical approach, stressing aesthetic beauty alone and appealing to audiences drawn from an initiated elite. Palaces, mansions and temples were the settings for its display, conservatism the source of its artistic strength. A lesser tradition was given expression through the folk theatre satisfying the tastes of the crowd. Simple rhythmic patterns, repetitive musical forms and dialect were in this case the basic elements of communication, and mockery of intellectual values an unwritten rule. The Asian clown has always obtained some of his biggest laughs by his parodies of classical stage form.[1] Nothing is sacrosanct for the crowd even though in the end they are the staunchest upholders of custom and the most conservative element of all.

Most of the great Asian theatre styles came into existence

over long periods of mutual exchange between the classical and folk traditions. Actors were wanderers and had to justify their existence; appropriations from either side of the fence were justified if they gave them more scope with their audiences.

The structure of Asian theatrical forms became highly systematized over the centuries. The actor, the musician, the stage hand – in fact everyone involved – was trained in a tradition and shared community beliefs. There were no problems of integration. The great strength of performance lay in the fact that the essential knowledge to make things work on the stage, at whatever level, had been handed down from generation to generation. Asian theatrical art sought its ultimate ideal through a personal transmission. The story has been told of the Japanese actor[2] who concluded instruction to his son about to carry on the family profession, with the admonition, 'and above all no originality'. The high standards of discipline imposed through these principles of continuity led to a remarkably intense communication between audience and stage. Theatre was an affirmation of solidarity, a recognized need in the life of the community and a break in the arduous work pattern of the people in feudal society. It was a festival whose ceremonial was helped by the deep sense of ritual that was always present in Asian everyday life and given expression in theatrical style.

Style is a word of many implications. Theatre is an art sprung from sound, rhythm and gesture arising from dozens of different indigenous sources and given unity of expression through the actor. His talent in the end results from a country's particular social attitudes and the way its people live and behave. Every country's theatrical style is the product of these factors.

Town life and manners have greatly influenced theatre development in Asia as they have in the west. A difference has been that until the nineteenth century Asian urban society was largely the product of autocratic government and agrarian economy. Peasants who formed the bulk of every population supplied most of the labour. They were at the base of a community stringently controlled through clearly specified class distinctions and dominated by relatively small but privileged groups of people for whom the city was the administrative apex. Theatre as a social art was inevitably an expression of the ideals of such a system as well as being particularly subject to its discriminatory code.

Literacy was the great indicator of rank and status in Asian societies, consolidating the power of the governing class. Their family origins entitled them to the benefits of learning. Even in China, whose ancient civil service opened its ranks to the commoner who studied hard enough, literacy became a supreme form of class distinction. The successful scholar was immediately set apart from the rest. Religion and education were in the hands of the literary elite, who formulated ethical codes, set standards, and preached conformity to the rest. Personal patronage and nepotism were normal methods for protecting their political interests and status. Polygamy, concubinage and the extended family were the favoured means of extending their kinship system and therefore the status quo.

In Asia the upper classes supported a wide range of non-productive workers, including an intricate administrative bureaucracy at their own level and a host of servants of every kind. It was a tried principle of Asian employment that a task was never assigned to one man where it could be shared by two, so that personal service was plentiful and expected and bestowed in every possible area of activity. This attitude existed all the way down the ladder and the first obligation of any pupil was to perform menial tasks for his teacher.

Craftsmen, artists and entertainers of every description congregated in the town areas for the good reason that this was where the leisured class, upon whom they depended for patronage, were concentrated. Kings, courtiers and princes were the protectors of the traditional arts in Asia. They maintained standards for the educated classes of society and by their own participation and direction often became known as artistic innovators. Most artists of calibre in India, China, Japan and south-east Asia were at some point dependent on the highborn to such an extent that they themselves were frequently given the status of palace retainers.

Dance and theatre were especially favoured in this way. Imperial courts and princely mansions maintained their own groups of performers as well as the musicians and teachers required for their training and activities. Courts also exercised their prerogative by combining artistic patronage with recruitment for the women's quarters. As supreme authorities and divine functionaries, most Asian rulers were constantly surrounded by women who carried out a bewildering array of duties, prominent among these being entertainment with song, dance and music.

An Indian scholar has suggested that women were so widely used in the ancient courts because their inferior status made them the more dutiful towards the throne, whereas men, being less subservient, presented a greater hazard.[3] An actress as a member of the royal harem was a safeguard, whereas actors could become a threat to the ruler's safety. The court entertainments of Thailand and Java, where women predominated, support such a theory. On the other hand, the use of courtesans as government spies in ancient India suggests a respect for feminine talents of a kind which have never been lacking in the history of palace revolts. The Chinese were in no two minds concerning the destructive potential of women at court, and voiced their feelings in the belief that a woman in power preceded the fall of a dynasty.

Whatever ambiguities surrounded the actress in her double function of artist and concubine, there was nothing imprecise in her subjection to the elaborate codes of ritual, etiquette and personal deportment which in Asia defined the life of the courtier as they did the commoner. Social stability was maintained by people obeying the rules and formalities which were laid down to meet every occasion in every walk of life. By honouring these, the paramount necessity of assigning everyone their proper place and obligations was served. The deeply ritualistic quality of ordinary behaviour resulting from this system was reflected in stage styles, where movement, gesture and manner of speaking were greatly affected by it.

Ways of speaking produced an uncompromising dividing line in Asian society. Honorific constructions and poetic metaphor derived from written forms were characteristic of the language of the ruling classes. Chinese and Arabic, for example, both had written scripts which were entirely independent of the spoken language of the commoner. Both languages represented supreme examples of communication for the minority in their emphasis on the beauty of the written form for itself. In most Asian countries the traditional ways of speaking depended on intricate forms of personal address. Superiors spoke to inferiors in special terms, and inferiors used suitably deferential equivalents in reply; women were described in derogatory terms to strangers outside their family; poetic allusions defined their physical charms; euphemistic terms were mandatory when naming forbidden pleasures; and so on. The permutations and combinations were endless, making language a protective barrier for conformity.

Theatrical speech and song were the children of this linguistic conservatism and its symbolic imagery. Some of the most revolutionary changes which occurred in Asian dramatic usage came about when more currently colloquial speech styles were used to counter stagnating literary conventions. Change in form rather than content marked progression in the Asian theatre; curiosity about the human condition, which became a motive for innovation on the western stage, affected it very little.

Just as the habits of citizens were the symbol of autocratic rule so was the architectural design of the city a result of its consequences. The traditional Asian town most commonly began as a walled or fortified enclosure built in the wake of territorial expansion to ensure protection of trade routes or religious faiths. Once established, these towns became centres whose kingly lawmakers, priests and scholars set the criteria for cultural patterns. Through the centuries each Asian city acquired its own aura and this was reflected in the behaviour, clothes and speech of its people. A man's origins became stamped upon him through an elusive amalgam of circumstances which immediately identified him as a native of a specific town and province. The mere mention of some city's name could conjure up an image in the public mind. Soochow, a centre of the silk and rice trade in eighteenth-century China, was a name on everyone's lips as providing the last word in taste and fashion. The city's wealthy merchants vied with each other as patrons of the actors and singing girls, who were sought everywhere on account of their origins. 'Heaven above and Hang and Soo below', ran the proverb, a lyrical reference to the town and the adjoining lake resort of Hangchow. The townspeople of eighteenth-century Edo, later Tokyo, reflected something of the swashbuckling warriors who governed their city. To be a 'man of Edo' was the proud boast of citizens who were impulsive by nature, prodigal in spending, and knowledgeable *habitués* of the 'floating world' of pleasure, presided over by the actor and the courtesan. Lucknow in India, noted for its architectural grace, was a centre of music and dance, renowned for the talents of its courtesans and the linguistic elegance of its literary men. The city's stylish mode of life at one time represented the quintessence of later Indian culture. As the man about town in Soochow, Edo or Lucknow differed in dress and manners but lived according to a common hedonistic philosophy, so too the city in which he pursued his pleasures functioned with a common social and economic system, whatever the outer differences due to national style.

Among the black and white of social distinctions there were many shades of grey. Human activity and status were compartmented by such concepts as the Four Castes in India or the Four Classes of Society in China.[4] It should not be overlooked that wealth eventually brought power to the merchant classes enabling them to overcome social distinctions to the extent of becoming patrons of the arts, a 'third force' as it were. The cities of Soochow and Edo just mentioned were notable examples of this phenomenon.

In a typical Asian city the less privileged, the poor and the socially ostracized were the furthest removed from the heart of the areas housing the palaces, temples and great houses of those in power and authority. The city itself was usually a congested area in which as much buying and selling was conducted on the streets as indoors. Trades and occupations were concentrated so that one street or group of streets housed the members of a particular craft or trade. In the ultra-modern city of Hongkong it is still possible to walk along a street occupied exclusively by Cantonese goldsmiths, a lingering reminder of a mercantile past.

Segregation in this way had its practical purposes for it simplified trading where transportation was slow and primitive. Moreover the guilds who were at the heart of the commercial system encouraged this open demonstration of solidarity. The guilds controlled competition, maintained standards, and protected their members rights. They also acted as entrepreneurs and sponsored a great deal of pageantry and theatrical entertainment, especially during religious festivals and for community celebrations. The localizing of urban districts also enabled the authorities to keep an eye on the stranger within the gates, as well as control subversive elements among which the theatrical profession usually ranked high. The theatres and the licenced quarters were invariably confined to special neighbourhoods and were usually contiguous. Actors and prostitutes were people of whom the ordinary public spoke in the same breath.

It is difficult to define this situation by other standards for the close connection of prostitutes and catamites with the theatre was the result of a social situation different from the run of western communities. The segregation of women in the interests of domestic propriety, whether it was in Hindu, Confucian or Islamic society, led to the acceptance of a class of women who were trained in the arts and social graces and taught to associate with men. Home life was kept strictly hidden from the outside world. A wife was accorded authority in her designated environment but she was not expected to be literate or indeed to be concerned with anything except raising children and domestic occupations for which she had been trained and prepared from adolescence. The emphasis in her case was on decorum, chastity and duty to her husband. Elaborate codes of conduct laid down for her guidance prevented her straying from the path of orthodoxy.

Because of this unyielding surveillance of women there were no opportunities for young people of opposite sexes to meet or have any kind of social contact at all except in their own families; and even there a certain distance was preserved. It was not unusual therefore for men to seek their leisure in the licenced pleasure quarters which were found in every Asian town. The professional women entertainers of these areas were regarded as fulfilling functions for which there is no exact equivalent in western terms. The courtesan was not regarded as a woman who had evaded the law or transgressed virtue. She was simply someone who both by personality and outlook had been trained to take her place in an environment to which other women did not have an entry. She was treated as a necessary element of the social system. Being educated, artistically talented, and amusing, she had immense advantages over the ordinary married or unmarried women who were carefully guarded from all male company. At the highest level the courtesan was the associate of scholars and statesmen and served as a model of deportment and courtly behaviour.

That is not to say that the pleasure quarters were populated solely by these paragons of charm, for the women found there

could be classified all the way from the highest class of entertainer down to the lowest common prostitute, but these areas
were always under control and run with circumspection. The
social segregation of ordinary women and the professional
training of the courtesan as an entertainer made the theatre a
forbidden area for the first and a natural habitat of the second.
It was not altogether surprising that the actress and the
courtesan were synonymous in the public's mind although the
really talented courtesans were in the minority and not every
one was necessarily connected with the stage. Moreover, the public
appearances of the actress-courtesan frequently resulted in repres-
sive measures by the governing authorities concerned about public
order.

As a result of these circumstances the theatre was constantly
starved of actresses, a situation that affected the trend of
theatrical entertainments until very recent times. The catamite
served as a substitute and became increasingly important to the
development of stage technique. The acting of women's roles
by men was in many ways a gesture of self defence on the part
of the theatrical profession. Dramatic art by its very function
has tended to condone the presence of the transvestite so that
his indispensable services to the stage and the lack of actresses
can be seen as interlocking factors in encouraging homosexuality
in the Asian theatre world in the past.

The growth of theatre as a social art brought a corresponding demand for improved stage techniques. From being sanctioned
eroticism in its early stages, female impersonation became a
polished and highly formalized art whose practitioners have included some of the greatest actors on the Asian stage. The artifice
of men playing women's roles has repulsed many visitors to Asia
because for them credibility on the stage is entirely a matter of
literary and visual logic, but Asian theatrical communication has
never depended on realism of this kind.

A majority of ordinary people in Asian countries were illiterate. Farmers, peasants, workmen, tradesmen and a great part
of the female population relied on memory as an effective aid to
dramatic receptivity. They were accustomed to sensory communication as a method of stirring their deepest emotions and such
factors had a definitive effect on theatrical styles. The development of these in any Asian society would have to be sought through

an intermingling of religious rites, court ceremonials and the seasonal festivities of country people. Within the framework of these activities song, dance, recitative and puppetry were first used as the accessories to sacred ritual and religious instruction. As they were gradually diverted to secular purposes they provided a structural basis for theatrical expression.

Two seminal influences in Asian theatre growth have been the storyteller and the puppet show. The combination of their methods has provided invention for acting methods. The storyteller was one of the first professional entertainers and he has carried on his calling with constantly renewed vigour throughout all Asia. He is still a familiar figure who can be seen entertaining the crowd in public halls, temple courtyards and village market places. Appearance on television seems as though it may give him a new lease of life as the public institution he has been.

Formerly storytellers were one means of diffusing information to the ordinary people as well as entertaining them. Communication by word of mouth was often the only way of transmitting information in feudal society and the storyteller became a kind of living newspaper. He was also responsible for passing on the words of the sacred texts and great epics and so ensured continuity of the beliefs and practices which bound a society together. Although exaggeration and embellishment were also the tools of his trade he was an indispensable source and one who provided the link between the nonliterate commoners and their literate superiors.

The storyteller, through long practice, learned the value of experimenting with new ways of gripping his audiences' attention. From being simply a man of words he took on some of the functions of the actor, the musician, and the puppeteer, and these people in their turn were sometimes given new insights through the storyteller. His use of mimetic gesture is often seen repeated in the actor's performance. Naturally this kind of exchange has been reciprocal but it is only necessary to watch the Chinese clown wagging an admonishing finger to a rhymed patter directed at the audience to understand how deep the storyteller's influence goes.

The old-time storyteller who is still at work in a few of the traditional variety halls in Japan embodies the skill of them all. The typical performer makes his entry on a low stage before which his audience sits on a rush matted floor, although this is now often superseded by modern theatre seating. Kneeling on a cushion placed centre stage he puts his fan carefully on the ground before him and prostrates himself in a deep bow to the expectant crowd. There is almost a nonchalant air about his opening gambit but it is deceptive and soon he is in full swing. His face becomes extraordinary mobile; he cocks an expressive eyebrow, and like the famous old English music hall star George Robey, he 'stops and he looks and he listens'. He is incredulous, shocked and angered in turn, he grows agitated and carries on a heated conversation with an unseen partner. The company on the stage grows, conjured into being simply by his changes of expression; they agree only to disagree, but he cows them all with a final sally. He gives a wink and a nod, he makes a sly point to the audience who are now convulsed with laughter as they follow his gaze towards an imaginary interlocutor. He mutters an aside to his invisible accomplice again and the audience are in stitches a second time. The electric atmosphere is a testimony to people's whole-hearted participation in the imaginary events on the stage called out of space for their entertainment alone. This is the true art of the Asian storyteller, a master of total communication with nothing more than his voice and a compelling gesture. Commentary on the current scene has not surprisingly been his great strength, although his witty barbs have not always endeared him to the high and mighty by whom he has often been belaboured. Mimicry of his countrymen's foibles has been in the best tradition of the Asian stage.

Both as an entertainer and a propagandist of the social code the storyteller was a unique artist who replaced the obscure speech of the scholar with colloquial expression for the market place where he forever polished his wit.

The puppet show in Asia represents a strong link between theatrical magic and religious rite. It is almost impossible to attribute the puppet's origins to a specific geographical area although contesting claims have been made. Puppetry has been a peripatetic affair, covering up its own tracks along the tortuous paths of Asian history. It seems clear that the puppet has very ancient origins in Asia, where it developed as a relic of tribal ritual in a distant age and from primitive attempts by man to reconcile his existence with a spirit world.

The shadow puppet[5] which many people think may be the oldest kind of all, was given a legendary origin by the Chinese. According to them, an emperor who reigned some one hundred and fifty years before the Christian era became heartbroken at the death of a favourite concubine. The necromancers were commanded to recall her spirit from the other world. One of them acceded to this request by projecting the shadow of the dead favourite on a curtain and the incident has been immortalized in Waley's classic translation

> Is it or isn't it
> I stand and look
> The swish, swish of a silk skirt
> How slow she comes!

Whatever the basis of fact for such legends it is feasible to think they were the result of early attempts to reach beyond the conscious world. Men everywhere have been hypnotized by the shadow and its mysterious effects of autonomous movement revealing a dream world of shifting nuances. 'An attic window on the supernatural world' was how the nineteenth-century French writer Lemaître described the shadow show.[6] In its fashion the shadow play forecast the art of the film. It was an early form of manipulating space-time where events could occur simultaneously without regard for logic and overflow into fantasy at will. Its cinematic action conjured up regions where human beings were a species rather than individuals, manifestations whose forms fused with the environment and whose continuity of motion implied space far beyond the limits of the screen. The shadow theatre captured the limitless flow of the visible world.

The Asian puppet in all its variety has also been the true guardian of acting form. Gordon Craig had this in mind when he once mischievously called for a theatre whose actors would be replaced by puppets, thereby freeing the stage of what he called 'the triumph of riotous personality'.[7] The actor and the puppet must have been old partners in the Asian theatre, with each learning from the other. Obviously the actor came before the puppet who took life from his creator but the Asian actor has consistently recognized the puppet as 'the symbol of man in the great ceremony' and measured his acting criteria accordingly. The puppet is precise, incapable of false statement, and cannot relapse into affectation. Its functional command of space and characterization drawn from the imagery of the collective consciousness is capable of instantaneous communication. To watch an Asian actor whose every gesture is composed, with each facial expression an extension of his physical being, as he transfers the onlooker's concentration from one part of his body to the next, is in effect to watch the puppet whose influence on formal acting styles has been incalculable.

Western classical theatre in its use of language has sought a balance between the fusion of verbal music, intellectual communication and suggestive power. It is possible to read a majority of western plays with satisfaction and never see them performed. They are effective as literature in their own right. The emphasis on language has been different in Asia, where few plays in their original language are satisfying to read when divorced from performance. The power of language to suggest imagery, its quality as pure sound together with the many possibilities in rhyme, juxtaposition, alliteration and the use of devices like puns, have been the ingredients for the Asian playwright. He has used these elements as complementary to the mime, dance and formalized gesture which make Asian performance a total sensory and emotional experience.

The particular characteristics of Asian languages have made them very adaptable to such theatrical purposes. Sanskrit, the medium of the classical Hindu theatre, contains numerous word endings which can be changed for grammatical purposes and offer the poet or playwright a choice of infinite variations in the word order. It also boasts an immense vocabulary with hundreds of synonyms and the most complex rules pertaining to choice of metrical patterns and fixing the length of stanzas. As harmony of metrical form depended on harmony of word imagery, the Sanskrit playwright was greatly concerned with mood, induced through an impeccable command of the rules of style. The power of dramatic suggestion was dependent on this knowledge and on a minute regard for the nuances in the transmission between stage and audience.

A different illustration of the same theme is offered by the

Turkish language. This has a distinctive vowel euphony and a devastatingly subtle but expressive system of prefixes and suffixes which leave a wide margin for interpretation. Turkish has in consequence abounded with puns, conundrums, double meanings and flowery metaphor. Like the Arab from whose vocabulary he freely borrowed, the Turk has never been sparing with superlatives. It was not for nothing that the Turkish name for a storyteller was derived from an Arabic prototype meaning eulogist. The Turkish language was God's gift to the storyteller. As soon as he opened the proceedings with some remark like 'In the olden days when the camel was town crier. . . .'[8] his audience settled back contentedly, anticipating the wit and innuendo which only a master could provide for listeners sensitive to cunning word play.

Chinese is yet one more case of how linguistic form dictates dramatic content. It is a language containing an abundance of syllables which are pronounced identically but have different meanings. In addition each syllable is pronounced in one of four fixed pitches differing in length and movement so that one could say that Chinese has a built-in musical foundation. Sound pattern has thus been given tremendous emphasis in poetry and song; in many forms of Chinese verse, rhyming is an essential preliminary and alliteration and onomatopoeia are skilfully stressed.

In the traditional Chinese theatre, song is used all the time to convey mood and emotion. The exposition of events is simplified by this method though it also results in a redundancy of sentiments and the rhyming patterns underscore these with their cadences. The dramatist had to be thoroughly familiar with the technical conventions in composing his pieces and worked with a prescribed system of rhyming keys which had fixed rules for their application. Through the use of devices like these the dialogue and music of the Peking stage were easily memorized by people for whom learning by heart was the natural way of mastering their very complicated language in the first place.

Pantomine and gesture have been exceedingly important accessories of language in Asian theatre styles. From the earliest times gesture has been a way of transmitting human thought and emotions. The question as to which came first, sign language or speech, has been as controversial a topic as the chicken and the egg. With gesture there is no ambiguity because the relationship between the idea expressed and its sign is plainly visible. It is for the most part impossible to say why a word we use means exactly what it does.

In the west, thought and feeling are expressed outwardly through facial expression largely; in Asia the hand has been trained equally to respond to mental states and reveal what the face would conceal. Gesture in the Asian theatre does not supersede language but it often carries on where language leaves off. Action on the stage and the reaction of the spectator are not intellectually separated; there is an immediate and total sensory impact.

Gestural techniques have a long history in Asia and enquiry inevitably leads back to India as a primary source. In her own dance drama styles the technique of gestural language has been developed to a point of ultra-refinement. Performers use their hands singly or in combination and at different spatial levels, but naturally these hand movements have to be coordinated with other bodily action even though they are often the climactic point of visual involvement for the spectator.

Gestures can be representational, that is to say pantomimic versions of everyday actions, or interpretative in suggesting qualities or feelings, or else simply decorative by embellishing choreographic patterns. All three functions are served in performance. There are single and combined movements of the hands to be learned by the dancer and these in effect represent a vocabulary of emotive expression. Correct positioning of hands and fingers are not the only requirement. An identical gesture used in a different way could mean both nectar and poison, for example, while the mood portrayed can again result in different interpretations of the same gesture. As this no doubt makes clear, gesture in its most developed form is an art of the initiated, but in spite of this the ordinary Asian theatregoer has always accepted the basic principles as a normal method of expression.

The fleeting quality of gesture aptly symbolizes the transitory nature of its history for which there are no consistent records. Religious ritual and everyday activities have both contributed to its composite qualities. The natural gestures peculiar to the people of different areas have been important influences. A Japanese mother beckoning her child, for example, gently waves one hand with down-turned palm in a vertical motion at shoulder height, a gesture which can be seen over and over again translated as dance gesture on the stage. Similar instances could be found in every Asian country, indicating how people's ordinary actions have contributed to theatrical style.

Gesture is inseparable from dance which in Asia has been the medium for celebration and commemoration. At the highest level dance has been both a divine art and a sacred ritual and at its most sensual the accomplishment of the courtesan. In palaces and mansions dance has been the recreation of nobility and in the field or along the seashore it has relieved the labours of the fisherman and peasant. Dance was a way of reconciling man's spiritual being with the Eternal as well as a physical display of the sheer joy of living. Court and temple dances were the creation of centuries of sophisticated application, the work of connoisseurs and specialists. In contrast to this the ordinary people everywhere in Asia have danced without benefit of patronage or scholarly favour, simply because occasion demanded an outlet for their emotions. In the words of an old Japanese folk dance: 'Those who join the dancers are supposed to be fools, and so are those who look on; if I am bound to be called a fool, better be one who dances.'[9]

There has always been a close relationship between manual labour and dance as a way of promoting energy and alleviating fatigue. Through the accompaniment of song, music and chanted choruses, the natural work movements of men and women planting, hauling or rowing were transformed into dances. Their spontaneous rhythms often became a fertile source of invention for stage choreography.

The Balinese say that 'dancing is not there to be looked at nor music listened to; both are only to be seen and heard like trees in a wood'.[10]

Like western classical ballet Asian dancing is deeply concerned with correctness of form. Fluidity is achieved through a more calculated restraint and what can sometimes be an unbelievable economy of energy. Harmony of sequence and gracefulness of line are realized through a meticulous concern for detail including mime. This is never separated like cream from milk as it often is in the west. The Asian dancer tends to treat ground space less prodigally and be less concerned with aerial effect. More important than any of these technical differences is the fact that dance and drama have never been considered as separate in Asia: the one begets the other. The changing rhythms of movement and gesture have been used to convey dramatic content in preference to any other way. The dance is theatre.

Feats of sheer technical bravado have always fascinated the Asian audience, and the juggler and the acrobat have been no less important as dancers. Chinese theatregoers delighted in that moment when the stage suddenly became transformed into a quivering pattern of somersaulting, high-diving figures whose breath-taking antics recalled a troupe of gibbons. The Asian performer indeed learned a great deal from the movements of animals. The Monkey God[11] has been equally recognized on the stages of India, China, and south-east Asia as a theatrical character who has fascinated generation after generation with his agile trickery and mischievous acrobatics which have seemed to mock the earth-bound human.

Combat forms are found in most Asian dance repertoires. The sword dance and sword play are characteristic of many theatrical styles. On the Asian stage it is often hard to draw the line where duel becomes pure dance and performance in duet becomes combat. In a great many Asian stage techniques physical training and dance training are one and the same thing. Dance is the essence and physical training the incident. The arts of performance and methods of combat are reconciled.

Representation of animal form has been an obvious function of the mask which in Asia has retained its hypnotic power, turned to good account in many theatrical ways. As both a sacred object and a means for making the wearer sacred the mask has a long history. During its transition from religious to secular usage the mask has been developed in an infinite variety of ways although the dividing line between the two functions has always remained shadowy. In the actor's case the mask has provided an effective way of emphasizing mood and archetypal characterization while maintaining a complete detachment from naturalistic behaviour. The actor wearing a mask is no longer the prisoner of his own ego or inhibited by the conventions of everyday speech and movement. Energy has to be directed in such a way that every gesture must tell and every movement be realized with a bold economy of effect. In the mask's most ancient function, the symbol became transmuted in the imaginations of those participating in the rite, the wearer becoming the other being, an impersonal force whose compulsive attraction induced awe of the supernatural. The actor in the mask becomes larger than life, imposing his theatrical will on the imaginations of his audience. Wherever one turns in Asia the mask has inspired some of the most powerful and telling dramatic devices of their kind.

Music, it need hardly be said, has with dance been indispensable to every kind of theatrical performance in Asia. Whether as song, percussive and instrumental accompaniment, chanted narrative, or a combination of all these, music has been completely integrated with the acting on the Asian stage, not simply incidental to it. There is a passage in the ancient Sanskrit *Doctrine of Dramatic Art* which says: 'One should first of all bestow care on songs. For songs have been called the resting place of the drama. The song and the playing of musical instruments being well executed, the performance of the drama does not encounter any risk.' It is a precept that has been implicitly honoured throughout Asia, where song has been used on the stage in every possible way, whether it was to continue the movement of speech and gesture, convey the unspoken thoughts of a character, suggest atmosphere and mood, or merely provide a cue.

In the Chinese theatre the actor sang his way through a greater part of the action, stressing climax and emotional tension by this means as well as explaining his actions to the audience. In the *kathakali* dance drama of south India, a singer provides the themes for the bizarre figures of the actors. Portraying the gods returned to earth they dance out the sung story without uttering a word, conversing only with their hand gestures, which become a fluttering extension of the dance in the light of the oil flare which illuminates the open-air stage. On the Japanese *noh* stage a chorus chants commentaries upon the scene of action or interpolates reminders of events long past. The sung narrative here links up the introduction, exposition and denouement which characterize the play structure, and leads the audience on.

Most dramatic techniques in Asia rely heavily for effects on the literary bias of music. The importance of elements like rhyme and metrical construction in stage speech was stressed earlier, and these are no less significant in the case of music. The poet has always been master of the composer in Asia. Literary emphasis in musical composition was such that the dance often became primarily the means of telling a story. Even in the Indian temple dance, so much concerned with rhythm and timing as the purest form, the dancer from time to time relapses into brilliant mimetic passages as she interprets the sung narration of the musicians.

The idea of mood conveyed through modal systems is characteristic of a great deal of Asian music. It is fundamental to Indian, Chinese and Japanese musical composition, as it is to that of Islam. The Arabs use four primary melodic modes in their music which they say influence the human spirit. One pacifies the soul, a second fills it with grief, a third induces courage, and the fourth simplicity. In Indian music certain arrangements are associated with hours of the day or a particular season. There is a story quoted in the Indian musical histories of the musician whose royal patron commanded a song with a modal pattern suggestive of fire. The protesting musician had no option but to begin and as his song proceeded he burst into flames which were not extinguished even when he leapt into the river! In the popular Peking theatre limited musical patterns are used to induce peaceful sentiments, noble or inspiring moods, alluring and captivating qualities, despair and sadness. These are the broad lines from which the dramatist works and from which he is able to suggest familiar sentiments in accepted situations.

In the Sanskrit *Doctrine of Dramatic Art* it was also laid down that 'a player of drums who does not understand the correct functions of rhythms and the treatise on the subject is merely a striker of hides'.[12] Of all instruments used on the Asian stage the drum is one of the most compelling, not only for the vitality and intensity of its expression but also for the manner in which it is used to control the flow of movement, create tension, and force emotional climax. In India drumming reaches its most developed expression through the complexities of a time-rhythm system unsurpassed for its brilliance in any area of music.

The intricacies of rhythmic pattern developed between a dancer and drummer working in perfect unison provide a dazzling display of form. The dancer's feet move with more and more speed and precision and the small bells attached to her ankles jingle in coordination as the drummer anticipates every step taken. Drummers use a system of onomatopoeic syllables representing the subtle variation in sound made by fingers and palms on the drumhead and these are chanted aloud during performance. This fusion of syncopated drum sounds, vocalization of the syllables, and the beat of the dancer's feet attains a climax that envelops the audience.

On the Japanese noh stage the slow metallic beat of the shoulder drum played before an actor makes his entry develops a mounting intensity of sound which is all the more penetrating because of the utter silence and emptiness of the stage. Anticipation is brought to a tense pitch by this restrained percussion and the throaty cry of the drummer. This has none of the quality of the Indian drummer's chant but is harsher, almost hoarse in its effect. The cries usually occur in measured progression at regular beat intervals. They pinpoint attention on the rhythmic variations, control timing, and sometimes intensify mood, especially in the spirited working up to the dance climax which usually ends with a noh play.

Noise as a musical dimension of sound is no new discovery in Asia and has been treated in many effective ways on the stage. The noh actor when dancing often brings his raised foot down with a stamping movement that has a feline grace in its suggestion of controlled force. The powerful reverberation on the polished stage has an isolated quality which asserts strength and arrests the mind for a fleeting instant, an instant which is immediately overwhelmed by the dream-like flow of continuing action. In the kabuki theatre there is always the point in a play where the actor moves from the stage out on to the runway which passes right through the auditorium. Posing at the head he draws himself up into a rigid stance and the tension of the audience is now high. There is a sudden beating of a drum and the actor moves off down the runway, his acceleration of speed matched by a rapidly rising tattoo of sound beaten out with a wooden clapper off-stage.

In Asia the aural and the visual have always been treated as

complementary in dramatic techniques. In visual space the eye
must focus and distinguish, but sound has no boundaries and
comes at the spectator from every direction. Its emotive impact
is unavoidable. Similarly the quality of silence has been
exploited to the utmost on the Asian stage. It is recognized that
silence is not negative but always there, existing without sound,
although sound does not exist without silence from which it
emerges and to which it returns. In some Indian musical
compositions there occur moments of silence which can be even
more evocative than sound to the receptive mind. One Indian
music critic[13] described this silence as portentous: 'it hovers
over the composition threateningly. It prowls about the turns
and cornices, the dead ends, the attics and the basement of the
mode, always imminent ...'. Silence on the Asian stage is
approached in much the same way and it is often taken to such
a pitch that it seems to pass the boundaries of logical
communication to many western people, for whom the difficulty
lies in their being unable to abandon themselves to situations
which are not verbally rationalized but dependent on a total
provocation of the senses.

Description so far has been concentrated on a traditional
Asia whose lands and people for centuries remained relatively
secluded from major disruption of their ways of living and the
economic systems which reinforced them. During the last hundred
years all Asian countries have undergone massive and sometimes
violent changes due to their confrontation with western industrial
civilization. From the end of the eighteenth century Asia became
the focus of a commercial power struggle culminating in the high
noon of nineteenth-century colonial expansion by the western
powers. Whether the contact with the new ideas was enforced,
expediently sought out, or resulted from a gradual process of
infiltration, the effects were continuous and cumulative. They
affected the structure of the old societies to such an extent that the
hierarchy of class relationships became fragmented. The balance
of life as it had always been lived was irrevocably upset. New
classes of society arose who were no longer inhibited by the past
and sought to use western-derived methods to bring about change
in their own countries. This is of course a simplification; metamorphosis has been an intricate process that is anything but complete today. Nor have Asian societies entirely abandoned their own

ways, the old and the new continuing to exist side by side. This duality is found in even the most advanced areas of westernization, and it is indeed inevitable in any attempts to create a new identity that is neither a downright imitation of the west nor incompatible with Asian resources.

The clash resulting from the confrontation with western culture has been especially reflected through the theatre. Western stage techniques with their realistic portrayal of contemporary events and society made a quick impression on the younger Asian intellectuals and reformers. They soon began to experiment with the new-found methods for there was a growing impatience with the old-style theatres and their conservative adherence to the old ethics. These had begun to seem too remote from the pressing realities faced by an awakening generation. A new spirit of enquiry was abroad, nurtured from the social and political systems of the west and echoed in the ideas and attitudes of educated young men throughout Asia. During the late nineteenth and early twentieth centuries the first active signs of a modern theatre movement imitating western methods could be found in cities as far apart as Cairo, Beirut, Bombay, Calcutta, Shanghai and Tokyo. The human basis of western drama with its positive emphasis on real-life problems seemed to offer to many young Asians the hope of a revitalized theatre dedicated to the issues of the day in their own countries. Moreover it was seen that drama could be a double-edged weapon, effective not only for attacking the old ways which were a bar to social progress but also the colonial masters, then at the crest of their power.

Women's position in society, the power of the extended family, and the tyranny of arranged marriages were especially burning issues, hotly contested and discussed by the young who were so immediately concerned. The new-style theatre offered a ready way of protest against these issues and the question of the emancipation of women particularly provided themes for scores of new plays. India very early became a lively centre for some of these theatrical experiments, especially the cities of Calcutta and Bombay. The extent of colonial domination there and the presence of groups of wealthy and interested patrons were tremendous factors in providing impetus.

Wherever it took root in Asia the new westernized style of

B

theatre became a medium for protest of one kind or another and to a large extent it has continued to serve that purpose in many areas until present times. Calcutta, consolidating an earlier reputation, boasts one of the most acutely political theatres in India, although it is only mildly so compared with China where the nation's theatre has been totally transformed and now serves the political state to the exclusion of any other purpose. But protest and revolt have not been the sole motives behind the growth of western-style theatrical methods among the Asians. Their passion for dance, music and spectacle has been indulged with the lighter side of entertainment. The showy but highly disciplined girls' revues of Japan[14] are a case in point and the stage thriller, the domestic farce and the musical all have their adherents and imitators.

The meeting with western civilization has been an uneasy and often incongruous business. Western customs and fashions, social behaviour between the sexes, kissing, drinking, and so on, though acceptable in the west were often bitterly resented among orthodox Asian communities, and in some cases still are, as being offensive to their own particular codes of public behaviour. On the other hand many Asians have not scrupled to exploit the new attitudes in the interests of sensationalism and profit. By and large, Asia has become more tolerant today, most noticeably in attitudes towards the sexes, although many areas of deep prejudice still exist. Objections to women going on the stage continue to be encountered, if on a diminishing scale.

One major stumbling block to the rise of a new theatre in Asia was the desperate lack of trained actresses, indeed of any kind of actress at all, both on account of the social segregation of women and the consequence that theatre was considered solely as the vocation of the courtesan. Even those hardy spirits who eventually rebelled against this state of affairs were faced with a lack of training facilities of the kind to induce confidence in would-be aspirants. There were no acting schools or conservatories in the western manner; theatre was a closed shop whose trade secrets were handed on within the confines of isolated groups. Directors who could coordinate production in the western way were simply nonexistent, and knowledge of lighting, stage machinery and all the technical paraphernalia

needed for western theatre and opera was virtually nil. In the
early nineteenth century, when a wealthy Calcutta dilettante
staged a play in his own residence, he went to great expense
importing equipment from England to simulate thunder and
lightning. In an unkind way this could serve as a comment on so
much early involvement with the western theatre; it was the
thunder and lightning which captured the imagination rather
than anything more significant.

In fairness it must be said that the late nineteenth century
was not the golden age of western theatre. The heavily declamatory styles, the lurid melodrama, and the preoccupation with
ornate display characteristic of the Victorian era did not offer the
most desirable models for theatrical styles which were often over-
endowed with such tendencies in the first place. Few Asian
people ever had the chance to see anything more than the
utterly second rate in western dramatic accomplishments. Such
performances as came their way were largely at the level of the
foreign communities' amateur dramatic clubs or school
performances. While there was nothing to sneer at in that –
interest was often stimulated by such productions – it meant
that in the long run a new Asian theatre started out lacking
high criteria by which to measure its own groping search for
standards. Colonial societies in general were not unduly sensitive
towards the arts and there were no national sponsors to send
the best of European ballet, theatre or opera east of Suez in
the nineteenth century or even the first part of the present
century. Any troupe that went further than Suez in the
old days had little to offer a new Asian generation as a theatre
of social significance.

A greater problem than any of these for the innovators was
the fact that in the end western methods were ineffective
for communication with the non-western-educated members of
the community, who always far outnumbered the rest. Attempts
at literal translation and direct adaptation were only partially
successful even among an intellectual minority and only plays
fully sympathetic to the Asian ethos seemed the answer for a
new theatre. How best to provide these has continued to be a
highly controversial topic. The creation of a theatre in keeping
with a new age and yet preserving the integrity of its own
origins presents a problem that has so far remained unsolved.

The film-makers have perhaps been more successful than the dramatists here.

Reappraising tradition raises some many-sided problems in the theatre and they can be as self-defeating as they can be constructive. The cry is constantly heard for a new theatre of the people but the question there, as always, is who decides what is for the people? Their fondness for entertainment has never been in doubt at any time in Asia. The need was met, and how it was done depended on the particular society, but the conflict between good and evil was always involved. The crowd were not too concerned who was evil so long as it was not themselves and the entertainment was there. This principle has been reduced to startling elemental proportions in contemporary China.

There were always those who tried to outlaw theatre or confine it. Islam perhaps went furthest in this respect, while others worked to give it some kind of standards by which to measure it in its social function. What those standards should be today raises the most furious debates of all. Confusion is present because there is a reluctance to admit that theatre is neither a democratic art nor progressive in the scientific meaning. It is a phenomenon of recurrence which always reverts to the same starting point. The contents of plays are adapted to current social behaviour, and technical resources are improved with the growth of scientific facilities, but theatre is a movement up and down rather than one of continual horizontal progression and this is the greatest dilemma of all for Asians.

War, revolution, and emancipation from colonial rule have between them forced sweeping social changes upon Asia during the last thirty years. Deeply conscious of their need to catch up with western technology, and irrevocably committed to the course of industrial advancement, many Asian people today sense a loss of cultural identity. The western pragmatist argues that the only salvation for Asia lies in economic and political growth, the rest being irrelevant. Most Asians are fully agreed on the first two necessities but are less convinced that the benefits of western industrial civilization satisfy all the needs of a national consciousness.

Cultural identity can be a baffling phenomenon, sustained from many sources not necessarily compatible with one another.

Questions of language, race and class differences add to the difficulty of reconciling the old and the new. In every society there are the fundamentalists who wish to perpetuate the past unconditionally and the iconoclasts who want to reject it entirely. The westernized Asian intellectual often has his own cross to bear in all this. As the earliest opponent of colonial domination and traditional conformism in his own society, he now faces an unforeseen quandary. With the battle against colonialism won and the old values hopelessly fragmented, the pursuit of modernism in itself does not necessarily compensate for a lack of that indigenous cultural depth which is the measure of a nation's innermost being. There is a vacuum, and the gnawing question remains, must the great levelling process of social and economic advancement sweep away the gold as well as the dross of tradition? It is a vexed issue of contemporary Asian society, and the theatre which has been the magnificent child of tradition now mirrors in its uncertain course the restless search for communal identity in a new age.

2

INDIA

The spiritual quality of Indian life and art has been so heavily and often misleadingly stressed in the west that the layman could be excused for picturing all Hindu society in a perpetual state of meditation. The intensely devotional nature of Indian culture is incontestable but so are the qualities of materialism and sensuality which have equally given it character.

Palace societies and a privileged literary elite have shown a fastidious taste for worldly pleasures, and financial shrewdness has marked a hard-bitten commercial class. The literary image of a nation of religious ascetics is not borne out by the realities of human behaviour.

The sheer antiquity of India's history has weighed heavily on all aspects of her culture. It explains to some extent the over-emphasis that has been given to the spiritual. In fact surprisingly little is known about early Indian society. The ages who have kept the records were largely indifferent to life as it was lived. Speculation on the metaphysical nature of human existence together with maintaining the theories of divine origin, fundamental to all Hindu priestly teachings, replaced a concern for historical fact. The anonymity of the human element was emphasised.

A central tenet of Hindu belief has been the sublimation of individual thought with a timeless, universal spirit. It came from the deeply held conviction that man was a part of nature, neither its master nor its slave, but fundamentally united with it. Anonymity was therefore in accordance with a supreme truth and the great achievements of Hindu art have been anonymous and collective. Even the two great literary epics, The Saga of Rama, or the *Ramayana*,[1] and the Story of the Great War of the Bharata, or *Mahabharata*,[2] whose influence

on the Hindu spirit and imagination has been comparable to
the Bible on western thought and reasoning, were the joint
compilations of many unknown poets and bards.

One literary source that has provided some unusually
realistic commentaries on ancient Indian life and manners is
the Doctrine of Prosperity, or *Artha Sastra*,[3] whose principal
contribution was reputedly the work of Kautilya, minister to
the Emperor Chandragupta in the fourth century BC. It is
now regarded as a compilation, parts of which are thought to
have been written no earlier than the third or fourth century
AD, but whatever the chronological discrepancies it gives a
vivid impression of manners and methods which shaped the Indian
social structure in later times, and it is a mine of information on
procedure and social customs.

The picture that emerges from this text is one of autocratic
monarchy beneath which a cosmopolitan merchant class operated
under organized trade regulations. Autocracy was backed by a
highly qualified administrative bureaucracy which supervised a
rigid land-tax system. The king's power was supreme in every
area of political and social activity, while at the same time a
priestly class maintained its superior and independent status
behind the throne.

A luxurious and sensual court was supported from state funds
and there the king was surrounded by women at all times. They
looked after his every need, acted as a bodyguard and performed
as actresses and dancers for his entertainment. Slave labour was
an integrated institution, women were treated as inferiors at all
social levels, and prostitution was organized and a recognized
occupation.

The people were pleasure loving and fond of processions and
circuses; dancing and pantomime shows were popular and
troupes of strolling players worked their regular circuits. Their
members were regarded as socially inferior people requiring
strict surveillance but accepted as a necessary evil within the
scheme of things. It is in the *Artha Sastra* that a point of view
which has stigmatized stage performers for centuries in the east
is epitomized, in the ruling: 'The same rules shall apply to
an actor, dancer, singer, player on musical instruments, a rope
dancer, a juggler, a bard, pimps and unchaste women.'[4]
Although the descriptions in this text supposedly deal with a

transient period before the full flowering of Hindu culture, they
reduce things to human proportions, leaven the lump of
religious idealism and evince much that was absorbed into the
bloodstream of Indian society. It was one whose homogeneity
was attained through a culture that laid extraordinary emphasis
on the sacred nature of class distinction. The whole of Hindu
society functioned by means of a system in which the work,
social status and family life of virtually every individual were
preordained by birth into a designated caste.

A classification of society was first laid down in sacred
texts before 600 BC.[5] The poet-priest, the warrior chief, the
common people and the slave workers were defined as the four
main orders of society issuing from a divine creator. It was
the nucleus of a system destined to develop as a vast stratification of human activity of every kind. At the apex of the
system stood the Brahmin, the priest-scholar and protector
incarnate of the sacred law, *dharma,* to which every aspect of
daily life related. As a divinely sanctioned principle it induced
established order in society and represented the universal law of
nature. It also provided a code of conduct for the group and therefore the individual. It was a code of sliding values, depending on
the caste into which a man was born. There was no absolute. The
supreme religious duty for anyone was unswerving fidelity to the
code of his particular caste. No concept of moral sin comparable
to western belief could be applied to such a scheme of social order;
violation of caste ritual was the only criterion.

The ideal theory of caste ruled that certain duties were
common to all, while others were the privilege of a few. Specific
means of livelihood, therefore, were allowed to some people and
forbidden to others. The first of the four main castes lived
by teaching and officiating over temple ritual; the second caste
was concerned with administration; the profession of arms,
agriculture and trade were the occupations of the third caste;
while the fourth provided service for all the rest. From this primary
grouping endless divisions and subdivisions developed over the
course of time, categories and sequential relationships multiplied,
always with purity and uncleanliness as the polar distinction of
class separation. The result of this was that certain trades, occupations and professions became hereditary in certain caste groups.

The Brahmin caste, as the transmitters of sacred knowledge,

became ultra-conscious of purity of blood. An elaborate system of taboos was devised to avoid pollution by intermarriage and social contact with the impure lower groups. This attitude was echoed among these lower groups, who sought the advantages of the system to establish their own respectability, and so the process multiplied downwards. It encouraged a concern for the details of caste ritual as the basis of social behaviour.

The multifarious groupings which resulted from the original separation of classes meant that more and more castes were created as time went on to embrace the ramifications of social status and occupation. Each group within the four main caste divisions acquired its distinctive name, and family names within these subgroupings indicated occupational distinctions. The temple dancers in the Madras area, for example, belonged to the great fourth caste of lowly service, the *sudra*,[6] but they were recruited from families bearing the names Vellala and Kaikolan whose traditional occupations were cultivation and weaving. Occupational names varied from province to province, as did caste customs, but the basic principles remained rigidly the same.

Castes and sub-castes had their own governing bodies which were tribunals for enforcing the ethical, professional and economic rules of a particular group. The exclusiveness of caste ritual was nowhere more strongly upheld than among the occupational castes, where rights and privileges were jealously guarded. This ousted competition as well as inhibited change. At the same time it fostered a group pride in professional discipline, for the stricter the discipline the greater the power of ritual. And ritual was not easy compliance with usage but close attention to detailed and punctilious rules. This kind of discipline in dance led to very high standards of training and performance for both in effect represented the carrying out of ritual.

Dance and drama in India were the dynamic accessories of a culture entirely dependent on a grand scheme of hierarchical ritual affecting every phase of living and given total realization in the community through the institution of caste. As the supreme celebration of ritual it can be said without exaggeration that dance has there attained qualities of dramatic intensity unsurpassed in any civilization. At all stages of human development the social function of the dance has been to communicate aesthetic imagery and to stir collective feeling for a specific purpose, whether it was inspiring valour, dispelling fear, celebrating sex ardour, or serving similar motives. Interpretation rather than representation was the dancer's function and carried to its climax in India this meant a communication of emotional experience which could lead to a more intense revelation of existence itself.

A bronze four-armed figure, seen everywhere in India and familiar to the west from countless illustrations in the art histories, is the sculptural symbol of the origin of movement in the universe. The lord of the dance, as portrayed in this figurine, symbolizes the recurrent cycle of creation and destruction which operates eternally through the universe.[7] The dance created by a performer has a unity that cannot be isolated in a measurement of time; it has been danced, is being danced and is going to be danced at any given moment for the performer and onlooker. Through the interplay of sound, movement, rhythm and beat variation the mind is aware of infinity. In Indian thought the universe was regarded as consisting of vast cycles of motion and repose involving the idea of perpetual change. Humanity as part of the phenomenal world was affected by the same laws of rhythmic recurrence. The dance was considered a visible expression of the universal state of being and the dancer's performance a symbol of the indivisibility of time and eternity.

The temple dance of India carries visual expression of these ideas to a supreme point. The solo dancer's hand gestures range through a gamut of mood defined in the chanted verse of the accompanying musicians. The percussive throb of the drums rises to crescendos of rhythm in which the bells on the anklets of the dancer echo the beats or alternately jingle away in countermeasures given aural emphasis by the onomatopoeia of the drummer's cries. The dancer's every fibre contributes to an expression of pure form through which gesture is used at every spatial level. The rhythms twist and turn, advance and recede, but the dancer preserves an impersonal unity within her dynamic control of space. Gesture in this case is not individual interpretation, but in the timelessness of its perfection it becomes a compelling sensory force which lures the onlooker's mind into the total flow of movement.

Dancing of this quality was in the past an essential aid to temple ceremony and an aspect of the Hindu preoccupation with the processes of ritual. As the dance became a systematised part of temple practice, there grew up a body of women whose duty it was to dance in the temple and in the processions which took place during the numerous festivals marking the religious calendar. These women were dedicated to the temples in childhood, though in later times they were often recruited for service. As a class they became known as *devadasi*.

Conflicting accounts exist regarding the custom of dedicating girls as temple votaries, none of them very precise. Cave inscriptions and temple carvings attest the antiquity of dancers in a religious environment. A figurine discovered in the Indus Valley excavations has confirmed the existence of ritual dancers in India as early as 2500 BC.[8] Some authorities believe that temple consecration of young girls was a substitute for child sacrifice and that the very ancient rite of sacred prostitution was a development from this. In this rite three factors which later became entirely independent were united: religious ritual, mimicry, and harlotry. As prostitution became a social fact it remained protected by the persistence of religious convention and usage.

As the custom developed in India, a girl was bound to temple service through song and dance and had to be literate, formerly one of the few classes of women with that distinction. Because literacy was the prerogative of the temple dancer and the courtesan, ordinary women of even quite high birth once held that it was not respectable to be literate. The status and situation of a girl dedicated to temple service depended to some extent on the size and importance of the temple and the nature of her dedication. Daughters were dedicated in the first place as an act of devotion and as a sect obligation or caste duty. If their first child was a daughter people often dedicated her in the hope of divine assurance for a son next time. There were others who sold their daughters to temples out of dire economic necessity. Whatever the motive, the end result was the same; eternal 'marriage' to a deity meant that the girl renounced the normal ideals of chastity and domesticity, although no stigma attached to this fact.

After a symbolic marriage ceremony to the deity, which varied in different temples and regions, the training of the dancer began, usually at the age of seven or eight, although five was the minimum age in former times according to knowledgeable authorities. The training, which was arduous, lasted seven years and at the conclusion of her apprenticeship the dancer gave her first solo recital in the temple, usually in the presence of a ruler or other dignitaries, before she embarked on her full professional career.[9]

Eleventh-century records describe a great temple built at Tanjore in Madras state which had four hundred dancers attached to it.[10] They were given quarters in the area surrounding the temple and granted tax-free land out of endowments. Many temples had similar systems which were sanctioned by the state as well as by the temple authorities. The rise of the temple-dancer class in such an institutionalized form seems to date from between the ninth and tenth centuries AD when there was an active programme of temple building in southern India.

Temple dancers formed a special caste with their own law and special inheritance and adoption rights. Children born of unions within the caste were absorbed into the family profession. Daughters were brought up to follow the mother's vocation and were trained in dance, music and deportment. Sons became musicians who accompanied the dancers or instructed apprentice pupils. Dancers were in demand for all kinds of ceremonies and social occasions outside the temple precincts. Well-to-do patrons often maintained them as concubines but such arrangements were strictly bound by their own rules and decorum.

One of the famous old teachers of temple dancers in Madras state[11] has described professional conditions as they prevailed in the more recent past. Daily temple ceremonies were held at which both the dancers and the teachers assisted. The rites involved dancing to the deities. Such dancing laid great stress on symbolic hand gestures accompanied by the drums and cymbals of the teachers with the chant provided by the temple priests. A great occasion was the annual temple festival, which lasted for ten days. Once the temple flag was hoisted for this occasion no one could leave the village until the celebrations were over. Dancing went on every day for a considerable period both in the temple and on the streets, where the dancers accompanied the processions of the gods. The ninety-minute festival programme in the temple on this occasion was apparently very similar to the modern classical *bharata natyam*, or temple dance recital, performed under present-day secular conditions.

For their participation on these occasions and their other temple duties the teachers were paid between two and three rupees a month, the rupee then being worth about seven new pence or sixteen American cents. They were also given a portion of the cooked rice offerings which were made to the temple. The dancers received less than this but as they were able to attend weddings, private parties and other festivities, as well as take pupils, they were able to augment their income. The devotional character of the dance programme was not changed on these more private occasions although appreciation was then more often directed at the virtuosity of a performer. Because of the nature of the system, villagers no less than others learned to recognize the merits of good dancers and teachers and often travelled to other villages for the chance of seeing them perform.

The teaching routine of the girls and boys of the devadasi families before the system was abolished followed a severe pattern. The children began training when they were five. At that age some went to live in the household of the teacher, others came from home daily. A regular routine prevailed in the household, work starting at five in the morning with music lessons for everyone. Cold rice and curry was served at seven-thirty, the first meal of the day. From eight-thirty to midday the girls learned dance steps under the teacher's supervision with the boys following the proceedings by beating out the time with short sticks. If either the boys or girls made mistakes they were punished with a slap or a blow from their sticks. After their noon meal the children then went to another school between one and four where they studied language. Returning to the dance teacher they studied steps from four to six with more music from six to eight-thirty. From eight-thirty to ten they concentrated on mime interpretation. The day finished with rice and curry again at ten-thirty and then bed at eleven. These were tough conditions which few people could tolerate today but they certainly created dancers with tremendous power and stamina.

When a child reached the age of ten intensive professional

instruction commenced and lasted until about the age of thirteen. At the end of that time the pupil made her debut as a dancer with a special ceremony in the temple. The boys, however, had no special coming out, for they were assistants to the teacher and never performed independently. At the coming-out ceremony the teacher was presented with gifts by the pupils' mothers and others. Whenever the pupil performed in public for remuneration after that she was always accompanied by the teacher who beat out the rhythms on the cymbals. Half the dancer's payment was given to the teacher on these occasions. This was the basis of a system which followed a more or less common pattern in different areas.

If undue emphasis seems to have been given here to the temple dancer it is because she remained a perpetual symbol of the great Sanskrit tradition which overshadowed all Indian dramatic art and the social pattern from which it emerged. The philosophy of this tradition has been laid down in the famous treatise called the *Natya Sastra*, or Doctrine of Dramatic Art.[12] It has often been compared in a superficial way with the *Poetics* of Aristotle and has earned the same kind of reverence from Indian scholars that the Greek philosopher has commanded in the west. The Sanskrit is nevertheless so much more encyclopaedic in treatment that detailed comparisons only become confusing.

The *Natya Sastra* contains information and instruction said to have been handed down from the gods through a sage called Bharata, for whom so far as can be ascertained there is no historical evidence. This text has also been called the Fifth Veda in India, thereby placing it alongside the four primary scriptural sources of Hindu tradition which were presumed to have existed in their complete form from the beginning of time. Like most classics the *Natya Sastra* has frequently been more talked about than read. Repetitious emphasis of its mythological claims and academic obscurantism between them have done much to make it confusing and meaningless for the ordinary western theatre student.

The text, whose date has differed in the opinions of various scholars, has now been recognized as the work of many hands rather than the product of a single author, divine or otherwise. It is a compendium that has been added to through centuries and according to present thinking was probably compiled in its entirety between the second and eighth centuries AD. The text is divided into thirty-seven chapters which go into detailed description of aesthetic principles, metrics, theatre architecture, music, direction and production, plus the most exhaustive details of every kind of gesture and posture used on stage or in the dance. Even the desired character and physical qualifications of the performers are given at great length. The preoccupation with minutiae is so complete that the larger issues often seem to be obscured. It is necessary to remember for whom this document was chiefly compiled – the initiate and the perfectionist. The *Natya Sastra* is in fact a vast exposition in which the theatre is treated as only one aspect of life; not only drama is described, but a philosophy of existence expressed through sensory pleasures.

The rules were laid down for the aesthetically knowledge-able spectator schooled in appreciation of method. The patron of the Indian classical theatre was the connoisseur, the epicurean, for the drama was not a democratic art. On the stage were the professional exponents, technically trained to a high degree, and before them sat the educated audience with erudite critical standards and a refined judgment. Only those with such qualifications were considered competent to assess the meaning and beauty of aesthetic accomplishment, on the stage or elsewhere. The prologues of Sanskrit plays frequently lauded the spectator along these lines. The playwright sought the favour of royal patronage, and in striving for ever greater refinement achieved a hothouse artificiality which never thought to make a hero of a commoner.

The *Natya Sastra* seemed to state a more liberal function for the drama in that it purported to teach love and duty and to chastise the unruly,[13] but in the end the scope of theatre was restricted by the multifarious rules as to what might and might not be done upon the stage. The mere fact that the treatise was so rigidly systematized may be explained partly by the theory that at the time of compilation the Sanskrit theatre was already approaching its decline. The codification of orally transmitted principles of performance suggests the end and not the beginning of a period of creative activity.

The *Natya Sastra* contains many contradictions and it almost seems as though there has been an attempt to reconcile two traditions of dramatic expression, dance and dialogue plays. Nevertheless, the elaborate descriptions of hand gestures, postures, musical timing and rhythm clearly indicate a song-dance-drama form, whose spirit has been perpetuated in the southern Indian temple dance and the kathakali[14] dance-drama of Kerala, to name but two important styles.

The *Natya Sastra* is important to contemporary students for several reasons, not least because, in the theory of dramatic communication it lays down and the description of the physical means by which this is achieved, it provides what is tantamount to the seminal philosophy of Asian theatre in general. The practical information contained in this treatise is shrouded by what now seem like mythological irrelevancies used as a defence mechanism by a literary elite. The art of theatre is held to be transcendental, the product of a sacred art which liberates the spirit on a metaphysical plane. Allowing for this very characteristic Hindu concept, the treatise is essentially an attempt to explain what happens when a play is performed, to define the process which makes theatre work when trained actors and a responsive audience confront each other.

A stock theatrical troupe was described as consisting of the master actor, the clown, the musicians, the actor dancers, the crown maker, the maker of ornaments and garlands, the dyer, the painter and other craftsmen. Indian scholars believe this indicates that theatrical companies in the past travelled from place to place, as they still do in parts of India today. The inclusion of craftsmen of all kinds suggests that troupes were self-contained and equipped to put on new performances at each place they visited. The *Artha Sastra* confirms the existence of travelling companies with the comment that if a troupe arrived from another state it was required to pay five *panas* to the king before being allowed to perform. The pana was a coin valued at eighty cowrie shells which were used for domestic exchange in former times. Actors were paid three hundred and fifty of these a year while those who were 'conversant with playing on high class instruments were paid seven hundred panas yearly'. The same text ruled that it was the king's duty to provide teachers for actresses, who were to be instructed in the arts of singing, dancing, acting, writing, painting, playing on instruments, preparing garlands and ornamenting the body with different materials, the cost of all this instruction to be charged to the state treasury.

The fact that the *Natya Sastra* included a playwright as the regular member of a troupe has been taken to mean that there was no dependence on a fixed repertoire and that special plays were devised based on local history and legend to suit the tastes of a particular audience. 'Because he puts different sentiments, states and temperaments, as taught in the *Sastra,* in different characters, a person is called a playwright.'[15] In other words his duty was to compose a play on any given theme.

It is obvious from the *Natya Sastra* that actresses were essential members of theatre companies and that they also played male roles on occasion. 'A delicate person's role is always to be taken by women, hence in the case of women as well as gods and men of delicate nature women are to assume the roles.' One passage suggests there were troupes composed only of women. 'In temples, palaces and houses of army leaders and other prominent persons, dramatic performances are mostly held by women in men's roles.'[16] Presumably this was a matter of security, as mentioned earlier, as actors could always be potential assassins. In the *Artha Sastra* it says that the king used to employ actors, dancers, singers, musicians and storytellers as spies who would try to reach the enemy king.

Men also played women's roles. 'When a man assumes a woman's character the impersonation is called imitative in the best actors.'[17] Catamites are mentioned as a class of performers and recommended as attendants for the royal harem when it was portrayed on the stage. The *Natya Sastra*'s listing of character types for stage interpretation shows the early formulaion of a stylized role system which was a precedent for other forms of Asian theatre. The division of characters into three main types, superior, middling and inferior, subdivided into four classifications according to conduct, presages an acting philosophy which dominated many later theatrical styles. Dance and drama offer the most striking testimony to the way in which Indian aesthetics, as laid down in the *Natya Sastra,* provided a primary source from which many other tributaries flowed. Even China and Japan, who developed strongly individual forms of theatrical expression, evince so many basic affinities with Indian concepts, whether in aesthetic reasoning or performing aims, that it is hard to accept this as independent but identical development by three separate cultures. The inference is that Indian influences run very deep indeed, to the extent of providing a common link.

Be that as it may, the impact of the *Natya Sastra*'s reasoning on the theatrical arts of south-east Asia remains for all to see. The two great epics, the *Ramayana* and the *Mahabharata,* for example, have been an inexhaustible source of invention for the dance, the drama and the puppet show throughout south-east Asian countries and it is there that Indian scholars acknowledge the survival of old dance traditions long since vanished in India itself.[18]

How these traditions evolved there remains a matter for surmise. They matured only after centuries of population migrations, territorial annexation and Hindu-Buddhist religious conversion which set in motion a continuing process of absorption and reabsorption. The fact remains that in Java, Bali, Thailand, Burma, and Ceylon, dance and drama have flourished in ways which though expressive of their original environment bear the unmistakable evidence of a common Indian ancestry for which the *Natya Sastra* was the stem of the genealogical tree.

The *Natya Sastra* has a good deal to say about theatre architecture and is one of the rare written sources on the subject, though much of it is more concerned with now obsolete ritual than with architectural facts. Knowledge of these remains speculative for no building has survived from the past which could be described as a theatre, nor have archaeological excavations so far been fruitful. The need for theatre architecture in India was to some extent obviated by the fact that the temple was the community centre where most performances went on. Apart from this the temporarily erected open-air stage best served the needs of the crowd, as it continues to do today. The ancient kings had their pleasure gardens and places of entertainment attached to their palaces and there are references to the royal theatres in literature. As dramatic art, music and dancing were a necessary part of the education of the concubines, courtesans and women-in-waiting who made up a large proportion of palace society, there was obviously a need for theatres and dance halls. It was to serve the high-born and privileged palace audiences that theatres like those described in the *Natya Sastra* were constructed.

Three main types are described and classified according to size and shape. The largest was rectangular and measured ninety-six by forty-eight feet in area. The other two styles were square and triangular in shape, both having sides which measured forty-eight feet. According to one authority the triangular theatres were used for rehearsals. They were all roofed, faced east and west, and from the exterior presented a closed appearance with small windows at a high level and few doors. The interior was usually divided into two, with the stage and green room as one continuous area separated by a wall. Even in the largest theatre the maximum distance from the rear wall of the stage to the rear wall of the auditorium was only seventy-two feet so that the buildings were essentially intimate in character and provided the maximum opportunity for the audience to observe stylized gesture and expression in detail.

The theatres are thought to have been of framed construction with brick or stone pillars and brick panel walls.[19] The auditorium was built with wooden supporting pillars and a curved semicircular roof ribbed in teak and described as 'like a cave'. The stage was raised on teak framed supports which ran lengthwise and crosswise beneath it, providing resilience. The stage floor was made with a specially prepared mixture of earth and clay, the surface being smooth as a faultless mirror. The stage floor was inlaid with precious stones and the centre treated with gold. In the larger theatres the stage is believed to have been on two levels, with the rear a little higher than the front portion. The side spaces of the stage served as wings and the doors from the green room opened on to them, leaving a blank rear wall. The floor of the auditorium was built with rising steps nine inches high and eighteen inches wide. The orchestra was seated on the stage between the two doors of the green room at the rear, although according to a second passage in the *Natya Sastra*, 'The orchestra, related to actors and actresses of superior, middling and ordinary types, occupies different positions on the stage during production of plays'.[20] This seems analogous to Japanese kabuki practice, where the musicians in dance plays may be placed right, left, centre or off-stage.

Temples have been the real theatre buildings it seems, and
the places where people gathered at festival times to listen to
the storytellers reciting the epics, and watch the dancers, actors
and performers of many kinds. No important temple was without its pillared hall, where dances and dramas were performed
as votive offerings to the gods. One or two old temples still exist
in Kerala in the farthest south, with theatres which are similar
in detail to those described in the *Natya Sastra* but incorporating their own regional characteristics. A feature of these
buildings is the large sweeping roof surface which slopes steeply
down on four sides over a rectangular auditorium standing on
a heavy stone plinth in which a flight of four or five steps lead
to two entrances at either side of the building, one for men and
one for women. The roofs are two or three times greater in
proportionate height than the lower structure of the building
itself. They are supported by beams resting on pillars which line
the interior of the building on its four sides and which surround
an inner rectangle of pillars, in which the stage, usually square, is
placed to face the deity. The auditorium floor is one flat level on
which the audience stand or sit. The area in front of the stage was
always reserved for Brahmins in the past and was sometimes at a
slightly higher level than the rest of the auditorium floor.

The stage also stands on a heavy moulded granite plinth,
and four large ornamented pillars which frame the movements
of the actors support a roof built over the stage itself. The rear of
the stage is separated by a wall from the green room and two
narrow doors for entry and exit are placed in the wall. Between
these doors on the stage stand two large egg-shaped copper drums
on wooden stands. Although details vary in different temples, those
described here represent a common pattern. The present temple
theatres in Kerala are considered to date back three to four
hundred years but they represent a continuity of tradition which
goes back to the time of the *Natya Sastra*. There is a remarkable
affinity between this type of stage structure and those of the old
Chinese theatre and the Japanese noh theatre. It is possible that
with the old temple theatres of Kerala a long, long historical link
is preserved.

Drama as laid down in the *Natya Sastra* was a courtly
affair devised for a courtly society. It emphasized the harmony
between good and evil, it was romantic, and the sordid truths

of life were ignored. It had its own clearcut, formalized idiom of expression, acting was non-naturalistic, music, dancing and spectacle were major elements. Great attention was paid to literary construction and convention in the plays although the plots are often trifling. Ritual was essential to their staging.

Of around four hundred or so Sanskrit plays written between 250 BC and 1000 AD thirty or forty have been acclaimed as literary masterpieces but few of them are actable today. Though the tradition of Sanskrit remains a powerful cultural force in India, the drama that sprang from it, its refinements, its forms, and the very aesthetic which animated it on the stage, are only a literary memory. The polished verse and ornate speech became ends in themselves and hastened its end as living theatre. The most vigorous remnants of it are found today diffused throughout various regional forms which assimilated some of its traditions and methods and adapted them to local characteristics.

The temple drama of Kerala is an outstanding example. In this form single acts from Sanskrit plays are staged with the hieratic and ritualistic display which marked their performance in the past, according to the sacred texts. The Kerala drama is thought to be one of the earliest attempts to take the classical drama to people ignorant of Sanskrit. The performers come from two separate castes who remain in temple service and have been storytellers and actors for well over a thousand years. The caste which provides the actors formerly contained eighteen families who were traditionally involved, but only six remain today. From the second caste come the drummers and narrators for the stage and it is their women who play the parts of heroines in the plays, in itself a link with the old Sanskrit tradition of actresses.

The clown is a most important character in the Kerala theatre, again suggesting a link with an ancient dialogue drama. He works to a strict set of conventions and appears on stage at a specified time in the cycle of plays produced over several days. As the *alter ego* of the hero he is also a kind of social catalyst. He is the only character who speaks in the local vernacular, through which medium he explains to the audience the meaning of all the Sanskrit and ancient dialect spoken by the other characters in his presence. At one point he launches into a parody on the four aims of existence. The scene is laid in the Village of the Illiterates, whose priestly leader is distinguished only by his monumental ignorance of all that passes for learning. In this company the four ends of corrupt society are discovered to be food and gluttony, sensual pleasures, deception and sharp practice, and the currying of royal favour for personal ends. Stories and verse are used to embroider the themes and no one remains immune from the clown's sarcasm and wit. Verses on food and sex proliferate, and while explaining the hero's experiences to the audience he parallels them with his own, and since food and maidservants are his particular preoccupations there is corresponding hilarity among the audience.

The Kerala method of staging Sanskrit plays has been criticized by the literary pedants in the past for its many departures from codified procedure. It was pointed out that colloquial speech was permissible for poetic embellishment not for parody, and in one comic episode where Brahmins are mentioned as having illicit relations with lower-caste women a charge of obscenity was levelled. The censuring in this way of actors' innovations not sanctioned by the known texts on dramaturgy is one reason why the Sanskrit drama shrivelled inwardly upon itself, but the loud-mouthed, greedy and amorous clown still dominates dozens of different regional styles of performance. As a debunker and a constant reminder of a world where you live in order to eat he continues to pull down the hero from his poetic pinnacle.

The Indian folk drama had strong roots in the sung narrative of a minstrel class whose accounts of the great and mighty provided ballad material which was readily turned into dramatic entertainment for the crowd. In the *Artha Sastra* the bard was classed socially with pimps and prostitutes and it is a reputation that he has sustained in many parts of India. On the other hand in ancient Indian court life the bard was a palace functionary who acted as the genealogist of kings and warriors. He was the one person born of mixed castes, normally considered an evil thing, who came within the jurisdiction of the sacred law. It was the bards who provided the genesis for the great epics which have so profoundly influenced Indian society. Their descendants in mediaeval times,

particularly in Rajputana and Gujerat, were minstrels of autocratic style claiming high ancestry. It was a time of numerous
small states which rivalled each other in glorifying the exploits
of their particular heroes. The bards and court minstrels
flourished and popularized many of the themes as well as the
poetic metres and musical forms which passed into regional
plays.

The romantic tale was a perennial favourite with village
audiences. Though dynasties rose and fell old stories went on,
even if names and settings were changed to suit the times. Folk
performers drew freely on this material, popularizing it from
one region to the next and performing it in several different
languages. Folk themes were sometimes used to propagate
mystic themes particularly in Muslim areas where the figures
from the Hindu pantheon were discarded in favour of secular
personalities.

The Muslim north was equally rich in its folk traditions. In
the Punjab there was a caste which provided musicians for
ceremonial occasions, who were experts at the art of repartee.
They also sang the praises of families at weddings, recited
genealogies and kept alive the old ballads.[21] Their profession was
hereditary, but if their occupation had high historical precedents
they were a socially inferior caste who, though Muslim, could
not marry outside their own enclosed circle. Their women played
and sang but were more brazen than witty in their speech and
were known for their easy virtue.

A second caste having professional affinities with this one
produced singing girls, dancers and prostitutes who were
socially rated in that order. The men of the caste could not
engage in any recognized occupation because of their low birth.
Physical charms only were demanded of the harlot but dancing,
despite its low level in these circumstances, at least needed
training and a lithe body. The singing girl required talent and
training over many years for hers was a literary art; she
represented an elite and bestowed her favours only where she
chose. In these ways the values and prejudices of ancient society
were perpetuated and perverted through the caste system.
Whatever their regional peculiarities and ethical associations,
performers of this description were the architects of folk theatre.
Song, dance and the acting-out of mythical and historical tales

provided them with a common point of departure and an irresistible combination.

Acting was a miserably paid profession at best in rural India and as a class performers were little better off than agricultural labourers. Travelling troupes in the past usually worked on the basis that food and bare amenities should be provided for each actor. At the end of a performance a plate was sent round into which the audience tossed their copper coins or else nothing at all as their circumstances dictated. Rural troupes depended for their greatest income on wealthy landowners who, during a festival or for some special family occasion, would hire a complete company. The disappearance of this class of patron in modern India dealt a grievous economic blow to the old-style folk theatre.

Standards of professionalism varied but the folk theatre if nothing else was marked by its vigour and bombast. Training was more often through participation than any organized teaching system and the hereditary caste system created an ingrown expertise. The leader of the troupe was responsible for standards of professional supervision. Troupes travelled the countryside on foot or by bullock cart and upon arrival at their destination they either slept out of doors or were accommodated in the local rest house for homeless travellers. They erected their own temporary stage or simply beat flat an open area of ground which served as their arena. Performances usually began between eight and ten in the evening and often continued late into the night. A show might go on for two or three days, or as long as three weeks during a festival season. The advent of a theatrical troupe in a village was the occasion for an excited and clamouring crowd; whatever else the folk actor lacked it was certainly never an audience.

With few exceptions, women's roles in the Indian folk theatre have been taken by men and boys. In the mediaeval period, from the eleventh to the sixteenth century, there was an increasing move to drive women from the stage. One reason was the reaction on the part of some revivalists against the immorality of the temple dancers, resulting in the exclusion of women from the new devotional dance dramas. A much more general factor was the Islamic invasion in India and the consequent segregation of women as a religious tenet. Mixed troupes were debarred. Moreover, Persian aesthetics, upon which the Indian version of Islam drew so heavily, had long enshrined the young male as the object of finer erotic sentiment so that the use of boys and young men on the stage acquired its own rationale.

The setting for folk theatre of all kinds was simple, usually extempore and often primitive. Country fairs provided a natural focus and when fairs went on for several days several troupes might be found performing at the same time. The market place, the temple courtyard and the street corner took the place of any permanent theatre building. Temporary bamboo structures with palm-leaf matting provided the nearest approach and in some areas large canopy-like tents were used for all kinds of celebrations including theatrical performances. A temporary raised platform which enabled the audience to watch the play on three sides was one of the commonest forms of stage used by travelling troupes, while arena stages varying from a simple patch of open ground to quite elaborate uses of space have also been typical.

The grounds of the courtyard of a private residence provided folk theatre with a more intimate setting when some private patron decided to entertain his family with a show, not however without inviting in the neighbourhood as was the invariable custom. Rabindranath Tagore has left a lively description of one of these occasions in his father's house. It conjured up the excitement and bustle of the moment as seen through the receptive eyes of childhood. *Jatra*, the type of drama he describes, was peculiar to Bengal where it was an accepted institution familiar to the whole community.

Jatra performances used to take place in our house from time to time. But we children had no part in them and I managed to see only the preliminaries. The verandah would be full of members of the company, the air full of tobacco smoke. There were boys, long-haired with dark rings of weariness under their eyes and young as they were, with faces of grown men. Their lips were stained black with constant betel chewing. Their costumes and other paraphernalia were in painted tin boxes. The entrance door was open, people swarmed like ants into the courtyard, which, filled to the brim with the seething buzzing mass, spilled over into the lane and beyond into the Chitpore Road.

Then nine o'clock would arrive and Shyam would swoop down on me like a hawk on a dove, grip my elbow with his rough, gnarled hands and tell me that mother was calling me to bed. I would hang my head in confusion at being thus publicly dragged away, but would bow to superior force and go to my bedroom. Outside all was tumult and shouting, outside flared the lighted chandeliers but in my room there was not a sound and a brass lamp burned low on its stand. Even in sleep I was dimly conscious of the crash of the cymbals marking the rhythm of the dance.

The grown-ups usually forbade everything on principle but on one occasion for some reason or other they decided to be indulgent and the order went forth that the children might come to see the play. It was a drama about Nala and Damayanti. Before it began we were sent to bed until half past eleven. We were assured again and again that when the time came we should be roused, but we knew the ways of grown-ups and we had no faith in all these promises—they were adults and we were children.

That night however I did drag my unwilling body to bed. For one thing Mother promised that she herself would come and wake me. For another thing I always had to pinch myself to keep awake after nine o'clock. When the time came I was awakened and brought outside blinking and bewildered in the dazzling glare. Light streamed brightly from coloured chandeliers on the first and second storeys and the white sheets spread in the courtyard made it seem much bigger than usual. On one side were seated people of importance, senior members of the family, and their invited guests. The remaining space was filled with a motley crowd of all who cared to come. The performing company was led by a famous actor wearing a gold chain across his stomach and old and young crowded together in the audience. The majority of the audience were what the respectable would call 'riff-raff'. The play itself had been written by men whose hands were trained only to the villager's reed pen and who had never practised on the letters of an English copy book. Tunes, dances and story had all sprung from the very heart of rural Bengal and no pundit had polished their style.

We went and sat by our elder brothers in the audience and they tied up small sums of money in kerchiefs and gave them to us. It was the custom to throw the money on to the stage at points where applause was most deserved. By this means the actors gained some extra profit and the family a good reputation. The night came to an end but the play would not. I never knew whose arms gathered up my limp body nor where they carried me. . . .[22]

The name jatra literally means a procession but came to designate a type of folk theatre whose beginnings were in festivals held in honour of the gods. The jatra seems to have passed through a number of phases but accounts of these are often vague and confusing. Systematic knowledge of the development of the present form dates largely from the early nineteenth century. A note in the *Asiatic Journal* of July 1816 commented that 'jatras of this season were chiefly dramatic representations of the loves of Krishna and the *gopis* [milkmaids] performed by the boys of the Kuttack tribe of the Brahmin caste and appeared to us to possess great resemblance to the ancient chorus of the Greeks'. This was the basis of the form from which many later variations developed. Throughout its growth music and song remained the main motive for expression. Changes in the jatra were often synonymous with new musical fashions.

In the early nineteenth century it became a craze for wealthy Calcutta citizens to stage their own amateur jatra shows, creating a vogue that ran parallel with the more traditional shows. Tagore commented on this trend in the article just quoted. 'A little before our day it was the fashion among wealthy householders to run jatras or troupes of actors. There was a great demand for boys with shrill voices to join these troupes. One of my uncles was patron of such an amateur company. He had a gift for writing plays and was very enthusiastic about training the boys.'

Amateur interest in the jatra was replaced by that of professional entrepreneurs of a new kind. One such was an itinerant musician of talent whose songs captured the heart of a well-to-do *demi-mondaine*. They set up house together and began to run a jatra troupe which became exceedingly popular. Others followed suit and women troupe leaders and performers appeared. A typical jatra troupe of this period earned fifty to sixty rupees a night, of which the leader took one-quarter and any gifts that were lavished on the company.

Another personality of the period, Gopal Ooray, began life as a peddler of stationery but joined the jatra troupe of a wealthy Calcutta amateur where his voice and looks (he was said to be indistinguishable from the real thing when made up as a woman) so charmed the public that he was taken on at a salary of fifty rupees a week.[23]

Such players introduced a new and amorous romanticism into jatra and this often degenerated into bawdiness and indecency. One critic writing of the jatra trend lamented, 'Does not a father feel ashamed to hear such things with his son and daughter? What will they think of their parents when they grow old?" Nevertheless, the jatra survived. The rising interest in a western-style theatre stimulated new approaches in the jatra to the extent that today it has been recognized as one of the primary influences in the rise of the modern Bengali theatre.

Lyrical elements still take up about two-thirds of any jatra play, in which the characters burst into song on the slightest provocation. There used to be a chorus of ten to twelve young boys with high soprano voices who took no direct part in the performance but expressed through their singing the appropriate dramatic mood to move the audience at high moments. They also narrated events which could be shown on the stage and in general provided the audience with a thread of continuity. The singers were divided into four groups, each of which faced the audience on the four sides of the open stage and performed in unison. A leader of the boys stood behind them, playing a stringed instrument and alternatively encouraging their efforts or clouting them if they missed their cue, needless to say providing extra entertainment for the audience. The singers were all dressed identically as young maidens, court attendants, and so on.

The simplest of stage props were used and these were moved around in the presence of the actors. Changes of scene were frequently indicated by the actor's declamation. Other actions were mimed or simply described by the actor concerned. All female roles were taken by men and one actor often played both sexes in the same play. Incongruities abounded but audiences were accustomed to using their imaginations and quickly involved themselves in the action on stage.

Comic episodes were introduced at regular intervals and generally concerned low life and manners, affording contrast to heroic events. There was little attempt at constructing a tight dramatic plot; the performance was a kind of moving tapestry incorporating myths and legends known to everyone from long ago with the ideas, customs and prejudices of the ordinary people of Bengal woven in. Plays went on practically all night in the old days, as Tagore indicated, beginning early in the evening and ending about five or six in the morning. In more recent times they have begun at midday and ended at midnight.

Oil wicks burning in earthenware cups were used in the past, supplemented by torches tied to posts, but the ubiquitous kerosene lamp has replaced them today.

Bengal, the home of the jatra, in many ways reflects an exceptionally clear picture of the social history of modern Indian theatre, which is the subject of the rest of this chapter. It was Bengal where western influences made a very early impact on the Indian community and where attempts to create a new theatre were particular insistent. It was in Bengal also that a socially committed theatre became most active in the pre-independence years and where today a passionately political drama persists.

The British had their theatres in India as early as 1756 in Calcutta and 1770 in Bombay, the predecessors of a number which sprang up during the late eighteenth century and which were intended in the first place to counteract the boredom of British soldiers and provide entertainment and recreation for the merchants, officials and their wives and daughters. A notable example was the Calcutta Theatre, opened in about 1776 and built at the cost of a hundred thousand rupees raised by subscription among the British community. In its later days this playhouse was a centre of activity for a new Bengali drama. Miss Sophia Goldborne, an English resident of the period, has left a characteristic description of it.

The performers are all gentlemen who receive no kind of compensation but form a fund of the admission money to defray the expense of the house. It consists only of pit and boxes, to be admitted to the first of which you pay twenty shillings, to the last forty shillings. It is therefore no wonder that the house is about the size of the Bath Theatre and consists of pit and boxes only, the first an area in the centre, the second a range of commodious, enclosed or rather separated seats around it from one corner of the stage to the other. No expense has been spared to gratify either the eye or the ear; a very pleasing band of music saluted the present Governor on his entrance and the pit was crowded with spectators. It is lighted upon the English plan with lamps at the bottom of the stage and girandoles at proper distances with wax candles covered with glass shades as in the verandahs to prevent their extinction, the windows being venetian blinds and the free circulation of air delightfully promoted by their situation.[24]

A human and feminine note is introduced by a final comment which reads:

Several country-born ladies figured away [sic] in the boxes and by candlelight had absolutely the advantage of the Europeans, for their dark complexions and sparkling eyes gave them the appearance of animation and health the Europeans had no pretensions to and their persons are genteel and their dress magnificent, whereas on the other hand paleness and languor told the country of my birth and were not to be concealed or compensated by all that polite negligence or accomplished manners could do. The pit was full of gentlemen of every denomination. As for myself, my attention was so engaged by the piece that my heart several times asked if it could be possible I was at the distance of 4000 miles from the British metropolis.

This contemporary account, enlightening among its other details for indicating the presence of Hindu women at a foreign public occasion at a very early date, presaged a long introduction to western amateur acting for the Indians. The British were especially prone to amateur theatricals, which remained a recreational outlet in most of their colonial societies. If this meant that the Indians were continually subjected to the influence of Victorian ham acting, at least it could be said that it also did a little towards fostering a new interest in dramatic participation and helped to break down the social prejudices of higher-class Indian society against appearing on a stage.

The earliest known attempt to stage a modern Indian play, that is to say one given in the Bengali language, has been attributed to a Russian called Lebedeff. He was a bandmaster and violinist who arrived in Calcutta in 1787 and gave public performances. He was apparently something of an opportunist and with the help of a Bengali teacher called Das he translated some plays from the English and then started a theatre. It opened its doors in November 1795 with a performance by Bengali actors of a play called *Disguise*. Tickets were sold at the theatre costing eight rupees for boxes and pit and four rupees for the gallery. There was such a rush that on the second night the audience had to be limited to two hundred which suggests this was an intimate theatre. Prices were raised to a uniform forty shillings for a ticket and the house was soon sold out. 'The stage and auditorium were decorated in Bengali style', meaning presumably floral embellishments, and the play commenced with vocal and instrumental music called *The Indian Serenade*. There is also mention of a famous Bengali poet's verses set to music and introduced before the acts with 'other curiosities'. The audience were given a detailed synopsis of the story. It seems clear that novelty was the principal motive here and the aim was to catch public attention and sentiments through original effects rather than any attempt to write a serious play.[25]

It was 1857 before this happened, marking the more logical beginning of a modern Bengali drama. The play was by a writer called Tarkaratna, the prizewinner in a competition organized by a public-spirited north Bengal landowner and first advertised in the local press in 1853. The award was offered for the best play in the Bengali language exposing the social evils of a particular Hindu marriage custom. Because of the restrictions which hedged high-caste betrothals there was a dearth of bridegrooms and many Brahmin girls were confronted with the choice of marrying a man with several wives or remaining unwed. The latter was regarded as such a disgrace in orthodox circles that polygamy was condoned as a result.

The prize-winning play attracted much attention for its sarcastic criticism of Hindu arch-conservatism and its frankly propagandist aim. It was first staged privately in the house of a wealthy Calcutta resident, a form of patronage which was common in the early days of the new theatre when no proper stage facilities existed and participation was very much an amateur affair. Although this pioneer effort evidenced no originality in dramatic structure and was traditionally declamatory in style, it was a tremendous innovation in its day as one of the first attempts to harness theatre to social reform.[26]

While reform of the old society provided new Indian playwrights with a platform, they also took a sharp look at the follies of their own western-influenced generation. One result of a too hasty assimilation of English education was the rise of a class of young prigs for whom it became the done thing to denigrate everything Indian in an attempt at blind imitation of the customs and attitudes of western people. The new cultural snobbery was pilloried in a play called *So This is Civilisation*, by Michael Datta, a brilliant young writer who had himself received a sound English education and was by no means a partisan of classical conservatism. He was therefore well qualified to understand his own generation.

The subject of his play was the son of a traditional Hindu family, extremely conscious of his superior education. He was the centre of a group of kindred spirits who 'drank wine, ate ices and talked about the pressing problems of the day, female emancipation and widow remarriage. Their speeches, half in English half in Bengali style, were constantly punctuated with cheers and slogans like "Be Free" and generally ended in Hip Hip Hurrah. Then they ate their dinners served in English style and made merry until late at night with music and dancing girls.'[27] First produced in 1864, again by a private troupe in a wealthy patron's house, this was one of the earliest genuine social comedies of the new theatre movement, whose immaturity was compensated by the dedicated enthusiasm of its sponsors. It rapidly gained ground in the major cities, where language differences gave their own particular twist to the new productions.

In Bombay, for example, the Parsis founded a theatre which adopted nineteenth-century melodrama lock, stock and barrel for its own. A hotch-potch of song, music, romantic sentimentality and pious moralizing made it a highly popular entertainment, whose brash vulgarity was enlivened by the bold talents of the actresses who became the stars of this genre.

The introduction of English education and the development of the printing press in nineteenth-century India had far-reaching effects. A new knowledge of English literature inspired the development of prose literature in the various Indian languages which until then had been largely concerned with poetic expression. Shakespeare was taught in the new schools opened by the British and his hallowed position on the school curriculum meant that Indian schoolboys, like their British counterparts, were eventually subjected to a grounding in the works of the master not always calculated to inspire a love of drama. Nevertheless Shakespeare had a considerable impact on the Indian mind, especially after the founding of a university system at Madras, Calcutta and Bombay by the British in 1857, when a new class of educated youth arose. To some extent Shakespeare seemed more in harmony with the spirit of the classical Sanskrit drama, but it was the confrontation of concrete evils and passions on a human basis in place of conventional ethical principles which provided the greatest revelation to intellectuals. One effect of the new ideas absorbed through the study of English literary and philosophical ideas was the awakening of Indian introspection, creating a spirit of reform bent on changing Hindu ultra-conservatism. Political awareness was stimulated and the seeds of nationalism sown.

The first generation of English-educated Indians, dominated by the literary ideas they had absorbed, were filled with a desire to change the old ways of life completely along western lines. British political control and social reform were in the beginning seen as twin benefits. By the late nineteenth century a second generation had come to the fore who were more openly nationalistic in outlook. They were also more backward looking and turned towards India's past glory as an ideal. Though prepared to take advantage of western influences, resurgent Hinduism maintained that liberation from British rule came before social reform which would automatically follow political independence. These differing points of view were in both cases held by men who were largely drawn from the Hindu castes, upon whom British education had made the most forceful impact. The lower castes remained virtually unaffected. The Brahmins, who had enjoyed the highest social status in the past, continued to do so under the British. There was a transition through the literary elite.

Such intellectual ferment and aspirations were bound to seek expression through a western style of theatre. As a medium for ideas it awakened new possibilities, although there was inevitably a wide gap between intention and performance in pioneer theatrical ventures. A fondness for Shakespeare and for amateur acting in the schools were well enough in themselves, but as the major concessions to theatre in a colonial educational policy which was unadventurous in the arts and even wary of their subversive possibilities, they had their limitations. How great these were may be gauged from an incident in 1876 when the director and stage manager of a Calcutta troupe were tried and sentenced to imprisonment for staging an 'indecent play'. The offending scene was one in which an English official caused an Indian maidservant to jump from a balcony in order to

c

avoid his attentions. In the subsequent scene he appeared holding the injured girl in his arms.

Public opinion was squarely on the side of the actors and the sentence was later quashed by appeal, but the affair hastened the introduction of a Dramatic Performances Act which placed an unimaginatively administered censorship on public performance. As the Law Member of the Legislative Council phrased the motives: 'It had been found in all times and in all countries that no greater stimulus could be supplied to excite the passions of mankind than that supplied by means of drama and no feat was too difficult for a dramatist who could produce any effect he pleased on the minds of the spectators.'[28] This flight of rhetoric was possibly more flattering than true of the embryo vernacular theatre movement in India, which had few pretensions to being a cataclysmic force. The burden of its stodgy Victorian inheritance weighed heavily upon it, and the night fears of colonial administrators were intimidating, but there were other problems which sprang from nearer home.

Classical Indian dramatic tradition had evolved a form based on music, song, dance and poetic declamation and this remained constant in all successive developments irrespective of language differences. A non-naturalistic and conventional style of setting was its recognized mode of expression. The transition from this to a realistic style of theatre which could portray the social problems of Indian civilization was a difficult step to take. Ideally it demanded a sound knowledge of the discipline of form, which western theatre required no less than their own.

One criticism of the British system of education in India was its accent on a literary at the expense of a vocational approach. Though liberal it was not practical. This argument was not without relevance to theatre. After the establishment of the university system the influence of English literature was more intensively felt through the novel, the essay and the drama. Drama meant Shakespeare, and Shakespeare in the university meant literary form, a discipline in isolation.

Many Indian innovators fell between two stools, lacking as they did knowledge of that other discipline which no less defines the drama: the staging of a play involving a planned scheme of cooperation in movement and emotional expression. People became side-tracked through mannerisms and were handicapped by their lack of access to first-class western theatre. Amateur dramatic clubs were no substitute for the stage experiments taking place in late nineteenth-century Europe.

Ibsen, for example, with his probing of the hypocrisies of the middle class eventually had a tremendous impact on many Indian intellectuals, but it was questionable how far literary appreciation could influence new theatrical creativity. The problems of sex and the idea of a free and independent life for women were in any case near-revolutionary ideas in Hindu society and could scarcely be stated in such terms. Moreover there was something paradoxical about a theatre of social reform which could only procure its actresses from the ranks of 'unrespectable' women and then often only with violent public disapproval. Writing of one amateur theatre venture in 1870 an Indian critic commented: 'The present theatre had no female artists on the staff. This will soon be considered a defect and means will be sought to remedy this defect. Some of the prostitutes are trying to receive education. If a few of such educated women are secured, happy consequences will outweigh any mischief done.'[29]

One amateur theatre director of the 1870s became interested in social reform in a rather more active sense. After founding schools and newspapers he married an aged widow of another caste in double defiance of orthodox prejudices. He next gave his attention to actresses and decided to better their lot through respectable marriage. In 1875 he arranged the marriage of a popular actress in his company with a personable young man who was under obligation to him. The arrangement went well at first and a daughter was born to the couple but the young man sailed secretly as a cabin boy to England and was never heard of again. His wife was reduced to extreme poverty and when, to quote an Indian historian, 'all other honest means failed she was forced by circumstances to resume her old profession as an actress'.[30]

Some of these earlier actresses brought down the house with their Shakespeare adaptations, which they turned into popular melodramas. As a theatrical rather than a literary inspiration, Shakespeare was undoubtedly a mixed blessing and these adaptations of his works often pandered to a taste for romantic sensationalism. The difficulties in translation were prodigious and to convert Shakespearian metaphor and imagery into a form which satisfied Indian social prejudices, mythology, and dramatic conventions was a task to daunt the stoutest heart. The results were often unrecognizable as Shakespeare.

In one nineteenth-century version of Macbeth the lack of love interest was considered too great a handicap, so Macbeth was given a daughter called Malati who was deeply in love with Malcolm. Lady Macbeth, having plotted the murder, revealed the plan to her daughter and urged her to renounce her lover. Malati refused and secretly warned Malcolm. He escaped without Duncan who was shot by hired thugs during a garden banquet. Malcolm was later arrested for patricide and jailed. He received a late-night visit from Macbeth who was intent on obtaining the secret of a buried treasure known only to Malcolm, but Malcolm refused to divulge its whereabouts. Malcolm was later rescued through a secret passage at midnight by his sweetheart, with the help of Banquo, and the two lovers were finally crowned king and queen.

Yet Shakespeare fired Indian audiences with unbounded enthusiasm, even though it was often for all the wrong reasons. In yet another Bombay performance of Macbeth there was a tumultuous ovation for the sleep-walking scene, drowning out any further action on the stage. The actor playing Macbeth walked to the footlights and lectured his audience. 'This is not a music hall, where you can encore a song. If you persist you must realize such consummate acting cannot be repeated devoid of context. If we start the play again we need three hours to reach this point. It is already one in the morning but I have no objection if you get the necessary police permission.'

The last sally was in reference to the fact that under the 1867 Act no play was allowed to be given for public performance unless the script, which had to be submitted one month before opening night, had been approved by the police. The same rule is still in force today, but not only does the hapless producer of a play now have to wait until some police inspector approves and makes deletions from a script according to rule of thumb, he must also get a police licence for the theatre, for selling tickets, for using microphones on the stage and for distributing handbills.

By the end of the nineteenth century the distinction between amateur and professional was recognized and dozens of new companies came into being with their enthusiastic followers. As professional theatre, however, the new vernacular styles rapidly became entirely commercialized and when it is considered what happened to Shakespeare it is not difficult to imagine what went on lower down the scale. Theatre was largely a musical spectacle whose melodramatic ranting, sensational plots and quick changes of elaborate scenes delighted audiences who sought escape in such entertainment.

At the same time a truly indigenous dramatic mode struggled to find an outlet in several regional forms, particularly the Marathi and Bengali theatres, but the confrontation of two traditions was ill-balanced and insufficiently understood in a majority of cases. Indian unity lay in culture, not nationalism, and this culture was devotional, hierarchical and related to a static, predetermined society of which theatre and dance were the dramatic expression. The rise of nationalism, sparked off through the introduction of western ideas, demanded a radically different approach in the arts. In any country the arts are the product of successive phases of social development and cannot be assimilated ready-made.

The beginning of the twentieth century found Indian society in a state of transition and intellectual conflict. Ideas of self rule and national independence, the result of British liberal education, had already taken deep root. By 1900 there was a growing western-educated class who were ready to press for Indian participation in the governing of their country. Their problem was that as they grew in number they tended to judge India through the values absorbed from the west. They subscribed to a different intellectual tradition from that of the broad masses of the people, yet under the British they lacked the supreme power which would have made them a political force.

In contrast to this Indian western-educated intelligentsia there was a new body of thinking men who remained faithful to the Hindu tradition but wished to rid it of its superstitions and social abuses. They wanted to return to the original purity of its religious inspiration, but they were prepared to accept western reforms and Christian ideals without abandoning the fundamental ethical principles of Indian society.

It was this philosophy that gained ground and increasingly

influenced the course of events, enabling Gandhi to lead India to independence through passive resistance. His leadership was religious, predominantly Hindu but tempered with his interpretation of Christian ethics. He was traditionalist and backward looking but he was also a revolutionary committed to the idea of equality. Gandhi denounced middle-class urbanism and focused on village life. Throughout history the village had been the bedrock of Indian life, an autonomous unit which ran its affairs without outside intervention through its own committee drawn from the village elders. The village and its families were the dominating units of social organization. Gandhi used this society as the model for national regeneration; he wanted to restore the village council as the unit of political power and revive its dying culture.[31] The call for a return to the village was in many respects falsely idealistic, but Gandhi's political conscription of spiritual values was effective and the emotional appeal tremendous.

Gandhi was heir to some of the ideas of Rammohan Roy, an orthodox Brahmin born in 1772 who for a time served with the East India Company during the early nineteenth century. A brilliant intellect, he studied Islamic culture, as well as Buddhism in Tibet, and finally became immersed in western philosophy and religion. He was the first Indian reformer in whom the liberal ideas of nineteenth-century western thought were given mature expression. He founded his own movement, which sought a fusion of humanist principles with a purified and modified Hinduism. He also advocated western education as a source of new ideas but demanded respect for all that was true in the old Hindu culture. He was the source and inspiration of most of the reform movements which have since revolutionized Hindu society. He died and was buried in England in 1833.

Roy was the friend of Rabindranath Tagore's grandfather, who became his follower. Three generations of the Tagore family, therefore, became steeped in the ideas of India's great modern reformer and Rabindranath became the greatest propagator of them all. His grandfather was one of the most colourful figures of the early nineteenth century. He accommodated his mind to the new industrial civilization from the west and made a fortune in several industrial enterprises, including coal, sugar and indigo, as well as newspapers and banking. A Hindu and a Brahmin he nevertheless defied orthodoxy. His cultured sophistication, business acumen, energetic drive and rejection of conservative prejudices mirrored the ferment of ideas that arose from the meeting of two cultures, to be expressed yet more positively in the life and work of his descendants.

Rabindranath Tagore was a towering intellectual figure who dominated the cultural life of his country during the first decades of the twentieth century. He saw the problems of India in universal terms. Poet, philosopher, educator, dramatist, musician and novelist, he made a lasting impact on the intellectual attitudes of his times. He became internationally known as Asia's first Nobel prize winner in literature but he is perhaps most remembered for the experimental educational centre he founded at a country retreat called Santiniketan which had once belonged to his father. Here he created a world university on the traditional *asrama* principle of admitting a limited number of selected resident pupils. People from all over the world went there to learn, discuss and to pass on their own knowledge. Tagore travelled extensively and was at home in many countries. Wherever he went he preached humanism and internationalism. Like Gandhi, he advocated a reassessment of the place of the village in Indian culture and he called for an emphasis on programmes of community development, with the village as the cultural centre.

Many of Tagore's ideas have been criticized today for their vague idealism and sentimentality but that he was a man of immense creativity, with the gift of inspiring others, is beyond all question. He became a fresh force in the Indian theatre and his school was a centre for dramatic experiment. He staged and directed his own plays, for which he selected his actors after intensive tests. In the early days of the school he held his rehearsals before the whole community, using them as an educational exercise. One of his sons, describing these occasions, has written: 'It was not the individual artists so much as the effect produced by the spirit that moved the whole group of actors, which impressed the audience and convinced them of the sincerity of the effort and gave them artistic satisfaction.'[32]

Tagore's plays were social dramas embodying his mystical

ideas and though they were completely Indian in theme and background they were quite untraditional in their form. In the theatre as in his music Tagore sidestepped both Indian and western classical methods and sought to find a way between the two to bring about a new approach to Indian dramatic expression. He believed that music and dance were the natural means for the Indian mind to express itself and his plays made great use of both. (The more severe critics have dismissed some of his plays as being nothing more than settings for his songs.) He made many experiments with dance techniques and drew upon both the south Indian and northern Manipuri styles. A visit to Java made a deep impression on him and he applied some of the ideas resulting from his researches there to his productions. His desire was not to incorporate traditional techniques but only to take from them what he felt necessary to develop his own dance dramas. Rhythm, tune and metre were to him dramatic elements as important as the spoken words of a play and dance was as much a means of dramatic statement as any literary text. Tagore's dramatic compositions have been criticized for their lack of construction and loose forms, which some people have compared to a mixture of Bengali folk drama and western mediaeval mystery plays. Like other great teachers, Tagore's work in the theatre remains more important for the ideas and creative energy he inspired in others than for his own contributions. Through his experiments a whole generation learned to reassess tradition while at the same time honouring it. It is in his fresh approach to Indian culture as a whole that Tagore's reputation as a man of the theatre is most firmly sustained.

Satyajit Ray, the film director, one of Tagore's former pupils, has spoken feelingly of the insight into creative activity he gained at Santiniketan, where his artistic interests were first awakened in depth.[33] It is appropriate that Ray, who has brought a new integrity to Indian film-making, should have used some of his teacher's stories as material for his films. Tagore himself would have approved, for nothing has been more disruptive to his own aesthetic principles than the methods of the Indian film industry.

The rise of the film, and particularly the sound film during the 1930s, was a phenomenon that completely changed ideas of popular entertainment. Song and dance keyed to a mass audience of less discriminating standards, and the glamour of female stars with their catching 'hit songs', provided a new allure. While professionalism continued to lag far behind in the theatre, the cinema rapidly grew into an industry which soon offered far better remuneration to actors, musicians and writers than the theatre could ever hope to do. The theatre was quickly forgotten in the flood of what, in the jargon of the critics, were called 'mythologicals', 'historicals' and 'devotionals' on the screen. The names describe well enough the fare that the studios began churning out for an eager public. The never-failing formula has been irreverently described as consisting of 'a star, six songs and three dances'.[34] The jibe holds as good today as it did forty years ago.

Today the film reaches an audience of hundreds of millions in India. Tradesmen, artisans, civil servants and of course the English-speaking section of the population are regular cinema-goers. Women are still in a minority and in some areas special sections continue to be shut off in the cinemas for women although there is no such segregation in the large modern city cinemas. Films are widely shown in rural areas and a large section of the rural male public see films. By any box office standards the cinema has replaced the theatre in terms of public popularity, and what is more has begun to determine the nature of the entertainment that people now expect from the stage. In the Madras area, for example, one of the principal centres of the Indian film industry, there has been a long tradition of colloquial theatre performed by professional companies. Until the war they had a large following. The plays were historical and mythological, with social comedies for good measure. Plenty of music, together with an amount of melodramatic ranting, linked them with a tradition started by the Parsi Theatre in Bombay at the end of the nineteenth century. Songs and rapid scene changes were the basis of the recipe, and as many as one hundred and twenty changes of scene were advertised for one star pro-duction. This theatre continued largely unchanged from the nine-teenth century up until the second world war, with a standard repertoire adaptable for all kinds of melodramatic ringing of the changes. The individual actor or actress made the play, together with the quality of the music, while tremendous liberties were

taken with the scripts. Although actresses took part in its later
stage of development, at one time boys' troupes were common in
the Madras colloquial theatre and many of these boys who played
women's roles became early film stars.[35]

Today, theatre like this carries on against heavy odds and is
at the mercy of the cinema. Actors and actresses all migrate to
the film studios just as soon as they can and then return to the
stage for intervals to bask in the glory of their film reputations.
The troupes gain kudos through this inverse process so that
the popular vernacular stage has in a way become an extension
of film publicity. Popular theatre of this kind was in any case
always a form of escapism for audiences who had nowhere
else to escape to and in this respect it has never stood a chance
against the cinema. Indian films offer escapism on the grand
scale to all men at all times. The poverty and squalor in which
so many are condemned to lead their lives can be forgotten in
the screen's fantasy world of a mythical past.

Indian audiences have always been accustomed to stereotypes in their stage entertainments and the transition of this to
the cinema screen in no way impairs credibility and in many ways
enhances it. Though the films reflect modern images of traditional
life and ethics they are none the less traditional whatever the
flights of sensual fantasy added to aid communications. Indian
folk theatre in any case has always been concerned with presenting
religious mythology, historical tales and elemental comedy through
the medium of music, dance and song. The cinema has taken
over this function on a vast new basis and however bad some
films may be as cinematic art, as long as the songs and the dances
are there so long will the great Indian public continue to enjoy
them.

The appearance of Satayjit Ray on the Indian film scene in
the late 1950s opened up a new era in the cinema. His sensitive
but powerfully evoked studies of Bengali middle-class life were
far removed from the spectacular sensationalism of the popular
Indian productions. Ray was dominated by the belief that the
film provided its own criteria as a medium. When asked why
he chose Pather Panchali as his first film and what he thought
was its particular message for Indians, he answered: 'I don't
like morals or messages. This story says true things about India.
That was enough for me. It had the quality of truth...'[36]

This simple testament of faith and the work it has sanctioned raises the conjecture that Indian dramatic genius is more honoured in the creativity of a man like Ray than anything which has appeared so far on the colloquial stage. There the stumbling search of the last fifty years remains hindered by the fact that it has still been unable to identify truth.

Gandhi's emphasis on a village-oriented society lent its own colour to the cultural revolutionary fervour which was mounting in pre-independence years. In theatrical circles there was great attention paid to neglected forms of folk dance and music, though the sheer facts of group participation and political dedication to the cause were perhaps too easily accepted as justification for professional naivety and lack of skill. Folk theatre is one thing when it springs from the grass roots, it is quite another when it is transplanted to political soil.

There was a more spontaneous side to 'people's theatre'. In 1943–4 there was a great famine in Bengal and a group of amateur actors, musicians and dancers banded together as The People's Theatre Group and went on tour in aid of famine relief. Their performances were widely acclaimed and there was a sense of community engendered in the group itself which lent its own warmth and intensity to performances.

Another politically inspired group was the Indian People's Theatre Association in Bombay where a nucleus of dancers from the famous Uday Shankar's troupe joined it in 1944. His brother Ravi Shankar, the sitar player, now the idol of the western world, also joined the group for a period. It was apparently financed by the Indian Communist Party and the members lived and worked together in a pleasant old mansion outside Bombay. The atmosphere was highly creative and dominated by the spirit of national pride which was then approaching bursting point. Work in this period concentrated on the composition of a ballet called India Immortal, a kind of cultural and political history of India portrayed through the dance. It had a great success all over India and is a name that has nostalgic memories for many as being symptomatic of the leftist idealism of the period. Eventually the People's Theatre became increasingly subject to party directives, with more and more people joining whose prime motive was political rather than its creative potential, and Shankar and others broke with the group.[37]

The 1930s were a period when Indian dancing made its first major impact on the west and the foundations were laid for a long line of talented performers who have become known in America and Europe. Uday Shankar was one of the pioneers; after studying art in London and helping Anna Pavlova, the celebrated ballerina, produce two ballets with Indian themes, he decided to form his own troupe. The Uday Shankar Company of Hindu Musicians and Dancers set up headquarters in Paris in 1930 and embarked on a series of performances which were continued over several years in Europe and America. Uday Shankar, in the way that has become typical of most Indian dancers since, drew upon the many styles of Indian classical folk dance in his attempts to introduce western audiences to the elements of his art. He suffered a great deal of criticism in India from the purists, who argued that his art was neither traditional nor pure in any one technique. This kind of criticism is still levelled at all dancers who attempt any kind of synthesis today. Nevertheless, Uday Shankar was an innovator of his kind and his name today is firmly linked with a period which for the west at least opened up new areas of artistic knowledge.

In 1938 Uday Shankar returned to India and founded a cultural centre for performing arts in a mountain area of Almora. On about twenty acres of land, modern studios for dance, drama and music were constructed with built-in stages, workshops, costume rooms and rehearsal areas. Leading teachers of different schools of dance were brought in as well as musicians. The school was run as a combination of the traditional Indian *asrama* and a modern western workshop where the teachers and students lived and worked as a community. The centre had a short life, being compelled to close in 1944, presumably for financial reasons, and it was then that a number of dancers and musicians who had been at the school joined up with the People's Theatre group in Bombay.

The establishment of independence in 1947 marked a great dividing line between all that had gone and was to come in India. When the first rejoicings had subsided the new government turned to the task of promulgating a cultural policy worthy of a state which had suddenly become chief patron of the arts. The problems were immense and extraordinarily complex. The British had at long last gone but the revolutionary fervour which had impelled so much cultural activity in pre-independence years, particularly in the theatre, had yet to be directed into channels of new constructive purpose. Values had suddenly changed and there was almost a vacuum. The partition of the country in 1947 had resulted in bitter internal conflicts and the assassination of Gandhi in 1948 had been a traumatic experience for the nation. There was a sense of insecurity which was acutely reflected in theatrical circles where people were disorganized and felt a loss of identity. The increasing gulf between right- and left-wing factions introduced a different political note, bringing with it new personal alignments.

It would be fair to say that independence confronted the Indian theatre with an acute sense of its deficiencies at many levels. Though there was a burning ambition among many groups, and a deep sense of dedication to a national cause, the total means to move forward were lacking. In many areas the old classical dance and dance drama was still surrounded by the prejudices and ultra-conservatism of the past. A handful of brilliant artists who were internationally famous had given the traditional dance drama new status, but they were a minority whose hands were tied. Theatre in a western professional sense was practically nonexistent. Amateurism and political dedication between them were the ardent forces which had kept theatre alive. Personnel lacked technical knowledge and professional status and there was scant means for acquiring these. A majority of those who were involved in a new theatre were without systematic training and there were few who could regard theatre as their regular means of livelihood. Theatre buildings were notoriously lacking; a majority of towns had no theatre at all, school auditoriums and public halls which were used for every other kind of social function serving their inadequate purpose for such theatre as went on. In the large cities the cinemas offered the nearest pretensions to equipped auditoriums.

These were formidable obstacles and the amazing thing was the tremendous outburst of activity that went on in spite of them. There was a spirit of renaissance in the air. A body of talented and creative people were anxious to re-explore India's classical traditions in the terms of a new society and at the same time train and equip personnel in western technical knowledge. There was no lack of plans and ideas, it only remained to be seen what means were available to carry them out. The government's lead was awaited. In this questing period gigantic problems emerged to dog the government's own cultural plans. Some of them impinged heavily on the whole question of theatrical expansion and development. Undoubtedly the most pressing and vexed problem of all was the choice of a national language. In a country that recognized fourteen major languages plus English, which was the official medium of communication, the decision seemed bound to be controversial.

In 1949, the Indian Constitutional Assembly selected Hindi as their choice. This Sanskrit-derived language was written in a script used with slight variations for four of the other major Indian languages. The choice was based on the fact that it was a living language best representing the Indian cultural synthesis. The decision sparked off a violent controversy over Urdu, the language developed after the Muslim conquest of India. As Persian had been the court language of the conquerors, many new words were absorbed into the Hindi used in that period which became written in the Persian Arabic script. The literary form of Urdu became a highly poetic medium. There were thus two forms of Hindi, one which used Arabic script and drew upon a Persian vocabulary and the other which used a Sanskrit script and vocabulary. The spoken language of the ordinary people remained more or less the same in both cases whichever script was used. The general term Hindustani was used in the past to define both forms.

The bitter quarrel that ensued over national linguistic reforms was tinged with both religious and nationalistic prejudices. It was complicated by the fact that all educated Indians used English as their second language if they were not Hindi-speaking and for many of them reform meant the learning of a third alphabet. In the Madras area, for example, the centre of classical culture, Tamil, a highly refined and cultivated language, is used and a tremendous clamour arose there based on cultural pride and indignation at the national preference for 'debased' languages. The problem has so far proved insoluble and English, which was to have been ousted by 1956, remains the medium for all interstate and government communication. This is not fruitful ground from which a new national theatre can grow and the problem of a common official language has vast implications for the future. Though Hindi is used as a medium of instruction at the new national theatre training school in Delhi, the fact remains that every regional theatrical style is dependent for its most virile expression on the local language used, and this points up its own dilemma.

Language problems reinforced the inevitable debate as to the merits of the traditional past in preference to the westernised present. Rejection of foreign rule in India brought reaction in some quarters against every aspect of foreign cultural influence and a call for a return to the glories of the Hindu past. A more rational outlook tried to come to terms with the past in order to go forward and efforts were made to strike a balance. This was so in the world of theatre, which could afford to be – in fact had to be – eclectic. Even so, there was always a hard core who regarded Indian culture as Hindu culture, ignoring the fact that many elements, foreign as well as local, had created a synthesis.

Yet another difficulty faced by the government was in providing an adequate substitute for private patronage whose functions they had usurped. There is a difference between good intentions and the means to carry them out. Before independence the traditional performing arts had been heavily supported by independent princes, wealthy landowners and the bigger temples. Financial backing was often generous and sustained by deep local understanding and knowledge. These were advantages lacking to a government concerned with a more total sphere of effort and compelled to operate through an extensive network of bureaucracy and its accompanying red tape. There could not be the same direct relationship between patron, function and performer.

A notable example of the kind of palace patronage done away with by independence was the dance troupe maintained in the palace of the Maharaja of Baroda. The troupe entered palace service as part of the dowry of the maharaja's bride in 1879 and was under the control of a department of cultural affairs. Every dancer joining the troupe was entered in the palace records and all dancers were retired on pension. During their active career they were allowed four consecutive days of leave a month and three months leave during pregnancy. Two of the most accomplished dancers in the troupe came from a famous family of temple performers and between them drew a salary of 433 rupees a month plus a total of 272 rupees for their musicians. Performances were given twice a week before the maharaja as well as on special ceremonial occasions or during the visits of distinguished visitors. Any gifts to the dancers were divided among them by the palace superintendent, with a portion retained for the palace treasury. Two hours notice was the minimum required for a performance and the repertoire included the standard classical devotional pieces but with some more secular dances added for the benefit of visitors.[38]

Although these descriptions apply to only one of more than five hundred independent states which remained intact until 1947 they provide a glimpse of a style of court patronage which was quite common and which government could not hope to equal in terms of lavishness within its far greater area of activity. The state of Baroda was merged with Bombay in 1949 and the old palace control of the arts was abolished. One of the palace dancer's sons was appointed head of the new dance department opened in the state university of Baroda.

An early task of the new administration was the reform of Hindu temple customs. The temples were self-contained organic units and had formerly held a unique place in the social life of the community. In addition to being places of worship, they were often centres of education and recreation. Their importance as areas for dance and theatrical performances has already been described. By 1947 there was small doubt in the minds of the majority of forward-looking people that the temples stood in need of instant reform. The administration of temple property had become corrupt in many areas and historical structures were being allowed to fall into decay. Low-caste people were forbidden right of entry, and primitive and barbarous animal sacrifice was still carried on in some areas; the list of objections was a long one. None was more heatedly taken up than the functions of the devadasi, or temple dancer, who had been the subject of controversial debate for more than half a century.

Dedication of girls as temple dancers was first prohibited in the state of Mysore as early as 1909. In 1927 a bill was introduced in Madras, one of the most important centres of temple dancing, to do away with the ancient practices. Several attempts were made to push the bill through but it hung fire and it was not until 1947 that the measure became law. Not only dedication itself was forbidden but, 'Dancing by a woman with or without dedication in the precincts of a temple or other religious institution, or in any procession of a Hindu deity, idol or object of worship . . . or any festival or ceremony. . .'. All these were declared unlawful.

The ban has been strictly enforced on a national scale and society is now free of a system which undoubtedly condoned many abuses behind the screen of religion in a number of areas. At the same time a great tradition of artistry has disappeared with the rest, for despite its seamier side the devadasi system at its best preserved a continuity of expert teaching and perfectionism in performance. At this level the dance remained for many people an expression of a spiritual reality and a deep artistic experience, whose intensity is not matched by the increasing slickness of approach in present times.

The criticism heard from many knowledgeable dance lovers that the art today has lost refinement and that dancers are interested only in gains has some truth; there is probably more bad dancing going on in India now than at any time in its history. As one famous teacher remarked on going round her class, if she saw one ordinary student getting a single sequence right she felt it was worth it.[39] For the temple dance today,[40] that is to say its modern choreographic equivalent, has become a social pastime, the recreation of respectable young ladies who take up dancing as their western opposites once took to the piano. There has been a tremendous revival of the classical dance all over India at this level, and if nothing else schools and teachers are kept busy even though they are often in despair. Enthusiasm is inspired by a new pride in the old culture that has arisen since independence, but the dance has its own aura of contemporary glamour. The emergence of a new school of solo dancers who travel round the world giving international recitals has added fresh dimensions to the dance in youthful eyes. A more questionable factor is the film, which has been one of the great debasing agents of classical dance form and has created a taste for superficial showmanship which frequently becomes the standard of the great Indian public.

Nevertheless, there are many excellent classical dancers at work in India today, running their own schools in a number of cases, and there is a talented younger group of artists coming up. In spite of all the problems, the widespread interest and participation of ordinary society in the traditional arts is a happy omen and one which at least augurs well for their survival. To stay the course in Indian dance art, which requires at the very least five years minimum study, is not easy and great stamina and perseverance is demanded.

One important school engaged in educating a younger generation in the traditional dance and music culture is Kalakshetra, outside the city of Madras. It is headed by the famous dancer Rukmini Devi, who founded it in 1936. A high school and a teacher's training college are run in conjunction with the dance-music training centre. The students live and work in thatched cottages and buildings in a large compound which includes a permanent library, administration block and assembly hall-theatre. The school is fee-paying and administered on western education lines, although the teaching and philosophy of the school are entirely Indian. The aim is to train performers in traditional dance and music and to foster public understanding of these through the work of the school. The pupils live and work together as a community with their teachers following old precedents. Their diet is strictly vegetarian. The courses are stiff and thorough and students are only selected after a period of one year's probation. In the prospectus of the school the director has this to say of her aims:

There is a craze today to learn quickly. People think they can learn to dance in three months, that if they receive a diploma they are indeed great artists. In Kalakshetra we do give diplomas, but through right education we hope to make the young realize that this diploma is only the beginning, for the diploma on paper has to be put into practice in life and living. We do not believe in short courses, not because we think that people are not intelligent but because the body needs time. It shows a very poor regard for Art when parents feel that college education needs a minimum of four years to complete but art education needs only four months . . . . In modern days alas there is an idea that technique is unnecessary. Again it is a mistaken conception for without technique there is no mastery. Unless there is hard work the body will not do what the creative soul commands.

A school of a somewhat different kind but devoted to the same ideals is that of the dancer Mrinalini, a woman of high-born family and wealthy background and with a cosmopolitan education. The buildings are an example of modern taste and planning and were designed to the dancer's own specifications by a pupil of Corbusier. Situated at Ahmedabad in the grounds of her own residence, the school is a functional complex with both covered and open-air dance areas for use by the students in different stages of training. In spite of its contemporary flavour, the daily scene there is one that may be found going on all over India as it has been going on for countless generations. A male instructor sits upon the ground beating out the dance rhythms on a wooden block with a short stick while a woman vocalist chants out the verses to be interpreted by the dancers. Before them a file of young girls advance, retreat and sidestep in constant repetition of some passage whose dynamic footwork and gestural arabesques elude their mastery. Time after time they go over the details under the critical eye of the teacher. Mrinalini's school, besides its teaching functions, acts as a local cultural centre which sponsors a continuing round of experiment and dramatic activity. Although very different in character, both these schools in their separate ways pay homage to the artistic philosophy of Tagore. He was the intellectual father from whom they have derived their emphasis on communal participation, respect for tradition, and belief in experiment, tempered with an enquiring attitude towards new sources. It is these attitudes which characterize the better traditional training institutions in contemporary India.

Women like the two dancers described here are not without criticism, some of it quite vicious and ranging between degradation of their artistic talents because of their 'non-professional' background and their 'out-of-date' idealism. There are many who hold office in government cultural activities today by virtue of their political loyalties in the past rather than for any other qualification. It goes against the grain that anyone with wealth and independent standing can possibly do a job of work. The fact that private schools like these are often able to do a better job of teaching than certain government institutions just because of the nature of their support creates envy.

By the early 1950s the government began to organize its cultural activities on a more active scale although it was not until 1956 that a Ministry of Scientific Research and Cultural Affairs was created, to become responsible for three national academies established between 1953 and 1954, and respectively responsible for Dance, Drama and Music; Letters; and Art and Architecture.[41] The Academy of Dance, Drama and Music, the Sangeet Natak Akademi, is the central point of coordination, in theory at any rate, for regional activities, which are promulgated under local branches of the Akademi, each with their own officers. Research is promoted, festivals are sponsored and prizes are awarded for outstanding achievements in dance, drama and music. All these activities have in fact been sponsored with varying degrees of intensity, and there have been some outstanding achievements. The Akademi in Delhi also incorporates a National School of Dramatic Art in which production, directing, acting, and design are taught along contemporary western lines. The director, Alkazi, is a former graduate of the Royal Academy of Dramatic Art, London. During the early 1950s he made a name in Bombay as the forceful and imaginative director of a group named Theatre Unit which attracted enthusiastic audiences in that cosmopolitan city with its sophisticated production of western classical and *avant-garde* drama.

Alkazi was asked to take over the school in Delhi, which had begun disastrously after independence as a school of Asian theatre and foundered under the weight of incompetence and factional jealousies which frequently dog such ventures in India. Through energy and talent the new director has in the face of many odds built the school into a training centre capable of turning out students with a sound basis of modern western theatre disciplines. The school has an impressive list of graduation productions and exercises to its credit.

Again there has been much overt criticism. The director is said to be too 'western', not 'really Indian', while regional critics grouse about the school being Delhi-oriented and out of touch with provincial needs. Criticism among Indian theatrical circles is never-ending, rarely constructive and always one-sided. Satisfaction of this criticism for everyone is under the circumstances well-nigh impossible. In view of the many problems, including the major ones of language and insufficient financial support, the National School has at least provided a working base from which a great deal may be accomplished.

One trend in the 1950s was the expansion of the Indian ballet movement which put new wine into old bottles and inspired a number of dance dramas, based on fresh material and approaches, although still closely related to classical techniques. One of the more successful groups was the Bombay Little Ballet Troupe under the direction of Shanti Bardhan, who created a stir with his new dance version of the *Ramayana*. The ballet movement proliferated, though not always with such happy results, and the opening of an Institute of Choreography under the sponsorship of the National Academy was a measure designed to combat deficiencies. The institute is under the direction of Maya Rao, a leading *kathak* dancer who studied at the State Institute of Theatre in Moscow for two years under Indian government auspices. Like many government-sponsored ideas it is a good one inadequately supported.

To detail all the experiments and successes of the new Indian theatre movement and the personalities involved would be impossible in the space available here. Those names that have been singled out have been chosen because of their importance to theatre education and appreciation and not with any intention of extolling them as the only important figures. The story of contemporary Indian theatre in post-independence years has been one of multi-purpose. It boasts a tremendous range of activities and talents. Even so it would not be too great a generalization to say that Calcutta and Bombay were the two cities where a theatre of quality became most firmly established; not surprisingly, because both had always been centres of dramatic activity from the first days of the British and had their own proud vernacular traditions.

Government sponsorship of cultural activities is always a vulnerable target and the Indian government has inherited problems of unenviable magnitude in trying to keep all the theatre people happy and satisfying their needs. At the same time nothing can hide the fact that the government in India operates through a hidebound bureaucracy of the most formidable proportions. The provincial grumbles against Delhi are not without justification in the area of cultural activities and always they return to the same points. There is a lack of coordination from the capital; there is of course a lack of funds; all appointees in provincial cultural administration are politically chosen; but the complaint voiced more than any other is the professional ignorance of the people to whom cultural responsibilities are delegated. Certainly one of the more tiresome aspects of the Delhi scene are the officials with their files and their cups of tea. More British than the British ever were, their apathy . . . and obstructionism have done more to strangle the enthusiasm and the hopes of people actively engaged in theatre throughout the country than any other factor. The general position in the Indian theatre today differs in one respect from the past, that while amateurism is still a formidable factor, dedication to a cause has been corroded by disillusionment. The adequate means to move forward are as lacking as ever.

A much criticized example of the fruitlessness of the official mind was in the spending of large sums of money in the early 1960s to provide each provincial capital with a theatre on the occasion of the Tagore centenary. Nothing could have been a worthier and a more desperately required provision. In the event it proved a classic case of bureaucratic bungling. The theatres were designed and built by those who had no vestige of knowledge concerning technical requirements. They were given vast proscenium arches for which the sight lines of the auditorium were inadequate and the crop of attendant deficiencies was such as to make anyone engaged in theatre weep with chagrin for the lost opportunities. But that was not the worst. The hiring of these nationally owned theatres was conducted through a time-wasting system of forms and requests which defeated any possibilities of advance programme schedules, while rehearsal and performance fees were unrealistically high and quite beyond the means of either amateurs or professionals in a country where theatre has never been a commercial proposition. The result is that the buildings lie empty and unused as theatres. What could have been rallying points for a new repertory organization remain permanent

monuments to the fact that modern theatre has been denied
its true place in the community, except in a city like Calcutta,
where performances are carried on with the same old lack of
suitable premises.

The amateurishness of their modern theatre has long been held
up by the Indians as a reason for a lack of interest in it, either
as an entertainment or a business. As the latter certainly no one
in his senses could regard it as a money-making proposition and
as an entertainment it does not have the support of ordinary
society, who prefer the cinema. The intellectual elite of the great
cities are bored by the vernacular and would prefer to see plays
in English. Because of the limited nature of its appeal this kind of
theatre is bound to be dilettante, and it flourishes only where
English remains the living means of communication between
regional, linguistic and religious groups. They are the 'brown
foreigners' who talk in terms of international values. It goes without saying that they most often have the means to indulge their
inclinations without too pressing a thought for mundane matters
like the price of rice.

The young people in this group eagerly copy the latest trends
in western drama. If Beckett is the fashion in Europe then he
becomes the last word in Delhi and Bombay. Their belief is
that modern western drama, properly staged by Indians, will
provide their people with a new theatrical experience. There is
nothing wrong in being open to western influence and history
has shown that a study of the western theatre is important for the
modern Indian to understand his own, but the influence of these
trend-setters is questionable. At the other extreme are those who
stage classical Sanskrit plays in an attempt to give a dead drama
new life. As for the Indian language theatre itself, there is here a
solid middle-of-the-road style, with acting methods influenced
by western film stars and the psychological-naturalistic theories
of Stanislavsky combined. The western three-act play form is
accepted by most regional language playwrights, and the proscenium stage and the box set are firmly established elements of
stage practice. Indian family life and the individual's conflict
with society palely reflect Ibsen and others in plot construction.

Most modern regional language theatre is staged seasonally
and occasionally, as a part-time activity, with little organization
and even less money behind it. It is dependent entirely on

individuals with a minimum of resources, the old-time professional troupes of the earlier years of the century having been ousted by the competition of the cinema. Educated amateurs have replaced them and they are usually prudent enough to experiment with nothing stronger than Broadway successes or West End hits. Murder mysteries have been among the most popular productions. *Dial M for Murder* ran for hundreds of performances in Bombay and constituted something of a record in the early 1960s, being produced both in the Gujerati and Marathi languages.

The ordinary middle-class public who it might be thought would have supported a theatre has too little money to spend and too many domestic responsibilities to indulge in such luxuries. If they can afford a theatre ticket they often cannot afford transport costs and time. Theatres, or what passes for them, are often far from the centre of things, while performances are spasmodic; they are usually confined to weekends and are not repeated. In contrast to this, films have long runs of several weeks or even months in different districts. It is fairly easy to choose the most convenient place and time, where theatre offers no such advantages. Theatre loses a large potential audience as a result and ticket sales rarely exceed a few hundred rupees. The profit is negligible which means that there is little possibility of further productions.

The struggle to establish a permanent modern theatre has gone on for many decades. It succeeded more in Bombay and Calcutta than in other linguistic areas where theatre has never been similarly accepted as a tradition by a sizeable body of patrons over a long period. Even in these two cities theatre has been dogged by the perennial problems, lack of adequate working capital and the inability to provide full-time artistic employment for its personnel. The causes of the problems run deep and government control and sponsorship have been unable to come to grips with them. Bureaucratic bungling such as the case of the Tagore theatres has merely widened the rift between officialdom and the theatre.

Disillusion stemming from this confusion has given added strength to a highly active leftist theatre movement which has a complete disregard for tradition or even the revolutionary ideals of pre-independence years. Predictably, one of the most

prominent of these groups is active in Calcutta, with its headquarters at the Minerva Theatre where it operates under the
title of *The Little Theatre Group*. The Minerva Theatre has
a history of its own for it stands on a site once occupied by
the Great National Theatre, one of the most controversial
vernacular theatre groups of the 1870s. Its members drew the
ire of the British authorities and provoked legislation against
the theatre which is still in force today through a cumbersome
censorship system. The Minerva was rebuilt after a fire in
1922 and is now a small three-tiered auditorium seating six
hundred. Its hopelessly dilapidated interior is a grimy reminder
of a vanished age of colonial occasions and drawing-room
comedies.

The Little Theatre Group is headed by Uptal Dutt, whom
everybody acknowledges as an excellent actor however much
they detest his political opinions. He writes his own virulently
propagandist scripts, revealing in them that he stands far to the
left. He began his professional career as a member of a touring
Shakespearian troupe of the kind so subtly portrayed in the
film *Shakespeare Wallah*, which had a considerable success in
the late 1960s and in which Dutt himself played a role. He is
an admirer of Shakespeare and Brecht, although one Calcutta
critic tartly remarked that Dutt seemed concerned to show
that Shakespeare not only had a social conscience but was an
early party member as well.

Dutt has continued to draw people in with his plays, which
deal with every possible controversial issue, ranging from the war
in Vietnam and anti-Americanism to a disaster in a Bengali coal
mine. Melodramatic, heavily propagandist, and drawing extensively on folk song and music, Dutt's plays exploit all the fashionable techniques of political theatre to involve the emotions of the
crowd. In this they brilliantly succeed. His group is only one of
hundreds of a less permanent nature who perform regularly in
Calcutta with no less ardent support.

Calcutta is today a city where thousands live in abject
poverty and frightful squalor and where people die daily on the
streets. The fact that theatre of this kind is supported under
such desperate conditions is testimony to its catalystic power,
even though this is in part derived from preaching to the
converted. The Little Theatre Group of Calcutta is a sharp

reminder that India today is a secular state, where the religious attitudes of the past are not in themselves enough to change contemporary institutions. Until social and economic transformation becomes a reality for the community at large, so long does the new theatre seem destined to remain the beggar of the arts, justified only as propaganda.

3

THE ISLAMIC WORLD

The Islamic world is a convenient way of describing peoples of many different races and languages[1] who all, however, follow the religion founded by the Arab Prophet Muhammad[2] at Mecca in the seventh century AD. The word Islam comes from a root literally implying submission to the divine will and so has become a comprehensive description for the Arab religion and the culture it has created. Islam soon spread beyond its country of origin and eventually numbered more non-Arabs than Arabs among its followers, but the essence of its philosophy was drawn from principles evolved in seventh-century Arabia and Arabic has remained its sacred language, Mecca its holy city. Although proclaimed for all men, the message of Muhammad was specifically directed towards the Arabs and it is through the fundamental nature of their social customs that its effect on the theatre must first be followed.

As a religious system Islam claimed an authoritarian jurisdiction over every area of human behaviour, and by stressing ritual, abstinence and conformity it offered a psychological guarantee for all who submitted unconditionally to its principles of faith. In the event, it never succeeded in imposing uniform submission in the several countries which came under its spiritual domination and a serious sectarian quarrel early divided the Arabs themselves.[3] Political protection of the Islamic faith in all its territories eventually passed to the Turks who built a powerful military and commercial empire in its name. These are the principal historical factors underlying the discussions on theatre which follow.

The great achievements of Arab culture have been in the fields of architecture, poetry and the invention of an advanced musical system, all in their maturity representative of an urban civilization. At a first glance this suggests favourable conditions for the growth of a sophisticated dramatic art, but instead the religious proscription of secular art and the social taboos this invoked effectively stifled any such possibility. When compared with Indian and Chinese civilization, alongside which Islam takes its place as one of the seminal influences of Asian society, the Arab contribution to theatre has been meagre indeed. Although Arab scholars enriched Islamic culture through their translations of the most important Greek writings in the fields of science and the humanities, they significantly ignored the drama. This rejection of theatre was a glaring omission that can best be understood by considering the precedents for Arab social behaviour.

The geographical and climatic conditions of Arabia forced its people very early on to live to a fixed cycle of pastoral migration. Until Muhammad's day the spirit of Arab culture was epitomized in the tribal customs of nomads, who pitched their tents as seasonal pastures demanded and were fiercely jealous of their free existence. They were constantly ready to fight for their interests and blood feuds became a feature of their tribal organization. Scattered centres of caravan trade with their more static populations were regarded as legitimate prey for their attacks. Mecca, birthplace of the Prophet, but a symbol of Arab unity long before his time, alone remained immune because of its sacred shrine used for tribal cult worship.

The desert Arabs looked upon themselves as the aristocrats of their race, holding the town dweller in contempt, an attitude which created and perpetuated the romantic legend of Arab culture. Yet it was the desert nomads who first transmitted their social and ethical values to town living. Early Islamic society was both a desert and an urban creation. The desert nomads spread the Islamic faith through their conquest of towns, carrying their militant religion far beyond the confines of Mecca. In so doing they became part of the developing urban culture. A polarity developed by which the townsman and the nomad both came to despise rural values and the peasant who maintained them, a viewpoint which has persisted until recent times.

Today, although Arab society can still be broadly classified in this way there is a changed situation. The desert nomads are a rapidly declining community, caught up in the process of modern communications and technology. Although in many areas the tribe remains the unifying social unit their old functions and powers are no longer valid under the new state administrations.

The old desert communities were fond of song, recitative and dance as the most spontaneous way of celebrating tribal occasions in their impermanent way of life. They developed great skill and aptitude for balladry and poetic recitative, which became the basis for later literary developments while satisfying a racial passion for the play of words. Tribesmen who spent their days in the saddle, exposed to the rigours of the desert and constantly alerted for battle, understandably became adept at reciting heroic exploits in the awesome grandeur of their environment. Tribal morale was quickly stimulated by their stirring effect. A talent for poetic expression became so prized in their nomadic existence that the perfect man was held to be one who combined proficiency in eloquence, archery and horsemanship with the first-named praised as a supreme talent.[4]

Women, we are told, were well regarded in pre-Islamic society[5] and were not degraded in status as they later became. This has been true to some extent of Arab tribespeople in more recent days for they have always been less restricted than townswomen because of their hard life and its privations. These have necessitated greater liberty within the tribal community, where women have had their distinctive rights and responsibilities. It was the women in the old days who exhorted their men to go out and fight for a triumphal return. They rallied the tribe by letting down their hair, and with faces uncovered urged on their warriors with oratorical fervour from some vantage point. Arab women were often bards who sang of tribal achievements or mourned the heroic dead. Elegy became a special accomplishment and some of their dirges were of such lyrical splendour that women poets have been given an honoured place in the annals of Arabic literature.

The urge for poetic recitation was greatly strengthened by the fact that desert dwellers learned to rely on prodigious feats of memory as the one sure way in which their tribal histories could be handed down from generation to generation. An eleventh-century historian recorded a long-standing admiration

for tribal narrators in these lines: 'When there appeared a poet
in a family of Arabs the other tribes round about would gather
together to that family and wish them joy of their good luck.'[6]
By the time of Muhammad, Arab fondness for verbal display
had encouraged a method by which poets employed their
personal narrators. It was the duty of these men to memorize
everything for public narration and to ensure its transmission
for posterity in days when writing had not yet become a widespread practice. In time they developed such powers that they were
accepted as independent performers as well as living encyclo-
paedias of literary style and poetic usage. They were even known
to embellish the work of others so skilfully that their forgeries
were accepted.

The important social occasions of pre-Islamic times were
the great intertribal fairs which became a meeting place
for the desert communities. Among their other attractions they
provided forums for poetic displays in which rival talents were
matched in public. Then reputations were upheld before the
admiring crowds by the professional reciters and approval of
their skill was spread far and wide. It was remarked about
the most famous of these fairs, which lasted for twenty days,
that 'What Ukáz said today all Arabia would repeat tomorrow.'[7]
With such public encouragement of talent and every man
striving to outdo his neighbour in declamatory skill, recitative
must inevitably have encouraged a feeling for dramatization.
The art of the shadow puppeteer and storyteller, both of which
at a later stage became no less ardent if more plebeian expressions
of Arab eloquence, conceivably had ancestral links with the performers at the ancient tribal fairs.

Considering the racial talent for verse and rhetoric it seems
appropriate that Muhammad, the founder of Islam, should
convince the Arabs that his divine visions were genuine through
a series of inspired and poetic utterances. So great was the
power of words in his case that within less than twenty years
he had welded his countrymen into a new religious community
whose impact on human affairs was to become worldwide.

The sacred book of Islam, the Koran, remains the supreme
testament to Muhammad's oratory and the high point of an oral
tradition which has been the compelling force of Arab culture.
It is reputedly composed from the sayings of the Prophet as

they were recorded by his followers but they were only put into written form after his death. Essentially devised to be read aloud, the Koran cunningly embodies stylistic prose and inter-spersed rhyme in a manner whose utter perfection to Arab ears seems befitting to the word of God. It is both a religious testament and a didactic treatise which lays down the rules of society and stipulates the correct personal conduct for the true believer. Although it abounds in contradictions and in-consistencies of reasoning, as an example of classical literary style it has remained unsurpassed and honoured for the beauty of its form.[8]

With Koranic style accepted as the height of linguistic purity, beyond which no man could go, poetry, the mark of the cultivated person, developed particular limitations. Excellence was seen to lie in emulating what had already been achieved through the strict rules of rhymes and metre governing classical composition. Rhymed prose was second only to poetry in the respect it commanded and was used for biographical and historical recording, which again never attempted to exceed the boundaries of hallowed stylistic tradition. Language moulded by strictly formulated canons became an end in itself and for the Arab an elegantly constructed verse or proverb was more effective than logic. No statement of fact could ever make the same impact as a passage from the Koran.

If the Koran epitomized Islamic veneration for the power and quality of classical language this was in striking contrast to the hostility it encouraged against any possibility of dramatic usage. Where total submission to the will of God is demanded the idea of conflict, which was so central to Greek drama, perforce remains stillborn. The dogma of Muhammad's creed and its later interpretations by his followers smothered any Arab potential for dramatic composition. It is true that the storyteller and puppeteer emerged as theatrical offshoots of the Arab talent for eloquence, but in Islam they never became the precursors of a high sophistication on the stage as they did in some Asian countries. They were limited to a prescribed range of entertainment in which mimicry was reinforced by the tricks of a language highly conducive to stylistic nimbleness. Imitative representation never went beyond the oddities of human speech and appearance, or sexual aberrations. Reptetition and descriptive detail, the well-tried aids of narrative juggling, were certainly carried to a high point but Islamic social prejudice remained the final bar to any deeper exploration of the psychology of theatre.

The theologians who followed Muhammad were not only militantly protective of language as a sacred medium, they were also violently critical of any artistic representation of the human form, holding this to be a blasphemy against the divine creator. Theatrical activity was doubly discredited on this account because of its mockery of God and potential for deriding his spokesmen. The elders of society both scorned and feared the professional entertainer because where the written word is the supreme agent of religious conformity the actor is suspect as a subversive; he distorts the sacred tenets and thereby unsettles the people.

There is often a margin between theory and practice in religious aspiration and the fact that the storyteller and puppeteer flourished at all suggest the triumph of irrepressible human nature. Whatever the loophole, nevertheless prejudice and religious prudery overruled every other consideration. Theatre was deprived of growth in a manner unparalleled elsewhere.

The nearest approach to an active theatre in Islam came from the Turks, who were not related to the Arabs at all, although even they never reached the level of high drama because of the restraints imposed by Islamic dogma. Their contribution to the history of popular entertainment has nevertheless been considerable. In the twentieth century the Turks have been in the forefront of all Islamic communities in creating a new national theatre.

The earliest history of the Turks is shrouded by many uncertainties, but it seems that they were nomads and fighters who sprang from central Asian tribal groups having a common language. They became frontier converts to Islam with its call to wage war against the infidel and remained unswerving in their religious allegiance. Among all the shifts in political power which occurred in Islamic history none was more spectacular or far-reaching in effect than the Turkish capture of Constantinople[9] in the fifteenth century. As the climax to years of territorial conquest and religious brigandry the event stunned all Europe and changed the balance of power. The fall of the capital of

Christendom was the first stage in the creation of a great empire dedicated to Islamic unity and controlled by an intricate and autocratic social system which, in principle at least, endured until the first world war.

As the new capital of Islam, Constantinople became the meeting point of cultural influences, among which the Turks' own Asian ancestry, Greek-Roman antecedents, and Renaissance Europe added something to the quality of living. The conquering sultan of Constantinople, which now became Istanbul, threw open the city for repopulation, saying that whoever wished should be allowed to enter and become the owner of houses, vineyards and gardens.[10] They were given to all who came and Istanbul expanded as a thriving centre. Many Greeks returned after the conquest and formed a new community, the Jews took refuge after persecution in the different capitals of Europe, and both Jews and Christians were allowed freedom of worship. European quarters sprang up, with merchants from many countries doing business there. The cosmopolitan nature of the Turkish capital's populace was later reflected in the art of the storyteller who gathered rich material for mimicry in the varied types who thronged the city streets.

Perhaps because of this diversity of cultural influence the Turks indulged an unusual liking for pageants and spectacles which were decidedly theatrical in impulse and at odds with the Islamic aversion to secular display of any kind. A European traveller who visited Turkey in the late sixteenth century recorded with some detail his impressions of the pomp and display which marked special celebrations in the sultan's palace where, in the words of this visitor,[11] 'Sundrie sortes of Playes and Pastimes were showne, it was marvailous great and large, wherein was created great Theaters and Scaffolds of woode, distinguished and separated into diverse parts, as if they were chambers appointed for everie Ambassador, places as well to banquet in, as also for to behold the Plaies and Pastimes'. Describing the entry of the performers the traveller went on to say: 'They were presentlie followed by Players, more in number than flies or gnattes, one sort masking wise, others having myters, like Popes, and crowns, bald and half shaven, theyr mouthes wide open, as if they would have swallowed up as many as looked upon them: some of them having theyr

D

garmentes all to broken, and as if they were tieade over theyr eares: others some halfe naked, and halfe covered, and others some altogether naked and shameless without measure. . . .' Certainly the scene presented here seems a far cry from Islamic prudery and decorum and is one which hints at the duality of things.

This duality becomes more obvious in the language and literature of the Turks. When they were converted to Islam they adopted the Arabic script although it was ill-suited to convey the sounds of their own language, whose structure was quite different from that of Arabic. Moreover, it was difficult if not impossible for the ordinary Turk to read Arabic script, which is complex and ambiguous, so that even educated people could readily make spelling mistakes. The result was two separate languages, that of the Turkish governing class, which was written rather than spoken, and that of the ordinary people, which was spoken but unwritten.

After their conversion to Islam the Turks came under the strong influence of Persian culture generally and literature in particular. Persian poetry, which had absorbed a great deal from Arab sources, attracted Turkish writers, who imitated its style and metre. Flowery simile, rhetorical embellishment, symbolic allusion and a mystic homosexual ideal were qualities which could be understood only by the initiated, thus creating a gulf in communication between the intelligentsia and the ordinary people. From the start of their rise as an Islamic power the Turks were faced with linguistic complications. Arabic remained the medium for religious prose for a long time, while Persian was used for more worldly themes with Turkish gradually replacing it, but it was not until the fifteenth century that Turkish was used at court as a literary medium. By that time Persian exoticism and Arabic scholarship had moulded usage to such an extent that they continued to dominate Turkish ideas until the nineteenth century.[12]

The Turkish people were heirs to a rich folk tradition and at first there were two tendencies in their literary development, the classical style, imitating Persian literature in form and content, and a more popular indigenous form, derived from oral folk literature. This last trend became completely submerged beneath the preponderant Arabic-Persian styles favoured by the governing class. Although they were conscious of their racial individuality and made some distinction between their adopted culture and their ethnic origins, as empire builders and followers of Islam they created a discriminatory class structure, whose learned and refined members called themselves Osmanli and not Turks. This last name was reserved only for illiterate peasants and in usage implied rough and crude fellows who spoke only the vernacular.

The Turkish folk heritage was rooted in a long tradition of storytelling, ballad singing, recitative, mimicry, fantastic tales and improvised poems sung to instrumental accompaniment. These simple and direct but often powerful methods of communication reached deep within the consciousness of the ordinary people and provided the impetus for methods of stage expression which even Islam could not subdue. Although the Turks never achieved a drama through the marriage of literary intellect with popular tradition, any more than the Arabs did, they at least supported a theatre of laughter whose early portrayal of ordinary society and improvised comedy was reminiscent of the Italian *Commedia*. It was known as Orta Oyuna. The origins of this form of theatre are obscure and the derivation of the term has been debated by scholars but there is evidence that the *Commedia*-like performance was known in the late seventeenth century, or at any rate a prototype was known from which the later style developed.[13] There is a strong similarity between this creation of human actors and the shadow theatre of Karagoz, both in terms of general characterization and stage business. Probably there have been mutual borrowings and influences, though which preceded which is not clear.

Performances were staged in the open with a minimum of props and the audience seated round the performing area. The cast of characters was headed by two clowns, Pisekar and Kavuklu, whose slapstick comedy, salty wit and sly impersonations enlivened simple comedies of manners. The stock plots were divided into episodes on which the changes were rung according to the actors' whims and audience reaction. There was a good deal of improvization and adaptation.

A full Orta Oyuna company contained about twenty-five to thirty members including the musicians and dancers. They were

headed by a senior actor from whom the troupe usually took
its name. During the 1890s there were about five hundred
active performers divided among ten different companies. In
later times these began to perform in roofed theatres with
raised stages. During the winter they played at taverns and
occasionally in the mansions of the wealthy. Administration of
the troupes was flexible but the word of their leaders was law
for the actors. Earnings were always meagre being dependent on
voluntary contributions. The money was shared out according
to the actor's rank. Pisekar commanded three shares, Kavuklu
two and a half, the minor actors getting as little as half a share.

The troupe leader always played Pisekar and it was he who
first entered the stage, which he seldom left. He introduced
the plays and addressed the audience among whom he sat
when awaiting his turn. He used flowery language and had
a penchant for poetic recitation. He wore a yellow gown, red
baggy trousers and a nightcap of many colours. He carried a
cudgel in one hand with which to strike the heads of those
who argued with him. His companion Kavuklu usually came
on accompanied by a hunchback dressed like himself and ready
to start an argument with Pisekar. The hunchback has been
a stock figure of fun in several forms of Asian entertainment.

Kavuklu's costume was a travesty of old style Turkish dress.
His form was enveloped in a long flowing red gown and a wadded
coat reaching to below his knees, as well as baggy red trousers.
On his head he wore a monstrous turban. Costume in Islam
had a deeply symbolic significance and as the turban was a sign
of Islamic orthodoxy, worn by high-ranking religious dignitaries,
its use by this pair of stage clowns speaks for itself. Their non-
sensical repartee, play on language and stereotyped impersonations parodying the human scene around them were in the
great tradition of thumbing the nose at respectable society and
all its taboos.

The Turks, as masters of the shadow show, also gave the
Islamic world Karagoz,[14] who is assured his place as one of
the great buffoons of theatre history, the central character of
an entertainment that is now obsolete in Turkey. His origins
have been the subject of much speculation. The Egyptians seem
to have adopted Karagoz although they had their own shadow
show with its separate history.[15] They also had an acutely

developed sense of mimicry, which had it been encouraged to progress beyond the scope of the puppeteer and the street entertainer might even have fertilized the seeds of a theatre with Molière-like possibilities. As this would have presumed the reconciliation of classical language with popular usage the obstacles against such an interesting possibility were overwhelming.

For the western world the use of the word theatre implies the presence of an audience and a language understood by everybody because it is accommodated to them, an impossible conception for the Arab world, where language was a privileged mystery revealed only through the chosen few. For them language was associated with a divine source and any utilitarian diversion of its function would have been unthinkable. Language in this case was a sign through which society accepted its fate. Faith, prayer, almsgiving, fasting and pilgrimage were the five pillars of the Islamic religion as decreed by Muhammad. He seems to have tried to make a distinction between the old excesses of Arab life and a more reasonable continuance of practices. His austere principles did not exclude recognition of human fallibility, but like many spiritual attempts to regiment mankind they were vulnerable to the charge of social inconsistency.

In nothing does this seem more so to the western mind than the Islamic attitude to women. The Koran bluntly states that God made men superior to women who must be treated accordingly.[16] The whole pattern of Islamic social behaviour has been based on this principle. The subjugation of women and their active exclusion from the world of men was clearly an insuperable obstacle to theatrical development. Although in other Asian societies women have been socially set apart, with considerable implications for stage practice (the use of the female impersonator here readily springs to mind), Islamic discrimination against women was carried to such a classic extreme that the possibilities for theatrical compromise of any kind did not arise. Even women's costume became a cumbersome accessory of physical segregation, both in and out of doors, and a bar to any kind of physical expression and certainly stage performance.

There is nothing at all in the Koran about women wearing the veil, yet it has been mandatory for all Islamic women. It seems to have become an arbitary regulation enforced by the theologians. The custom possibly grew out of the purely practical habit of swathing the face against dust and sandstorms, which both men and women who spend their lives in the desert are in the habit of doing. Even so, wearing the veil became with all the other accessories of women's costume the effective symbol of virginity and marital fidelity.

The style has varied in different areas from being a thin muslin scarf drawn across the lower features of the face to a kind of mask with eye holes. In all cases the veil has been supplemented by voluminous and enveloping garments whose primary purpose has been to conceal the bodily form.

Wearing the veil was less rigidly enforced among some of the desert dwellers and peasant communities, where the women were expected to labour in the fields and at other tasks. In these cases the veil might only be worn when they went into the village or town or on a formal occasion. Turkey was the first country to abolish the veil when she became a republic, and Java the one country where Islam became dominant and women never accepted the veil.

In general, the veil has been related to sedentary living and the arch-conservatism of Islamic town life. Nevertheless, few women escaped and a majority spent their lives concealed in this way. Female costume became the visible affirmation of the obsessive concern for privacy which was again evident in the architectural design of Arab cities. There the residential quarters, with their blank walls, tortuous streets and segregated quarters were intended to preserve a jealous defence of family privacy and enforce the personal and racial segregation which was demanded by religious dogma. Low buildings were characteristic and conformed to the belief that height symbolized a pride in display to which only the house of God was entitled. Durability of dwellings intended for man did not matter and the use of perishable materials was a sign of the negative regard for human existence. A standard domestic layout consisted of a house with quarters centred round a courtyard, facilitating family segregation by an extension in size and number of courtyards according to the status of the family. Concealment within concealment was the operating principle.[17]

The mosque was the centre of the town and village, the one significant concession to architectural decoration, and a place for public gathering. Even here women were ostracized. Urban life in Islam had a fragmented and secretive character. There was no recognition of a unified collectivity nor means for its expression. The factors which make theatre a sociable art were lacking. Any form of entertainment was necessarily inhibited when communal prayer was the only acceptable form of public gathering and the dignity of man's existence was upheld through iron concern with sexual distinction. Under such restraints theatre could only be a vagrant art at best and in the traditional Arab world it was often scarcely that. It sought its chief outlet in the shadow play and the storyteller who at times attracted the intellectual by his skilful literary gymnastics, and entertained the court, but in the main these pastimes were directed at the commoner for whom bawdy tales and knock-about comedy were perpetual reasons for laughter. Music provided the greatest stimulation to the Arab intellect, replacing the need left by the lack of theatre to some extent and ranking with poetry, to which it was closely linked as an art. Although music was reportedly condemned by the Prophet his prohibitions were largely wasted, for music remained intimately a part of Arab life. Religious feeling and profane emotion have both been given expression through its practice. Music satisfied a racial sense of mysticism as well as a taste for mathematical inventiveness fulfilled in the permutations and combinations of rhythmic patterns and modal systems which characterize classical composition.[18]

Music was also held to have therapeutic powers, not merely because of its soothing effect on the mind but because mathematics, astronomy and music were interrelated through an elaborate metaphysical concept whose proportionate combinations indicated ways to combat sickness. Music was also equated with Arab philosophical reasoning based on a cosmic system designated as The Fourfold Things. The four strings of the Arab lute, for example, were related to the elements air, fire, earth and water, as well as humours, planets, constellations and perfumes. In the Thousand and One Nights Entertainment a Baghdad porter quotes the lines:

> Seeest not we want for joy four things all told
> The harp and lute, the flute and flageolet

And be they compared with scents fourfold
Rose, myrtle, anemone and violet
Nor please all eight and four thou wouldst withold
Good wine and youth and gold and pretty pet.

A somewhat hedonistic invocation of this power of numbers, but it was the relationship of music to this fourfold scheme which provoked the invention of an intricate musical system in which every mode acquired its own emotional and psychological function. The names given to the modes served as a kind of sensory guide to the initiated.

Whether it provided a healing aid for the physician, a revelation for the mystic, or was simply the accompaniment of worldly pleasure, Arab music was highly emotional; through its direct impact on human consciousness it provided a substitute for dramatic experience.

Music and oral literature were closely related in Islam, and recitative with instrumental accompaniment was a developed art whose lyric themes were based on life, death and love, as well as on the exploits of heroes and saints, with animal fables and riddles for lighter measure. Two important practitioners were the male minstrel, an accomplished singer and instrumentalist, patronized by high society, and the woman singer, a characteristic figure of Arab social life, without whom both public and private occasions were not complete. She was often a freed slave, an ex-singing girl who had reached maturer years. Lastly there was the singing girl herself, perhaps one of the most legendary figures of Arab society where she had been an established institution from very early times.

Long before the Prophet's day it was the custom for men of position to keep slave girls of non-Arabic extraction as personal musicians who catered for their pleasure.[19] It is not clear how far the Prophet condoned the practice; he certainly accepted slavery and the Koran contains no direct censure. He is even credited with the saying, 'Allah listens more intently to a man with a beautiful voice than does a master of a singing girl to her singing',[20] suggesting tolerant awareness at least. Sterner commentators attributed harsher feelings to him and relegated the singing girl and her music to the area of forbidden pleasures. Music was banned for a period of twelve years after the

Prophet's death, although in fact the ban probably operated more in theory than in practice. The Arab sense of forbearance remained adroit in adjusting moral reasoning to the logic of human needs.

The accession to power of the Baghdad caliphs[21] in the eighth century encouraged the rise of a powerful merchant middle class under a social autocracy which paid little attention to the ascetic puritanism of the Prophet's early followers. Power encouraged luxury, and the singing girls were patronized by the wealthy on a scale unknown before. Music was promoted as an authorized field of study with poetry and the sciences.[22] By the time of the Caliph Harun-al-Rashid of Arabian Nights fame the court was sponsoring the most elaborate displays. It is reported that on one occasion two thousand singing girls presided at a feast given by the caliph.[23]

Instructed in her vocation from childhood, the singing girl was generally bought at the slave market for the palace or private household to become an 'aristocrat' in that sexual hierarchy which has often mystified the western mind but which found easy acceptance in the Asian social outlook. Highly trained and often a very talented artist, the singing girl was treated as a concubine. Islamic law in theory sanctioned marriage to a slave but made it difficult in practice.[24] Concubinage on the other hand was freely allowed so that the status of the singing girl in Islam was somewhat analogous to her Chinese equivalent or to the Japanese geisha.

The social standing of the concubine was hedged with rules and etiquette to be observed by those with whom she co-habited. Though a morally inferior being in the eyes of the law, to all intents and purposes a human chattel, she frequently attained a position of privilege. Children by her patron were born into freedom, a ruling which applied for all slaves. Princes, scholars and connoisseurs of music were often rivals in their claims on the singing girls' accomplishments. The past glories of the singing girl have been lavishly recorded in The Thousand Nights Entertainment and a Night. Fictional though these tales are, and censured by Islamic moralists for their sensual bias, Sir Richard Burton made it clear in his monumental translation that they provide considerable documentation of social practices in mediaeval times.

Personal patronage of singing girls was, needless to emphasize, a pastime of the wealthy but they were of different classes and the ordinary public were also entertained by their presence. 'The masses were no different and even they set the fiats of the piously minded at naught where the intriguing singing girl of the tavern was concerned. All and sundry were prepared to fritter away their silver coins where a pretty face and alluring song prompted. . .',[25] comments H. G. Farmer.

In like vein, a nineteenth-century traveller, William Holt Yates, described Egyptian dancing girls: 'They sing and dance near the coffee houses for the gratification of the licentious; similar performers but of a much higher grade are still to be met with at the banquets of the luxurious. . . .' Obviously disapproving of the custom, Yates nevertheless conceded that 'the extremes to which they carried the dance proved that it was only to be acquired by much study and practice'.[26]

The women performers of these descriptions were typical products of town life, their profession one of degree, ranging from the artist from whom both long years of training as well as talent were demanded, to the harlot who relied chiefly on her physical charm. A slave was always a slave; a combination of many social circumstances decided her ultimate fate. For the ordinary townsman, singing, dancing and prostitution went hand-in-hand, and the lower down the social scale one goes the more difficult it would be to say where the line was drawn in the mind of the public.

Circumstances were different in the desert communities, where song and dance were inseparable from tribal ritual and custom and were in fact an ardent celebration of the forces of the human cycle. Moreover, women in these communities lived a much more active existence, prostitution was unknown, and their song and dance activities were directly related to their duties and responsibilities within the tribe.[27] Among the Touareg tribes of the Algerian desert, oral recitative and narration are exclusively the province of the women, from whom the men learn the legends, poems and ballads which are handed down from generation to generation.

The performances of Arab tribespeople have been sparsely recorded, particularly their dances. Writers' descriptions are often the only source for the brief but frequently vivid glances

we can get. From among many such accounts two are worth
repeating here for the picture they evoke. The first is from an
English political officer who spent many years among the desert
tribes of Iraq.

On the occasion of the Festival of Sacrifice celebrating the
annual pilgrimage to Mecca a unique dance was performed by
the unmarried girls of the Bedouin desert tribes. They entered
a large tent, let down their hair, took off their veils and there
danced in their bright coloured undergarments, moving with
'short, straight-legged jerks' and at the same time swinging their
heads from side to side with a circular impetus which kept
their long tresses in flight. As they danced they covered the lower
part of their faces with their hands or part of their sleeve, or
else they held up a small cane supported by its tips between
the two hands. The dancers usually performed three at a time,
each dancer carrying on until she sank down exhausted and
another took her place. In the towns at the same festival,
women gathered together to hold their private dance parties,
the difference here being that the performers remained in a
seated position as they moved their heads round and round in
a circular sweep, those with the longest hair being the most
successful performers.[28]

The second description is by a young Arab who became a
government official in Saudi Arabia and wrote down in
English a simple but heartfelt account of his desert boyhood.[29]
It presents a vivid picture of tribal life. At one point a description is given of a celebration where beneath a lamplit tent a line
of young men danced in a row to the rhythmic clapping of
their hands. In front of the line stood two other male performers
who carried on a question-answer sequence in chanted verse
with each stanza repeated in chorus by the line of dancers.
Between the two narrators stood a woman in a long full dress
who danced with a sword clasped in her hand, she being vested
with the tribal right to strike down anyone who touched her.

Dances like this obviously had deep ritualistic implications,
though the observers in both cases offered no explanation, being
solely preoccupied with the sheer visual excitement of the
occasions. It is precisely because they convey this so well that
they have been singled out here. Performances such as these
are indicative of how much remains undiscovered concerning

the social implications of the dance among Arab tribespeople.

A distinction must be made between authentic tribal customs and the so-called 'belly dances' of the harem which largely colour the western imagination at the mere mention of Arab dancing. These suggestive performances, which possibly originated in long-forgotten fertility dances, are more likely in the form seen today to have descended from the performances given in the Turkish sultans' palace harems. Such displays were often staged for the palace women as a relief from the intrigues and jealousies which riddled their exotic communities.[30] Today they pander largely to the commercialized eroticism of the night clubs frequented by tourists.

William Holt Yates' description of coffee houses as a magnet for itinerant performers draws attention to a social phenomenon and an institution which, other than the mosque, was the only place where anything remotely resembling a regular audience gathered. The coffee house was one centre where dancers, story-tellers, musicians and shadow puppeteers were sure of turning an honest coin.

During the sixteenth century, when it was first introduced into the Turkish capital by enterprising Arabs, the authorities began to bewail the fact that addiction to the coffee house stopped people from going to the mosque any more; it was said that there was nobody left who did not drink what one poet called the 'negro enemy of sleep and love'. According to one historian of the period:

Those who used to spend a good deal of money on giving dinners for the sake of convivial entertainment, found that they could attain the joys of conviviality merely by spending an asper or two on the price of coffee. It reached such a point that all kinds of unemployed officers, judges and professors, all seeking preferment, and corner-sitters with nothing to do, proclaimed that there was no place like it for pleasure and relaxation and filled it until there was no room to stand.[31]

The scene has really changed little during the centuries and the coffee house remains as popular as it ever was although it has not entirely escaped the changing trends of modern life with innovations like radio and coca-cola invading its privileged territory. As a symbol of male gregariousness, the coffee house has been a great informal 'club' for the ordinary classes. Apart from the mosque, it was the one place where communal affairs could be discussed, opinions given and decisions made. In the coffee house the water pipe was passed round, with refreshments served in a pulsating atmosphere of social gossip, business deals and backgammon. It goes without saying that it was a prime centre for intrigues, combining the functions of a newspaper and a telegraph office in the speed with which information was disseminated from its smoky interior. Every town had its coffee houses which became the haunts of specific coteries in which seniority was paid deference and a man was accorded his regular seat in the daily parliament which ruminated on the issues of the day. It might seem on this evidence that coffee was a minor consideration but this was far from being so. Coffee drinking in the Arab world[32] was a ritual, like the British passion for tea, and a preliminary to every kind of social intercourse.

As a centre of conviviality, where men could expand their social identity after the restraints of the mosque, the coffee house was a natural pitch for the itinerant performer. The storyteller found there a ready-made audience of regular *habitués*, a heaven-sent opportunity for an artist who depended on retaining the interest and suspense of his listeners from one day to the next. An eighteenth-century description exists of a large coffee house which was popular with the Turkish sultan's troops. Inside the house there were stools placed in a semicircle for the audience, who were served with water pipes and coffee as they waited expectantly for the storyteller to mount his platform, which was situated against a window. Once in position he clapped his hands three times to announce he was about to begin and through the ease and fluency of his narrative soon had his audience spellbound. Having whipped up their suspense to breaking point he suddenly stopped and, seizing a coffee cup, stepped down to collect his dues, a cunning psychological move which sent him back to his seat well recompensed.

In more contemporary times it has been a practice for a crier to stand ringing a small bell at the entrance to the coffee house where a storyteller was appearing. Tickets were sold by an assistant seated at a small table and the price sometimes included serving the patrons with coffee and different sweets. Value for money has always been a first principle of the Asian theatre audience and eating and drinking the normal accompaniment to entertainments of most kinds. The storyteller himself sat in a corner nearest to the entrance of the coffee house and announced the opening of his tale by beating the floor with a cudgel which was also used as a stage property with many different functions.[33]

Literary stylist, comic mime and local wit all rolled into one, the storyteller was a solo performer who might have an apprentice assistant but whose appeal lay in the extraordinary self-contained quality of his talent and ingenuity. He was usually a superb mimic, who brought down the house with his gallery of local characters complete with their peculiarities of gesture and speech. He paraded these one after the other until his audience needed no further convincing that they were present before their eyes.

Not every storyteller was king of the coffee houses; there was a hierarchy as in every field. The lesser members of the profession could always be found on a pitch in the market place or under the shadow of the village mosque, where they simply sent round the hat or its equivalent with all the guile at their command. The more sophisticated performers had their arrangements with coffee house owners on a contract basis. The proprietor might simply charge a rental or, in the smaller houses, be satisfied with the extra business he pulled in because of the attraction. Famous storytellers even bought their own coffee houses and so got the best of both worlds.

Throughout Islam the storyteller has been a figure of respect and a man to be treated as such. Those who offended fair practice in their dealings with him were liable to find themselves publicly mocked. He was always a member of his professional guild, often a large and influential one with its own patterns of protocol and procedure. A list of Cairo guild activities in the late nineteenth century, for example, names two guilds of storytellers as being subdivided into groups each having the exclusive prerogative for certain kinds of stories.[34] The guilds cast their nets wide and deep. There were always the performers who gained a reputation among their audience for a particular genre or style of interpretation. Whatever his particular bent, the guiding principle of the storyteller everywhere was summed up in an interpolatory line much used by the Turkish narrators, 'I was there also'.

The coffee houses reached the peak of their business during Ramadan, the sacred ninth month of the Islamic calendar during which time every true believer must go without food and drink of any kind between sunrise and sunset. The evenings in consequence were always a time for relaxation, and when dusk fell many people made their way to the shadow shows which were especially popular during this season. In the coffee houses where performances were held, a tightly stretched linen screen was erected behind a light wooden barrier, in front of which sat a small group of two or three musicians. The audience crowded themselves in between the musicians and the entrance. The puppeteer stood behind the screen, operating his camel-hide figures against the light of an oil lamp. Sometimes a large coffee house had a garden attached and the show was given there, while many a puppeteer throughout Islam simply set up his screen on a convenient street corner.

Wherever it was, the spectators were equally attracted, although it was in the smoky confines of the coffee house that the shadow show was at its most typical, adding its oily smell to the tobacco-heavy atmosphere. The onlookers remained indifferent, for they were united in their expectation of an entertainment provided by one of those inimitable comic partnerships[35] which have enlivened the theatrical scene from time immemorial.

Karagoz, the protagonist of the pair, was portrayed as a bearded, shaven-headed incarnation of the ordinary Turkish man, a realistic affirmation of national character emerging beneath the borrowed plumes of an imported culture. Always short of cash and plagued by the eternal struggle to make ends meet, he was the butt of the crowd, yet good natured withal and sharp witted in a downright fashion. Constantly bemused by the tortuous reasoning of those who governed he poked fun at bureaucracy and jibed constantly at pretentious learning. Never averse to a lecherous wink and a nod, or a ripe obscenity, he was nevertheless a staunch upholder of family virtues and the social taboos so fiercely defended by his kind. Like all great clowns Karagoz left no doubt at all that he was one of the crowd.

His foil, Hacivad, shared his partner's troubles and the common lot but he was different in being educated, knowledgeable and pedantic. His speech, as the spokesman for high tradition, was larded with classical Arabic-Persian allusions. He did not scruple to pander to higher authority if it suited his purpose and he was constantly involved in keeping his impulsive partner in his place. Through their contrasting personalities this famous couple appealed directly to a public whose problems and inhibitions they shared. Their antics symbolized in their own fashion the confrontation of Islamic urban autocracy with the less complicated Turkish strain. This was revealed in the cross-talk of the two clowns. Karagoz spoke in the unvarnished idiom of the Turkish man in the street but his eloquent companion was skilled in all the fanciful nuances of an alien literary culture and was always ready to show up his less erudite friend.

A Turkish scholar[36] has pointed out that the Karagoz screen did not simply portray a world of fantasy but a panorama of city life whose characters revealed the old Islamic urban social structure. Turkish cities in the past were divided into autonomous districts, each with its own mosque, community dignitaries and of course coffee houses. They were guarded not only by watchmen who went their rounds, and packs of fierce roaming dogs, but 'by a sort of collective conscience which, ever alert to what was going on, kept constant vigil over the honour and welfare of all'. Each district was run along identical lines to its neighbours so creating a tightly interlocking pattern of behaviour controlled by decrees handed down through the palace and mosque. The life of every individual was regulated down to the minutest detail by these well-defined observances.

An important official was the judge, who besides his legal duties supervised the mosques, appointed school teachers, set the prices for food and grain, and in general represented the complete bureaucrat. Each city judge was helped by a special legal expert, a private scholar, in theory unpaid, who interpreted the sacred law for his superiors. This system became notorious for its corrupt practices and to the ordinary people typified the age-old comparison of 'them' and 'us'.

Until the nineteenth century Turkish education was exclusively controlled by religious leaders and by a special class of officials known as Men of Learning. Schools were attached to the mosques. There was nothing comparable to a western university or high school for the majority of the population. The pride of the ancient Turkish educational system was the palace

Karagoz of the Turkish shadow theatre, one time idol of the coffee house

The Chinese stage clown as storyteller

The storyteller in the puppet theatre: Takemoto Tsunadayu, a famous narrator of the Bunraku, Osaka

The legacy of India: legong dancer, Kedisan village, Bali

Immediately below: Cantonese puppeteers, Hongkong, a vanishing race of artists

Below right: Song, dance and music: Shanta Rao, the Indian dancer, in performance

Above: An Indian *kathakali* actor using mudra, symbolic hand gestures

Left: High ritual: *kathakali* actors of India

The player of women's roles: Chang Chün-ch'iu, a famous actor of the
Peking theatre, in a pose typical of the virtuous women roles

school,[37] an exclusive establishment with a small enrolment specifically founded to train palace and government officials. The aim of the school was to produce soldier statesmen, loyal to Islam, who were at the same time men of letters, polished in their speech and meticulous in etiquette. Training at the school took approximately fourteen years and only a selective minority completed the full curriculum.

The old Turkish literary elite was jealous of its power and sought to monopolize education by preventing the spread of learning among the ordinary people. The first printing press was not sanctioned in Turkey until the eighteenth century[38] for it was considered that printing the sacred scriptures would destroy their potency, a somewhat perverse interpretation of the power of oral tradition.

The privileged classes were the palace and its extensive bureaucracy of administrators, the military commanders and feudal landlords. The peasants represented the largest social group but the gulf between village and city life was so great that it virtually defined two separate forms of existence. Wars and revolts caused great shifts of population throughout the greater Turkish empire which comprised an extraordinary diverse fusion of nationalities and cultural backgrounds. As a result, people of every race and creed were attracted to the Turkish capital. In Istanbul there were large Jewish and Christian communities, as well as Greeks, Albanians, Hungarians, Persians, Armenians, Tartars and gypsies rubbing shoulders on the streets. This kaleidoscopic array of nationalities produced many stock characters for the shadow screen as well as providing incentive for the storyteller's mimetic talents.[39]

The extended family was the basis of Turkish society, providing both personal and economic security as in other Asian communities. Women were both publicly and privately segregated in accordance with Islamic practice and were completely subservient to the male members of the household. Polygamy was a recognized institution and at the palace level one which has received a considerable amount of historical attention. The western imagination has been definitively coloured on the subject by Turkish custom. The sultan's harem was a complex hierarchy, with every woman occupying an accepted position according to a strict protocol, the whole administered by a staff, which made it a realm of its own. The notorious eunuchs guarded this secret world, presided over by of all people the sultan's mother. It has been said that the Turks, while knowing that a man could acquire and discard many wives, also realized he could only have one mother. She, therefore, assumed the high position which only death could dispel. The harem was the source of endless intrigues and as in all societies where concubinage was sanctioned the very nature of women's status provided means for unbridled power. Shrewdly wielded it could make them the real controllers of men's affairs.

The style of the old Turkish social structure fostered particular attitudes among the people. A sense of fatalism induced by Islamic dogma accentuated a hedonistic approach to living on the one hand and indifference to diligence on the other. Feudal autocracy bred a deep suspicion of all authority, which was treated with a mixture of dread and humility while being fair game for every kind of graft. Bribery and corruption were the normal processes of existence and the peasant saw himself as the eternal victim of it all.[40] In the more intimate areas of daily living homosexuality and lesbianism were intensified through the unnatural separation of the sexes and provided material for a good deal of erotic jesting from both the shadow stage and its human counterpart.

This was the world that Karagoz and his supporting cast of characters were engaged in presenting. Through showing a cross-section of human absurdities they parodied the larger issues of life as it was lived. Religious, military and civic dignitaries were predictably sacrosanct from the irreverences of the shadow screen but symbols were readily devised to defeat restrictions. There was such rich material from which to create stereotypes that these were all the more effective as theatrical butts instantly recognized by everybody. In the person of Karagoz himself the ordinary man's daily struggles to get round life's problems, which seemed deliberately aggravated by the men who ruled, provided constant fascination for those who knew them only too well.

Karagoz embodied the essence of human failings, distilled with cunning for the entertainment of the crowd. He provided a release for some of the deeper psychological social conflicts underlying Turkish life. Mystery surrounds the origins of the ubiquitous Karagoz. From the available facts it seems reasonable to suppose that the Turkish shadow play had indigenous roots. Karagoz in a developed form has had a great influence on other Arabic-speaking countries, even though Egypt may have been a source of contribution at one point.[41] What seems clear is that Karagoz became a uniquely Turkish creation, artfully suggesting the more intangible characteristics of his countrymen for the mass of whom he spoke with uninhibited gusto.

Until the early years of this century the Karagoz shadow play was a kind of half-way house, which in a sense encouraged a feeling for theatre as a public art by its use of a colloquial medium intelligible to the crowd, who found the language of their rulers incomprehensible. By the end of the nineteenth century the continued use of the Arabic-dominated language of official Turkey had grown into an issue which aggravated the consciousness of a new generation. Finally it sparked a movement which ended in total language reform as the basis for a new national identity. Karagoz, with his mockery of literary pretentiousness, had in a way been a prophet of change although it was inevitable that as the mouthpiece of the old parochial society he would become outdated for a westernized generation. Though the coffee house that knew him remains a part of social life, the radio comedian has now replaced his presence, which lingers only in the memories of the middle-aged as a figure from the faraway days of childhood.[42] His name, however, still adorns the title page of a popular political weekly, a defiant reminder of his one-time function as a social commentator.[43]

Karagoz was a symbol dividing an old world from a new which is in turn seeking its own symbols. Nostalgia, hope, and a fervid nationalism mingle as the new dimensions of Islamic society. The twentieth century has been one of political and social upheaval for the Arab and Turkish people alike, with the Turks most completely rejecting the past and becoming a secular state on western lines.

The nineteenth century fostered overt resistance in the Arab world against western influence and colonial domination while in Turkey it was rather a protest at the failure of Islam to offer an effective confrontation with the powerful pressures resulting from the impact of western industrial civilization. In both cases the climate of the times fired new literary aspirations. They inevitably led to the first attempts in Islam to create a theatre with a social message. In Turkey such early dramatic experiments were the bubblings of political-social undercurrents which finally swept the old order away and severed centuries-old bonds.

In the Arab world the situation has been different. Although literary experiments there were also the signals of a mounting movement for political independence, profounder and more complex conflicts were present through the discord between religious aims and practical progress. Tensions were heightened by the increasingly obvious need for a solution based on a reciprocal evolution of both society and its language. In Islam the ethical and emotional restraints imposed by the combination of religion and language have been all-powerful. The problem has dominated the minds of many Arab reformers since the Napoleonic invasion of Egypt and the subsequent arrival of European specialists in increasing numbers. Until then classical Arabic had been the undisputed medium of expression for all Islam.

The evocative power of symbolic suggestion found in Arab prayer and poetry is in marked contrast to its usefulness for transmitting exact information. The arrival of Europeans induced the first realization of inadequacy in the revered language if it was to meet the demands of a new age. Unwillingly the Arabs conceded a need to learn from the west in order to counteract the west, whose literature in the nineteenth century was increasingly studied. European writers in this period had put aside the classical approach and become pre-occupied with ordinary man and his problems, including analysis of his individual emotions. New Arab writers were much affected by this trend, which was reflected in their embryo works. These tended to use themes of past glories rather than contemporary confusion. In striving to align themselves with the west through language, Arab writers were constantly faced with the fact that they not only had to change style, but the medium of language itself, and this problem has continued to be a bone of contention for the various literary schools which have arisen.[44]

Arabic still retains its classical structure but it has lost its most intense association with sacred ritual. The more the need for strictly practical communication has grown, the more

Arabic has adapted itself to new functions. The gap has widened between the concern with religion and the material demands made on language as the social symbol through which the community has sought identity. The period of evolution is still far from having run its course. On the one hand, language has become the weapon of modern progress, and yet it is still regarded as a means by which the Arab world must establish continuity with its past. The theme of adapting language without compromising Islamic individuality has inspired different advocates and induced a literary divisionism which also embraces the theatre.

The problem could have offered new scope for the dramatists were it not for the fact that the play, like the novel, has been a completely alien form for classical Arabic style. The flurry of new literary activity during the nineteenth century largely represented attempts by Egyptian writers to emulate western techniques. Their aim was first to demonstrate their mastery of the forms even when they attempted to mirror a concern for their own social values. Their plays and historical novels were stylistically imitative by intention.

The first to venture into the field of playwriting in this sense were the Syrians, whose country in the nineteenth century comprised the present day Syria, Lebanon, Israel and Jordan. The area had been subject to both Catholic and Protestant missionary infiltration since the beginning of the century, resulting in the first Arab nation with a Christian majority. Printing presses had been introduced and the missionaries' pupils proved extremely receptive to European cultural influences. By the middle of the nineteenth century the first fruits were being seen in literary trends which were directly responsible for the rise of a modern Arab theatre.

At Beirut in 1848 a somewhat free adaption of Molière's *The Miser*, translated into Arabic, was staged by a young man called Marun al-Naqqash, the son of a rich merchant, who had travelled in Italy and Egypt and who spoke fluent French, Italian and Turkish in addition to his Arabic. The play was performed on an improvized stage built in the playwright's home.[45] Even under these circumstances prejudice was so great that no woman dared venture on to the stage and the female roles were played by men. The author was a Christian, so that in one sense the dramatic impulse could not strictly be called Arabic, but the young man understood the tastes and ideas of his audience and he has earned his niche as an innovator. His play seems to have been part comedy and part operetta, one historian[46] describing it as having an orchestral-choral accompaniment whose songs and tunes were not necessarily related to the contents of the play, a foretaste of a musical trend which has persisted on the Arab stage until present times.

Arab fondness for music possibly received new stimulus from the fact that early western contacts came from Italy by way of Egypt, especially the cities of Cairo and Alexandria. Both places had large Italian populations who were frequently entertained by visiting troupes from the homeland. Italian prestige reached a peak in 1869 when the world premiere of Verdi's opera *Aida* was performed at the newly built Cairo Opera House, the Egyptians' own version of the celebrated La Scala.[47] The opera had been specially composed for the occasion and both events marked the momentous opening of the new Suez Canal. The Emperor Louis Napoleon and his consort had travelled in state to be present and attended the first night surrounded by a glittering retinue of European celebrities.

Small wonder that Cairo appeared as a centre of cultural sophistication, towards which many of the young, western-influenced Syrians turned their eager steps in a search for a favourable environment in which to continue the experiments begun by al-Naqqash. He had continued his first modest success by writing a second play, based on material from the Arabian Nights, entitled *Abu'l-Hasan the Idiot,* regarded by historians as the first original Arabic modern drama. It was staged in 1850 in a small theatre which al-Naqqash had built adjoining his home and for which he had obtained an official order allowing him to put on his plays.[48] His third play was an adaptation of Molière's *Tartuffe,* renamed *al-Hasud,* and is said to have resembled an opera bouffe in verse and rhymed prose. The sudden death of al-Naqqash in 1855 was a set-back for the embryo Arab theatre. A nephew followed in his footsteps but decided to leave Syria for Egypt, where he staged his first production in Alexandria in 1876. A notice in the Cairo newspaper *The Egyptian Monitor* for 17 November of that year described the company as including actresses. An Italian teacher who visited Beirut in 1875 saw the second play of al-Naqqash re-staged with actresses in the female roles so that the 1870s appears to have been a time of innovation in the new Arab theatre.

There were other experiments in Damascus, where a young man called al-Kabani, born in 1830 and a student of traditional Arab arts and music, staged his first play in public around 1865. The governor of Damascus encouraged his theatrical venture, which led to the establishment of the first Arab theatre in Damascus, named the The House of the Arab Theatre. It is recorded that two actresses called Bibe and Myriam joined the company. Difficulties soon arose with religious authorities and in 1884 al-Kabani too left for Egypt.

Among other young Syrians tempted by the intellectual sophistication of Cairo was a young actor called al-Khayyat, who first arrived in Egypt with the nephew of al-Naqqash. Attracting the notice of the viceroy he was invited to appear with his troupe on the new Opera House stage.[49] Unluckily for him, the play chosen for his debut, *The Tyrant*, was taken as a personal affront to the viceroy and the ill-fated actor and his troupe were sent back to their own country. It seems that official feelings had already been exacerbated by the dramatic production of a young Egyptian Jew, James Sanua, who had studied in Italy and become very active in Cairo politics as a journalist.[50] He turned to playwriting as a political medium and staged his productions in his own theatre where they played to full houses.

As may be gathered, sponsoring early theatre in the east was very often a question of being a one-man band, and productions were obviously only possible on an intimate scale. Sanua's plays were written in colloquial Arabic, an unheard-of practice at the time, but his ideas touched some sensitive spots and his theatre was forced to close down through official intervention. His plays continued to be published in the Egyptian press even though their author was exiled in Paris.

In spite of all the reverses the new Arab theatre movement continued its halting progress, with Cairo and Alexandria as the main centres up to the first world war. The general pattern of performance which emerged was a kind of hybrid musical theatre, the most popular actors being those who sang well.

The early introduction to *bel canto* possibly had something to do with this but it was much more attributable to the true nature of Egyptian public taste.

Theatre assumed more public proportions as new halls were built, in contrast to the private settings of earlier experiments. Actresses began to appear, although they were always of Jewish or Christian origin and not from the strongly segregated Islamic class.[51] Indeed, theatre generally was still largely the concern of non-Islamic people, whose ideas were mostly above the heads of the ordinary Arab public. Their tastes demanded a different kind of appeal, and these were first met in the early years of this century when a new star called Hijazi[52] appeared on the scene. He came from a poor Egyptian family and first gained fame by his recital of the Koran and by singing popular songs at private celebrations in time-honoured custom. In 1905 he formed his own troupe at a Cairo theatre[53] where he built up a tremendous reputation among Islamic audiences, not only on his home ground but in Syria and North Africa too, where he took his troupe on tour. The secret of his success lay in his decision to make music central to every dramatic consideration, and his own vocal talents were a great advantage there. A precedent was created which had a deep influence on the future course of Arab theatre.

After the first world war, which brought the Egyptian public into closer proximity with European customs and ideas, there were new social trends whose effect was not lost on the theatre. Most important was a growing movement towards the emancipation of Muslim women, a number of whom were emboldened to take up stage careers. This was a revolutionary move in orthodox circles, where any woman associated with song and dance was automatically assumed to be a harlot. The women who were attracted to the stage in this period were untrained in a strict professional sense, but if they were more conspicuous for their favourable appearance than for their talent, at least they paved the way for a new attitude towards their sex.[54]

There were no schools for training stage people in the early days. Actors and playwrights (the two were often one and the same person) depended on their natural talents and on acquiring experience. Some, of course, had studied abroad, where they had been able to absorb new stage methods. The

first Arab to study dramatic art in this way was a young
Syrian, George Abyad, whose talents induced the viceroy of
Egypt to send him to the Paris Conservatoire then directed by
Sylvain.[55] The story goes that Abyad went to Egypt in 1896
and became station master at a place called Sidi Jaber. Arriving
there on a visit the viceroy was met by the impetuous railway
official who thrust a letter in his hand saying that he wished
to devote his life to theatre. Whatever the facts, he duly left for
Paris in 1904 and returned to Cairo in 1910 at the head of
a French company. For two years he presented French classics
to Cairo high society. He became accepted as the doyen of the
Arab stage and did a great deal to arouse interest in the
possibilities of classical production. According to another
account, his own vanity and love of the limelight prevented him
becoming the seminal figure he might have been. As against this,
an Algerian newspaper article in 1964 declared that Abyad's
failure resulted from his public's rejection of a theatre further
and further removed from national social problems. But it was a
remarkable failure. It indicated what the theatre meant to people
even then and the course it had to take.

Between the wars a proliferating number of troupes and
stage artists broadened the theatrical scope and there was an
increased interest in the drama among writers, poets and
journalists, whose contributions ranged over historical themes,
political plays, melodrama, social satire and comedy. Increased
intellectual awareness stimulated official awakening to the
national importance of theatre. During the 1920s playwriting
competitions were organized to stimulate talent, scholarships
being awarded for promising young men to study abroad. One
such was Zaki Tulaima,[56] who in 1924 was sent to the Odéon
in Paris and returned to make his reputation as a director and
teacher. In 1930 he became the principal of Egypt's first school
of dramatic art, a coeducational venture which was shortlived
but which led to later government support for an Institute
of Dramatic Studies.

During the 1930s annual grants were awarded to help
individual troupes and performers, though these were not on
a particularly generous scale, thereby incurring much criticism
for the niggardly treatment of indigenous artists. The wheel
turned full circle when a Popular Theatre founded by the

government in 1948 was granted a very generous budget. Nine years later it was being criticized because 95 per cent of the funds were being spent on administrative salaries, production being left to make do with the rest.

In spite of these familiar problems there has been a sustained move to develop popular interest in the theatre in Egypt. Every kind of genre has been staged, ranging from classical plays and puppet shows to comic opera. One government troupe has in recent times been led by Yusuf Wahbi, a veteran stage and screen star and among the most popular figures of his era. Born of a well-to-do family, he studied theatre in Italy against his father's wishes and founded his own company, the Rameses, in 1923. He quickly gained a national reputation for his talents in musical and social comedy. After unsuccessful ventures in classical theatre and business enterprises he has returned to the fore again and toured other Arabic-speaking countries with great success.

Politics and the new nationalism of the Arab world have increasingly invaded contemporary theatre and produced much dialectic argument and experiment among the new generation of intellectuals, many of whom are greatly attracted by socialistic ideas. A fashionable new genre was freely exploited after the Suez incident in 1956 when street plays, often based on the political and patriotic ideas of established writers, were staged a great deal in Cairo.[57]

There have been tremendous advances and many problems solved during the last half century but the quest for an Arab theatre still continues. The happy fusion of popular tradition and artistic integrity which is required remains a task of formidable dimensions. Whether it can ever be resolved to the satisfaction of the majority remains in question. Dominating everything is the necessity for compromise between classical literary expression and a style which will facilitate communication in a way that so far has only been possible in a western vein. A modern press, radio and the films have perhaps proved to be more potent aids towards a new humanism which the theatre has only partially attained.[58] At the heart of the dilemma is the question of what is really meant by theatre for the majority of the Arab people. The public, considering its size, remains only marginally involved and unconcerned with classic arguments on the differences between the taste of an urban minority and a peasant majority. Nevertheless, this is a theme which tortures the minds of Arab innovators no less than it has done other Asian reformers in the twentieth century. Should they turn to western or indigenous sources of inspiration in their hope of creating new forms of communication in tune with the Arab mind? The progressive argue against the backwardness of traditional forms, treating social progress as synonymous with the intellectual basis of European art; others seek salvation through a modern creative development of folk tradition as being the purest expression of the people.

The solution in the end depends more on the inner character of the people than on the theories of the few. Folk revivals so often end in only serving propaganda and western imitations are above the heads of a larger public. If Arab experiments with theatre in the present century have proved anything at all about national character it is that there is a spontaneously overwhelming response to mimicry and humour from the humblest minds, and also that music exerts a collective magic without which no attempt at a popular theatre can succeed. Every level of Arab society responds intensely to the emotive character of music. Whether it is through the classical rhythmic structure and regulated vocal modulation united in metaphysical function or the vitality and feeling of the peasant's work song, music has always been the direct way to the Arab mind 'making the heart respond as a needle to a magnet'. These were the words of a composer[59] who was a leading member of a group which from the 1920s on sought to develop the dramatic function of music, treating it as neither incidental entertainment nor individualistic expression but as the collective outpouring of a society.

Nothing has more forcibly typified Arab response during the last half century than the life and work of the woman singer, Umm Kulthum, whose vocal artistry has not only enchanted all classes of society but has made her a social phenomenon and a symbol of her race.[60] Born into a poor family, she early impressed everyone by the quality and depth of her singing and recitative. After serious study of the Koranic classical style she became a professional performer and soon made a name in Cairo during the 1920s. There she appeared at private social gatherings, always a legitimate field for traditional women musicians. Her reputation grew, and after her first broadcast in 1934 her popularity reached fantastic heights. She became a national figure. It is said that on the nights when she appeared on the radio the whole community from whatever strata of society tried to get to a radio by fair means or foul. It became fashionable to hold listening parties in order to hear her. Although she commanded fabulous fees, starred in films and tasted all the fruits of dizzy success, she remained bound by her strong sense of Islamic propriety and insisted on her moral as well as her artistic status. Within her talents and personality the sublime essence of Arab feeling was crystallized for her people.

Although she is in her late sixties, today her popularity is un-diminished and her magnetic presence continues to establish instantaneous communication with rich and poor alike. In November 1967 she performed outside the Islamic world for the first time in a concert at the Olympia Music Hall in Paris given for overseas Arab audiences. A press account described the occasion as 'part prayer meeting, part demonstration of patriotic fervour, and part riot'. Her repertoire had been specially composed by contemporary Egyptian poets and her audience was described as including 'students from the middle east, Algerian labourers working on a new subway line round the corner, and tall men from Dakar who sweep the streets round the Jardins des Tuileries. Hundreds of fans had flown in from all over Europe ...'. The emotional tension of the occasion, described as reaching fever pitch, was climaxed by an Algerian workman who shouted from his balcony seat through the wild hubbub of applause, 'I've been eating nothing but boiled potatoes for a week to come here!'

It is true that Umm Kulthum has come under heavy criticism from the intellectuals of a younger generation, who have accused her of being greedy for gain and of losing touch with the true spirit of the people. Such criticism of a popular traditional artist are predictable in the iconoclastic temperature of present times even though they are never entirely convincing. Although the Olympia occasion was a commercialized event which benefited from the pent-up emotionalism of Arabs in exile, it was also something else, a demonstration that although contemporary needs are rapidly changing the difference is not only one of intellectual fashion. The dynamic appeal of this old artist is a ready-enough proof that dramatic experience is still most forcefully realized in the Arab consciousness through the complementary nature of music and speech. Her art, though more vocal than physical, nevertheless achieves that alchemy of communication with an audience which the makers of a new Arab theatre still search for in vain.

All the same it would be foolish to deny that Umm Kulthum now presides over a nostalgic past, not because the new left says so, but because Arab society is undergoing a process of irreversible change. After centuries of negative conformism, the phenomenon of 'mass culture' which accompanies the process of westernization is beginning to penetrate every single area of social life. Increased education has created a mass market and a mass audience for popular journalism, cheap literature, radio, films and television to come. Industrialization has provided a new economic potential for a population who can now exercise a choice of the material advantages offered through the products of the new mass culture. Where before there was one standard for the upper classes and another for the lower, each insulated from the other as well as from outside influences, today their ways are beginning to merge along the same central path of easy sophistication induced through westernization and its products. The traditional past now only induces boredom. Under these circumstances the old folk culture is bound to disappear. The new ideologies of nationalism and socialism have laid a major emphasis on the tastes and needs of the ordinary people, and if the 'age of the common man' has not quite dawned for the Arab world its advent can not be retarded for much longer. A new theatre must draw upon these changing trends for its style and power of communication. It remains to be seen what will emerge. At present the film rather than the stage play appears to be the more flexible medium of expression and more sensitive to the social metamorphosis.

In Turkey as elsewhere the nineteenth century was an era when the voice of the reformer was constantly heard and when new ideas proliferated. By the end of the eighteenth century Turkish leaders had already grasped the need for westernization to recoup their country's waning powers, but it was not until 1838 that the reigning sultan promoted active reforms. Even more far-reaching decrees were promulgated in 1856, when westernization was pushed ahead. The equality of all citizens was advocated, tax systems altered and penal reforms proposed. A new monetary system was adopted, banking instituted, road and canal construction advocated. It is true, reforms were sometimes pursued with well-meaning intention rather than practical implementation but the seeds were being sown. An increase of revolutionary movements among intellectuals highlighted the ambitions of people anxious to speed the country's conversion.

It goes without saying that in this time of ferment theatrical activities became indicative of trends. As in all Asian countries, this amounted to nothing more than an imitation of western ideas following a first acquaintance with theatre as it was presented for the European community in Turkey. One result was a spate of theatre-building, and by the late nineteenth century the Turkish capital boasted a dozen or more play houses, music halls and café-concerts modelled on French patterns.[61] France was an early cultural influence and left her stamp in numerous ways on Turkey. Most of these places catered for the foreign community but they established a tradition of public performances which created precedents.

One of the first theatres to be built[62] belonged to an Italian entrepreneur and was situated in a fashionable quarter with a large Christian population. It has been described as an imposing structure in Italian style with six tiers of twenty-six boxes, each one accommodating eight persons, surmounted by a semicircular gallery. The auditorium was ornate with red velvet and gilt. Named the French Theatre it was also nicknamed the Crystal Palace because of the glass-covered entrance. In 1831 it was burnt down but was rebuilt again. A second theatre was opened by an Italian conjuror to house his shows which were licensed by the palace. It seated five hundred people and was also used by visiting foreign companies. The first play staged in Turkish was given at this theatre in May 1858. It was a translation of an Italian piece but the details are not on record.

A popular rendezvous during Ramazan,[63] the great annual occasion in Turkey, was the Ottoman Theatre, originally built for a French circus company in 1860. Seven years later it was reopened under its new name in time for Ramazan. Records describe it as built of wood in the shape of a huge tent, having an entrance supported by brick columns and a spacious foyer where patrons could play billiards and read the newspapers. The semicircular auditorium had ornate marble pillars and the seating consisted of stalls, three tiers of boxes, and a gallery. Large chandeliers illuminated the high square stage which was faced by a curtained box reserved for the sultan.

In 1868 this theatre began staging plays in Turkish, the first production being a translation of *César Borgia* from the French by an Armenian writer who did a series of such adaptations. The acting troupe were all Armenian, although their leader went over to Islam and applied to the sultan for a monopoly in the staging of theatrical shows. He was granted his request in 1870 for a period of fifteen years with the proviso that over specified periods he opened new theatres in other towns.[64]

Advertisements were placed in the press by the theatre asking for actors who spoke good Turkish and also for people able to write, adapt or translate plays, for which a 10 per cent royalty was offered. People responded and this theatre became an institution which at its zenith attracted the notice of Turkish literary circles and was patronized by an ambassadorial clientele as well as the grand vizier himself on a number of occasions. Molière adaptations were frequently staged but the plays in Turkish were the real attraction and they did a great deal to encourage Turkish playwrights.[65]

The Armenian acting troupe was maintained on a standing basis, their contracts forbidding members to perform elsewhere without express permission. During Ramazan the actors had to work a four- to six-day week, being engaged on a seven-months basis with no provisions for sick leave. Each actor was required to perform in any role allotted to him whether it was in Armenian or Turkish. Twice a year each player was granted a benefit, with the proceeds shared on a fifty-fifty basis, the play chosen having to be one not previously staged by the theatre which claimed all production rights. The director was empowered to cancel the contract of any actor at any time and there were no powers of redress in the event of such action. The troupe in its heyday numbered twenty-six actors and eighteen actresses, all of whom were Armenian.[66] No Turkish woman would have dared to go on a stage at this period for the storm she would have raised among conservative circles would have condemned her as a social outcast. Women were not even allowed in the theatres as spectators when they first opened and when the rules were relaxed a little it was only to set days apart for women only.

The Ottoman Theatre and its director ran into trouble in later years. On 1 April 1873 a play entitled *Fatherland or Silistria* was staged.[67] Namik Kemal, the author, was the editor of a radical newspaper, and an intellectual returned from political exile which had been imposed because of his revolutionary activities. The theme of his play was patriotism and the loyalty men owed their country, a novel concept for people accustomed to unconditional obedience to a sultan. The plot concerned the Turkish defence of the fortress of Silistria against the Russians in 1854 and the script was full of rousing sentiments. The play brought the audience to its feet and received acclamation in the press. Wary of public demonstrations aroused by political suspects the palace ordered the playwright to be arrested and he was deported with his associates; publication of their newspaper was suspended. He was granted permission to return from exile three years later and the 1876–7 season at the Ottoman Theatre opened with a performance of his play. By this time the director had become unpopular with some of the critics and a new theatre had opened its doors and was drawing away the audiences. Disgusted with the lack of public support, he finally gave up control of his theatre in 1880. It lingered on for an intervening period but eventually closed its doors for good, so ending an era.

The palace was not to be outdone in following prevailing fashion and in 1858 the sultan built a theatre adjoining his main quarters. A grand opening featured a visiting foreign opera company accompanied by a Turkish orchestra. According to records the theatre seated three hundred and was built with three box tiers, each tier having thirty boxes, with the sultan's close to the stage. The novelty quickly wore off. The theatre was little used and ended by being burnt down.

A new sultan built another theatre in 1889 and here regular performances were given. Several well known western artists, including the great Salvini, appeared there. It was said that the sultan was so scared by the convincing interpretations of the famous actor that he hastily left his seat in the middle of an act. This same sultan refused to see Bernhardt when she performed in Istanbul, as she did on three occasions, because her death scenes were too convincing.

This theatre seated between seven and eight hundred people and had a bridge connecting it to the palace harem, whose occupants had special boxes. These were faced with richly decorated lattice work to conceal the women from the audience. Rossi, an Italian actor who performed there, described the main structure as being rectangular, sixteen metres by ten. Columns two metres high flanked the stage and supported the balcony from which other columns both acted as a roof support and divided off the gallery into boxes. The interior seems to have been rather overdone, with gold and crimson hangings, heavy chandeliers and oil paintings on the walls. The stalls were usually empty, as to have sat there would have meant turning one's back on the sultan in his box, a grave breach of manners. Palace personnel had special seats in the gallery. The stage was reportedly well equipped technically and had a two-metre proscenium arch. The orchestra was placed to the right of the stage beneath the balcony and included both Italian and Turkish musicians.

The sultan's theatre was directed by a French conjuror and an Italian actor who also organized operatic performances. Every member of the theatre company was given military rank and wore uniform. Men played women's roles although there is mention of Armenian actresses appearing there later. Turkish plays performed by local actors from the Ottoman Theatre were sometimes put on in addition to those by visiting foreign artists. The sultan occasionally indulged his dramatic whims by calling for some item he had read in the newspapers to be dramatized on the stage. Practically everyone of any standing at all who performed before the sultan was decorated.

Political events put an end to the palace theatre. In 1908 a mutiny in the Turkish army led to demands for a revised constitution. In the following year the sultan was deposed and his theatre abandoned for ever. The palace entertainments, though reminiscent of some comic-opera setting, were nonetheless symptomatic of an age dominated by a desire for experiment, however inhibited by social prejudices these were forced to be.

E

Society's dallying with westernisation in its leisure hours was in itself a sign of the prevailing winds of change, although the time was still not ripe for the fulfilment of the theatre visionaries' dreams. The social practices of Islam and the violent prejudices they induced among the ordinary public raised too many obstacles. First on the list was the old dilemma of women's segregation. By the end of the nineteenth century the status of Turkish women had changed little since early times. They were treated as inferiors, requiring both personal and collective supervision to prevent them straying from the narrow path of Islamic virtue laid down for their protection. Physical concealment was one means to this end. When they were out of doors in the Turkish capital all respectable women wore loose-sleeved, cloak-like robes. The outer robe hid equally voluminous garments beneath, including baggy trousers. The head was swathed with a doubly fine muslin veil, one half of which was drawn across the bridge of the nose, the mouth and the chin, the other portion being taken over the forehead, leaving only the eyes exposed. It was considered bad manners to show the whole nose, the sign of a harlot or what was nearly as bad, an Armenian, the depraved type who even appeared on the stage in public, for it will be remembered the first actresses in Turkey were either Armenian or of gypsy blood. Though their inadequate pronunciation of the Turkish language did not provide a model for better stage elocution, at least their example later helped Islamic women to overcome prejudice against their sex. It was the same story everywhere in Islam; gypsies, Jewesses, Syrian Christians and Armenians pioneered the way for the actress. As infidels their skill in the forbidden arts was accepted so long as the pure spirit of Islamic womanhood remained un-sullied.

No Turkish woman could ever venture on the streets even by her husband's side. To have appeared on a stage in the company of actors would have seemed outrageous. If she went out with her lawful protector she walked at a discreet distance behind him, and of course heavily veiled. Women remained segregated on every social occasion in old Turkey; there was no mixing in society at all. They were not allowed to attend school, nor the first university which was opened in 1900. When they travelled on the ferries across the Bosphorus or in the new electric trams they were separated from the male passengers by heavy curtains. There was not an area of daily life where women were not controlled and restrained in the name of religious propriety.

It was scarcely a favourable climate for progress in the theatre. Even the most ardent reformers failed to break down the barriers of sexual prejudice in the early years of experiment. It seems ironically appropriate that the first western-style play written in Turkish was a satire on arranged marriage. It was a one-act comedy called *Marriage of a Poet*, published in 1859 and written by Ibrahim Sinasi,[68] a journalist and poet educated in Paris. There appears to be no record of it having got beyond the printed page and had it done so there would have been formidable production problems.

Quite apart from the social bans on women there were no schools for training them in theatre methods. Actors learned their business on the stage itself, in accordance with well-established custom. Though this was in many ways an admirable principle, it left much to be desired when completely alien forms and techniques had to be assimilated. The illiteracy of the general public was again an insuperable problem when trying to gain attention for dramatic experiment. New theatre became a vehicle for the intellectual few or the fashionable pastime of the well-to-do, a state of affairs which was not of course peculiar to Turkey in nineteenth-century Asia.

Topping all these problems was the fact that a rigid government censorship tied the hands of the playwrights. Every manuscript had to undergo official scrutiny and palace spies attended all performances, noting down offensive material, a phrase with wide terms of reference in a political autocracy, and an Islamic one at that. Writers were in constant danger of banishment for their ideas, or even of execution. Foreign players were not immune and found themselves in trouble if their repertoires offended sensitive ears. The French actor Coquelin is said to have been so incensed by the Turkish censor prohibiting his best plays that after one performance he denounced the sultan's methods in a stinging monologue from the stage. When the curtain came down he hastily fled the capital.[69] The theatrical professional was nothing if not hazardous in old Turkey.

The opening of a new century saw the flowering of nationalism in Turkey, particularly among the students. Several groups gave impetus to a generation restive and anxious to throw off the shackles of mediaeval Islam. Among the many conflicts of opinion as to which direction progress should take there was unanimity in the belief that the Turkish people had to become westernized as the first constructive step.

In May 1889 a student group at the Imperial Military Medical School founded a new revolutionary society destined to play an important role in political-social reform. Named the Young Turks,[70] they were in fact the successors of an earlier group, the New Ottomans, first active in 1866. The Young Turks failed in their first attempt to dethrone the sultan, but they set in motion a train of events which had wide consequences and which led their heirs to political power in the years 1909–18. Though the Young Turks movement emerged as ideologically divided and unable to bring about a really democratic government, their period of ascendancy was marked by immense intellectual activities. Newspapers were founded, a new literature was born, and thoughtful opinion given a hearing where before it had been suppressed. The seeds were sown for educational reforms and the emancipation of women. The modernization of city life made great advances and from it all the efforts to create a new theatre gained strength and fresh resources.

By the outbreak of the first world war artistic resolves were given expression and it was decided to found a permanent theatre and a conservatory in Istanbul. It was a major step towards professional training facilities. Antoine of the Odéon in Paris was invited to become the first director of the new school. He accepted the appointment, which was widely acclaimed in the Turkish press, where advertisements were inserted to attract the first students. Sixty-three candidates were accepted from among the one hundred and ninety-seven who applied, all men needless to say. Before training could begin war broke out and Antoine was recalled to Paris. It was a severe blow but the Conservatory did not close and after some reorganization opened classes at the end of August 1915.

Courses in elocution and verse-reading were taught by veteran actors and writers, who at this point were the only instructors available. The period of training was set at four years but the new Conservatory seems to have been in a hurry. Their first performance, an adaptation of Fabre's *The House of Clay*, was staged in January 1916. There was a segregated audience, the evenings being reserved for men and the women allowed to attend only matinée performances.

The war and its impact held up constructive organization at the new Conservatory, where both teaching and administration languished for lack of adequate funds. At the same time the war did something to ease the restrictions against ordinary women in the cities. For the first time they were used to replace men in certain menial jobs; a women's labour battalion was recruited for street cleaning in the capital and this kind of work made the veil such an encumbrance that it was discreetly replaced by a long kerchief. This only covered the face if drawn across and its usage survived.

In spite of these advances there was still a long road to travel before women could attain true liberty of action. In 1918 women were admitted for the first time to the new Conservatory, although they were far from being allowed to become actresses. One of them was given an assignment as a stage prompter but nothing more. In 1919 a young girl appeared for the first time in a play in Istanbul but there was such an outcry that she was forced to withdraw after the first night. The first Turkish woman to appear regularly on the stage was arrested by the police after a two-week run and only released after the most protracted discussions. The signs of freedom in the theatre were still only signs. Happily, a more enlightened attitude soon prevailed and in 1921 the Istanbul city authorities agreed to allow women of the Islamic faith to perform on the stage. The way for the training of actresses was then open even though antagonism in the most conservative circles persisted for a long time.

In 1921 the six-year-old Conservatory was given a new constitution which emphasized its function as a civic theatre rather than a training school. A number of troupes were formed to develop touring activities and encourage national interest. Finally the turn of political events brought about the long-awaited official support for theatre.

The Turkish sultanate was abolished in 1922 and a republic

proclaimed in October of the next year. Kemal Ataturk, the
new president, was a dynamic personality, a military man who
had been at the heart of reform movements since his student
days. There had been two distinct tendencies then – advocacy
of equality for all subjects under a central government, as
against a call for Turkish supremacy in a political empire.
Separatist movements arose and one school demanded the
political union of Islamic Turks and those who had affinities
with the original non-Islamic Turkish culture. Ataturk stood
squarely for a uniform national state and flatly rejected any
other solutions. To this end he introduced sweeping reforms
and measures designed to hasten the westernization of his
country. Religion, education, language reform and the emancipation of women became immediate issues for which legislation
was pushed through and to which he gave his undivided
attention. Deeds rather than words were the order of the day and
Turkish society underwent a permanent transformation.

Theatre, for so long on the brink of acceptance as an
essential element of westernization, now received its due. In
1925 the Istanbul Municipal Council took in hand the
complete reorganization of the old Conservatory group and
decreed it should become a municipal theatre on a permanent
basis. They appointed as director Muhsin Ertugrul, one of the
first students of the original group. He had just returned from
study in Russia and was destined to become a father figure of
the modern theatre. In 1931 the new undertaking was granted
its official charter and this was eventually extended to include
a children's theatre. In 1934 the whole organization was
designated the Istanbul Municipal Theatre. Ataturk himself is
said to have authorized the next step of creating a national
theatre. The story goes that in 1930 Ertugrul had taken his
troupe to Ankara and staged a ten-day run with a different
play performed each night. Ataturk was present on every
occasion. The new Turkish leader, who had the reputation of
being a hard drinker, at the final curtain sent for Ertugrul and
exclaimed that the impossible had been accomplished – performances had kept him sober for ten nights. 'The theatre is
what Turkey wants', the president is said to have added,
followed by a demand as to what way he could help the
director. The answer was a request for a new training school,

at which, on the spot, Ataturk commanded his prime minister to provide a school.[71]

If the story has apocryphal overtones it is certainly in keeping with the character of the 'Father of Turkey', whose deeds invariably matched his words. At a meeting of the State Assembly in 1936 he announced the founding of a State Conservatory, though he did not live to see the 1941 graduation of the first batch of students. The German composer Hindemith was called in to advise on setting up the Conservatory and as a result of his recommendations the curriculum was arranged under three divisions: music, drama and the training of music teachers. Another German expert, Carl Ebert, was asked to coordinate dramatic and operatic studies. The first year's enrolment was a modest one by western standards – eleven men and five women students. Today about twenty-five new students are selected annually for training. They enter on a five-year course, which includes general education, and during this time they are entirely supported by the state, which provides tuition, board and lodging and even clothing. If they complete their course successfully they are engaged as salaried members of the State Theatre to which in any case they are obliged to give two years service for every year of their training. Drama students in Turkey are assured of an artistic security unknown elsewhere.[72]

In spite of a troubled national economy the State Theatre continues to receive its annual budget. Although theatrical production costs are low by western standards the salary sheet is a long one for actors and singers are treated as civil servants. Old tradition dies hard. A fledgling actor joining the State Theatre receives a first lieutenant's pay; after ten years of meritorious service he receives the equivalent of a general's salary. Bureaucracy must have its guidelines and doubtless state-controlled theatres suffer from all the problems usually created by official paternalism. But when all is weighed in the balance, the Turkish achievement of making theatre so essential an element of their national life is an astonishing one, commanding admiration.

It is a far cry from the founding of the State Conservatory in 1936 to present times. The Turks are today seasoned theatre-goers and the state caters generously for their needs.

The Municipal Theatre in Istanbul has carried on its long tradition and today controls four play houses as well as running an opera company. The State Theatre in Ankara controls four play houses in the capital itself and two more in the provinces; it also runs an opera and a ballet group.[73] As many as fifteen hundred theatrical performances are given by the state companies throughout Turkey during the year. Plays staged during recent times have included a wide cross-section of works from Russian and European repertoires. A major part of the productions, however, consists of plays by Turkish dramatists covering both historical and contemporary themes. Plays usually have a run of between seventy and eighty performances, with four to five productions staged during the season, which runs from October to May. Admission prices are kept low to enable the ordinary citizens to benefit, the average admission ticket costing about twenty-five new pence or sixty American cents.

In recent years classical ballet has become very popular in Turkey. Dame Ninette de Valois of the English Royal Ballet was invited to advise on the founding of a ballet school in 1947. For a time she travelled between her own country and Turkey, teaching and advising. The school was given official recognition in 1950 and moved to Ankara as an ancillary of the National Conservatory. The students work under exactly the same arrangements as the theatre students. They are completely cared for by the state during their nine years training, and on successfully completing the course they become paid servants of the state with free medical care, holidays with pay, retirement benefits – everything in fact that the modern worker enjoys in the west.

The instructors have mostly been English and have included people like Travis Kemp, Molly Lake (once with Pavlova's company), Claude Newman of Sadlers Wells and Anne Parsons of Covent Garden Opera Ballet. The new company, most of whom are still in their early twenties, have attracted considerable notice and an enthusiastic following. *Coppélia*, *Les Sylphides* and *Les Patineurs* have all been staged with *The Rake's Progress* as their *tour de force* to date. The story goes that on opening night the principal dancer in *The Rake's Progress* interpreted the mad scene so convincingly that several members of the *corps de ballet* missed their entrance as they wept with compassion in the wings, while in the audience there was genuine alarm lest the performer had really taken leave of his senses. There are echoes here of the sultan who could not bear to see Bernhardt die on the stage. During rehearsals of *The Rake's Progress,* according to the same source, the accompanist frequently dissolved into tears herself.[74] The Turks are highly emotional and project themselves totally if the work affects their sensibilities. While Turkish ballet at present must of necessity draw upon the west, it is the hope of all involved in this undertaking that the body of Turkish choreographers, dancers and musicians will eventually begin to create a new repertoire of their own.

One of the great dangers that face state enterprise when it provides such security is complacency and disregard for self discipline, both fatal to creative performance, which too protective an environment can easily encourage. This problem will doubtless require constant vigilance in the new Turkish theatre, although the talent and potential which according to those best able to judge has already emerged, is the best justification for the system.

A far graver problem is the general political situation[75] of the Turkish nation, whose economic and social problems have increased to such an extent in recent times that the question is being asked today whether these can be settled in the framework of existing institutions. Discontent in the army and labour unions, an explosive cost-of-living situation, and recurring conflicts between university students of right and left, indicate an all-too-familiar pattern. These dissensions point to a possible disruption of society in a way which could only be to the detriment of a state-run theatre.

4

CHINA

The traditional social order of China remained fundamentally unchanged for centuries, an order reinforced by a geographical and political isolation which led her people to think of their country as the hub of the world. As an agrarian nation, and with India the major cultural influence in east Asia, China remained indifferent to pressures from without and change from within. When she was eventually conquered by the Manchus in the middle of the seventeenth century, resilience was maintained through the continuity of tradition and her aggressors were accommodated to her own unquestioned ideology.

The uncompromising conservatism of her way of life, compounded by the ineffective rule of an effete dynasty, finally brought disruption and humiliation to China in the nineteenth century when a direct confrontation with western industrial civilization exposed her inability to withstand the ambitious forces of European colonialism. China was plunged into a period of internal strife, social confusion, and national degradation, until the relentless pressures of the west and the determination of a new revolutionary generation inside China – who were in large part the intellectual foster-children of the west – caused the collapse of the old civilization.

A republic was declared and a new era began. China now faced a turbulent period in which her people struggled to reconcile a hallowed past with a present demanding social and economic transformation on an unprecedented scale. Still dominated by the west, and a reluctant partner to commercial expansion incompatible with her traditional economy, China nevertheless drew many lessons from the new political, economic and cultural ideas with which she was brought into increasing contact. As a republic she faced the gigantic task of finding her place in a world from which she had withdrawn for so long. The continuance of western controls, and the failure of Chinese political leaders to view social and economic problems either selflessly or decisively, encouraged continuous political unrest, which was however offset by the tide of rising nationalistic fervour and cultural experiments among students and intellectuals. Japan's military ambitions finally halted China's struggles to become a modern state. A long war left her economically exhausted, politically divided and spiritually bankrupt. She seemed incapable of attaining that inner unity the lack of which had compromised all efforts towards a true national renaissance.

China's postwar transformation as a communist state seemed, to many who knew the country, to be the inevitable demonstration of cause and effect. Elimination of ineffectual government, which had been China's lot for so long, suggested drastic measures of uncompromising severity which have since proved to be the basis of a totalitarian control unprecedented in scope and aim. The new ruler of China has imposed his will on every level of society and demanded a complete severance with the past, confounding the many who believed that older values might eventually prevail as they have so tenaciously done in China's past history. Nevertheless, Chinese society is still in a state of flux. No country has been the object of speculative assessment from so many quarters and yielded so much that was unpredictable. Complex forces still contend with each other in a way which is difficult for the rest of the world to comprehend in view of China's new and self-imposed isolation.

The Chinese theatre has been a barometer of the traditional stability and social change so briefly noted above. Chinese theatre became a highly perfected form, whose vigorous acting conventions delighted the public; it remained sworn to a continuing tradition from generation to generation. Although westernization changed the face of Chinese society, and with it accepted ideas of public entertainment, the old theatre remained remarkably persistent. China without her famous Peking theatre seemed as unthinkable as China without her tea. The events of the times have shown otherwise; what follows in this chapter represents a survey of some particular aspects of Chinese society which have made the theatre what it was and also speculates on what it may become.

Ancestor worship and nature worship were two important forces which moulded Chinese thought and habit from early times. The consequences of the first were seen in an intense regard for precedent and a deep respect for the elders of society who represented the living link between the present and the past. Respect for age became a political as well as a religious measure, an aid to authority for preserving conformity throughout the community.

Nature worship may have preceded ancestor worship in point of time but it had a continuing influence on philosophy and aesthetics and encouraged a dualistic view of the universe. The phenomenon of nature was explained in terms of two polar opposites, Yin and Yang, the positive and the negative forces, representing the energy of life. Kept in a state of balance these ensured total harmony. This principle, expanded in different ways, coloured many aspects of Chinese life and the concern for harmonious relationships led to a passion for codification and ritual. A culminating point was reached in the fifth century BC, with the advent of Confucius[1] who, in a sense, imposed order on ideas long tacitly accepted. The code of conduct which was evolved from his teachings proved binding and conferred a remarkable homogeneity on Chinese society that persisted for centuries, the same values being honoured at all levels of the community with little deviation.

Society in China involved a sharp division between an educated but bureaucratically powerful minority and a peasant majority who provided the mainstay of the agrarian economy. At the pinnacle of the social structure was the emperor, whose mandate to preserve law and order in the land was regarded as conferred by heaven. Below him a tightly centralized body of Confucian scholars administered the illiterate majority. They were subdivided into occupational categories broadly defined as farmers, artisans and merchants in that order of importance. The fact that many of the early traders in China were foreigners may have helped to put them last on the list but in any case buying and selling were ruled to be incompatible with the moral obligations of a Confucian gentleman. He was selected for the governing class on the strength of an extensive series of examinations in the literary classics which demanded long years of preparation and effort. Once successful and rewarded with a post, the state looked after his material needs.

The despised merchant gained power in China, as elsewhere, through his control of money and this in turn enabled him to breach the boundaries of social status. When he prospered he usually invested in land and so assimilated himself into the gentry. Once arrived he often became a patron of the arts, including theatrical activities. The merchants, in fact, were important sponsors of theatre in China and to some extent helped its expansion as a public entertainment in the towns.

At the very bottom of the social ladder in Confucian China were the outcasts, a group which included criminals, bandits, scavengers, slaves, prostitutes, actors and entertainers of all kinds, categorized as having no claims on society under imperial edicts.[2]

The family was the cornerstone of the social and political fabric; indeed Chinese society was composed of families rather than individuals. According to Confucian reasoning, the well-regulated family ensured a well-regulated state, so that the family became the prototype for the nation at large. Outside his immediate family a Chinese had obligations to those related to him by marriage and through descent on the male side, so providing the basis for a clan system which became extraordinarily deeply rooted. Families in a clan bore the same surname, marriage within a clan was taboo, and women had to marry outside their parental group. Histories and genealogies were jealously guarded and preserved in writing, and ancestral rites were fundamental duties often shared by the various branches of a clan.

Naturally, in such a tightly knit family system, jealousies and disputes arose. Clan feuds were proverbial in China. Nevertheless, as a way of uniting large bodies of related people the clan system remained particularly effective.

The ordinary Chinese family included a man and his wife, his unmarried children and, wherever living accommodation made it possible, the married sons. Even in quite humble households there would be a dependent relative or a servant to round off the numbers. The Confucian ideal of domesticity was the extended family, although it was only economically possible among the higher classes, wealthy merchants and landlords. Such a family was headed by the patrilineal grandparents and beneath them a descending order of married sons, their wives and children, as well as the unmarried children of the family. All had their separate quarters but lived under the same roof. The servants, maids and kitchen staff required to keep a family of this size running were legion.

Age, generation and sex were the unquestioned principles which determined family precedence. Property was controlled by the male head of the family, who also supervised disbursement of any income brought in by the various members. A father was obliged to support his son and find a wife for him; widows and unmarried children were supported by surviving adult sons. No daughter could inherit from her father. The sexes were segregated to the extent that women were confined exclusively to domestic tasks, except in peasant families, and also in the larger households where women had their own quarters. In wealthier families tutors were engaged for the education of the sons and in more modest families the sons were taught whatever skill or trade the father followed; if only from the point of view of family survival instruction was thorough. Apprenticeships and outside employment were usually negotiated through family connections. The family was the major employment agency, so to speak, and the invariable sponsor for any form of personal advancement. Nepotism was a virtue rather than a vice in these circumstances.

When a son married, his wife severed all connections with her own family and went to live in her husband's home. Her first duty was to provide a male heir to carry on the family line and fortune and the birth of a first son gave prestige to her subordinate position. A wife had to submit to her husband at all times and to her son if she became widowed. If she was treated badly she could return to her parents but this was regarded as an inordinate disgrace and not necessarily acceptable to her own father. Suicide was the last resort of an unhappy wife. Marriage was a contract arranged between the heads of two families; it had nothing to do with personal affection or physical attraction.

These, very briefly, represent the basic principles on which ordinary Chinese society functioned and they provided material

for theme and characterization in scores of plays. The patriarchal family head, the filial son, the virtuous daughter-in-law,
the faithful servant or the scheming marriage go-between,
were all reproduced on the stage in roles whose well-defined
acting conventions made them as familiar to theatre audiences
as the originals which inspired them.[3] At the same time the
social taboos which kept women from the outside world operated more fiercely in the theatre than most areas and they were
replaced on the public stage by the female impersonator, whose
art was developed and perfected accordingly.

Even in Confucian China the pattern of carefully systematized
family relationships could be disrupted by the vagaries of human
nature. The shrew, for example, was no stranger to the Chinese
family, as the stage clown was quick to show. Her nagging
tongue could make a nonsense of hallowed male authority.
Women deprived of status in the outside world could redeem
their authority in the domestic environment. The mother-in-
law was a figure of dread to every newly wed bride and the
matriarch of many a large family was a disciplinarian capable
of quelling family opposition with a glance. The theatre provided
her with a role all to herself. The robust singing and forceful
characterization radiated the essence of family pride and
cohesion.[4]

The extended family, of which the stage matriarch was a
symbol, frequently had scores of people living under the same
roof, and although the principles of personal relationship were
the same as in smaller families the scope for tensions, jealousies
and intrigues was correspondingly greater, rivalling those of a
small town in their complexity. By the same token, celebrations
and festivities were on an equivalent scale and often very lavish.
Freed from the necessity of productive labour, well-to-do
families had ample leisure to cultivate the arts and these served
to alleviate the boredom and morbidity which arose from such
enclosed living.

There was a Chinese saying, 'a hall is not a room, a concubine is not a person'. The presence of a concubine was
nevertheless sanctioned by Confucian society, adding to the
complications of the extended family. In theory she provided
assurance of a male heir when a wife failed in that duty. In
practice she was a sign of social prestige, and a man might look

n his concubines as he did the rest of his property, as well
satisfying sexual indulgence. Concubinage was carried to
extremes in the imperial palaces, which swarmed with women.
The wives and servants resident in the royal quarters were all
designated with a bewildering array of ranks and title which
often provided no ready distinction for the uninitiated between
wives and servants.[5] Court concubines were usually trained as
musicians or dancers of one kind or another; possibly the supreme
example in history was the T'ang court, whose emperors ruled
from the seventh to the tenth centures AD; they retained literally
thousands of these women in their entourages.

The dancing girls of the T'ang court were said by some
authorities to have been responsible for the custom of binding
women's feet which reputedly developed in the ninth century.
One Chinese scholar has dated the custom as beginning three
centuries earlier; he has argued that the ancient Chinese dancing girls performed a kind of tap dance in a limited area, and
as the feet had to be shortened binding was devised.[6] A great
deal of speculation surrounds the whole question and if the custom
did indeed originate with dancers it can only be said that it
contravenes every known principle of dancing, where flexibility
of foot control is imperative.

Whatever the history of this ancient custom it became the most
perverse aid to social segregation, but a majority of Chinese
women tolerated it for centuries in the interests of fashion and
social status. The Manchus, who conquered China in the seventeenth century, forbade women to bind their feet but were unable
to enforce their regulation and withdrew it in 1668.[7] The custom
only completely died out in the present century.

Foot-binding was carried out in early childhood so that
growth of the foot was retarded by deformation of the bone
structure. The dwarfing which resulted was reckoned a mark
of physical attraction and social status, necessary for women
who expected to make a successful marriage. It got to the
point where parents approaching a matchmaker to seek a wife
for their son did not ask about a girl's looks but the smallness
of her feet, emphasising their belief that 'a plain face was given
by heaven but poorly bound feet were a sign of laziness'. For a
woman to have natural feet was regarded as unnatural, so
perverse can human custom become.

Women with bound feet developed a teetering step which was regarded as a mark of refinement and sexual appeal. The most seductive courtesans were considered those whose tiny feet made them sway from side to side with a hip movement regarded as highly erotic in Chinese eyes. Mimicry of this gait was part of the stock in trade of the actors who played female roles and who used a special device bound on to their own feet enabling them to simulate this way of walking.[8] The mere sight of a popular actor of women's roles in the old days, one hand on swaying hip and flicking a coquettish handkerchief, was enough to bring down a delighted roar from the gallery.

The custom of foot-binding contributed to the appeal of the actor who played female roles and provided him with new stage business. Apart from the fact that any ordinary woman would have incurred virulent moral censure by appearing on a stage in Confucian China, her physical disability would have placed her at a disadvantage in acting skill. This was one factor among the many others which hindered the development of the actress. The actor was able to develop mimetic and gestural techniques which were theatrically more powerful and visually more exciting because of his natural muscular control. The actress, whatever her charm as a courtesan and singer in the old days, was otherwise limited and at best reduced to pale imitation of the actor. There is something piquantly ironical about the fact that when actresses were publicly accepted in the twentieth century they had to learn all the artful devices invented by men to simulate femininity on the stage, including the technique which enabled them to imitate walking on bound feet.

The daily philosophy of the ordinary townspeople in old China was summed up in the maxim, 'the rich rely on heaven but the poor rely on the rich'. Artisans, workers and tradesmen, who comprised the majority of the urban population, lived frugally and put in long working hours for the minimum remuneration. Shop assistants and apprentices usually slept at their places of work and were under the complete jurisdiction of their masters. If they were bad masters life could be terribly hard, but under the better masters a strong sense of personal loyalty, familist in character, developed on both sides.

The great annual festivals celebrated throughout China provided the few occasions for leisure for the ordinary people.

Most important of all was the New Year holiday held in the first fifteen days of the old lunar calendar. It was a time of celebration, settling of accounts, and above all of family reunion. Every town worker who possibly could return to his native village on this occasion did so and in the towns themselves the shops put up their shutters and all work ceased except in the world of entertainment. This was the season of the year when actors were overworked, their services being in constant demand for both public and private occasions. Itinerant troupes set up their temporary stages in the streets for the benefit of the holiday crowds, whose women nevertheless remained well out of sight. All they could do was to peep at the show from behind screened windows, or if they were able to ride out catch a glimpse of the stage from a closed cart halted on the edge of the throng.[9]

Other great occasions were the Spring Festival, when offerings were made at the ancestral graves; the Dragon Boat Festival, in the fifth lunar month, with races on the rivers and estuaries; a festival for the souls of dead ancestors, held in the seventh lunar month; and the mid-autumn festival, held in the eighth month, a time of harvesting, match-making and moon gazing. On all these occasions the ordinary people, after observing the necessary rituals, let themselves go. There was always something to see in the streets and at the fairs where jugglers, acrobats and storytellers offered their entertainments and eating and drinking were the order of the day. Certain plays were traditionally performed at the times of the annual festivals and these were awaited by theatre audiences who anticipated their pleasures the more keenly because of this association.

In the villages the annual festivals were celebrated with equal intensity, if on a different scale. Village life was dictated by the agricultural cycle of ploughing, planting and harvesting; life was hard and everyone had to work from dawn to dusk, year in year out. There was very little time for relaxation. The landlord was a threat shadowing many lives, and the constant hope was that when his collectors had done their work there would at least be enough left to see them through to the next harvest. There was a very popular play on the old Peking stage which dealt with this theme.

A visit from an itinerant theatrical troupe was an auspicious occasion for any village society, on whose behalf the elders sometimes arranged these events, frequently with a religious motive – to give thanks for a bumper harvest, or to ward off calamity, drought or flood. It was often the custom for two or more villages to cooperate in sponsoring performances and then there were long and protracted discussions to decide on a mutually convenient site to erect a stage, a dry river bed being a favourite spot. Larger villages sometimes had stages in their local temples and then the audience gathered in the courtyard to see and hear the performance. The quality of the troupe would depend on the relative prosperity of the sponsoring villages, although even quite poor communities made a supreme effort to secure the best performance they could for their celebration. A show was a show to villagers starved of leisure through long months of backbreaking labour, and enthusiasm was never dampened because of an artistic lapse or two. The fishing communities had their theatrical occasions also, and in modern Hongkong it is still possible to see a performance given on a large junk moored to the harbour side, or at some temple dedicated to the fishermen's gods situated on the banks of a creek where the boats can pull in.

Some vivid accounts of travelling theatrical troupes have been given us by Robert Fortune, an English botanist who visited China professionally during the 1840s and 1850s. Describing one performance he attended during his travels he wrote:

The Chinese have a curious fancy for erecting these temporary theatres on the dry beds of streams. In travelling through the country I have frequently seen them in such places. Sometimes when the thing is done in grand style a little tinsel town is erected at the same time with its palaces, pagodas and dwarf plants. These places rise and disappear as if by the magic of the enchanter's wand but they serve the purposes for which they are designed and contribute largely to the enjoyment and happiness of the people.

On the present occasion I did not fail to accept the invitations which had been given in the earlier part of the day. As I did not intend to remain for a great length of time I was content to take my place in the 'pit' which I have already said is free to the public. But the parties who had gone to the play were too polite to permit me to remain long among the crowd. One of them, a respectable looking man dressed very gaily, came down and invited me to accompany him to the boxes. He led me to a narrow staircase and into a little room in which I found several of his friends amusing themselves smoking, sipping tea and eating seeds and fruits of various kinds. All made way for the stranger and endeavoured to place me in the best position for getting a view of the stage. What a mass of human beings were below me! The place seemed full of heads and one might suppose that the bodies were below but it was impossible to see them so densely were they packed together. Had it not been for the stage in the background with its actors dressed in the gay coloured costumes of a former age and the rude and noisy band it would have reminded me more of the hustings at a contested election in England than anything else. But taken as a whole there was nothing to which I would liken it out of China.

The actors had no stage scenery to assist them in making an impression on the audience. This is not the custom of China. A table, a few chairs and a covered platform are all that is required. No ladies are allowed to appear as actresses in the country but the way in which the sex is imitated is most admirable and always deceives any foreigner ignorant of the fact I have stated. . . .

Of a second performance he saw the same author said :

In the afternoon the play began and attracted in its thousands the happy spectators. As already stated, the subscribers of those who gave the play had a raised platform placed about twenty yards from the front of the stage for themselves and their friends. The public occupied the ground on the front and sides of the stage and to them the whole was free as their mountain air. Each man, however poor, had as good a right to be there as his neighbour. And it is the same all over China; the actors are paid by the rich and the poor are not excluded from participating in the enjoyments of the stage.[10]

An illuminating note on the economics of shows of this kind is provided by another nineteenth-century traveller and diplomat, Sir John Davis, who published a book on the Chinese in 1836. Concerning the Portuguese colony of Macao in south China he wrote:

To prove the rage of the Chinese for theatrical exhibitions we insert an account of the expenses annually incurred at Macao, which is a Portuguese town and contains few rich Chinese, on account of play acting. In front of the large temple near the barrier that confines the Portuguese, twenty-two plays are performed the acting of which alone amounts, without including the expense of erecting the theatre, to 2,200 Spanish dollars. At the Chinese temple near the entrance of the inner harbour there are annual performances for which 2,000 dollars are paid and various lesser exhibitions through the year make up the total expenditure under this head to upwards of 6,000 dollars or £1,500 among a small population of mere shopkeepers and artisans.[11]

The strolling player has been as familiar a figure in Chinese society as he has in the west, and in some ways more persistently active, if only because of the kind of public he served and the conditions under which he worked. No romantic mystique provoked a literary legend in his case, however, and the actor more often than not has been treated with thinly disguised contempt by Chinese writers. In the ordinary public's mind he was classified as a shiftless and immoral person, certainly not a respectable member of society.

The fact that actors and their families were forbidden to present themselves as candidates for the government examinations denied them any standing in the community. For the Chinese, the imperial examinations were the mark of an egalitarian society, a proof that a man's merit, irrespective of his origins, alone decided how high he could rise in the world. There has been considerable debate among modern scholars as to just how true this was; that there were anomalies is plain, but broadly speaking the examinations represented the way to success for every family, and to be denied access to it was not so much to be denied one's rights as to be set apart from the rest, an uneasy fate in a society where conformity mattered before all else. The stigma placed upon the actor put him beyond conformity. No self-respecting person would have dreamed of accepting an actor as a possible son-in-law. If an actor married it had to be within the inbred circle of his own community and this was a factor which made the theatrical profession a closed one.

The use of a generalization like 'the actor' must be qualified by the realization that in China, as elsewhere, the profession contained a varied range of people, talents and kinds of performance. Although in the social hierarchy actors were not distinguished from other kinds of performer it is the actor proper who is implied here and not the acrobat or the storyteller, even though the Chinese actor had to combine the talents of both of these. Not every one in this category was a second-rate player operating on the street corners, as accounts sometimes seem to imply, nor was the fact that actors in general were illiterate a necessary condemnation of talent. The majority of people in China were illiterate and while this might sound like a deplorable situation by contemporary standards it did not prevent either a carpenter or an actor becoming excellent craftsmen and craftsmanship was sought by the Chinese audience before all else. Though they had many reservations about the moral integrity of their actors they had absolutely none about the standards of stage discipline they expected from him. If he disappointed them, like his western counterpart he got 'the bird'. A few years ago a veteran Peking actor in his eighties made this comment on acting standards: 'In feudal China an actor's life was a hard one and an actor's training like a term in jail. But after you had been through an ordeal of seven years' training you still had to find a troupe to take you and joining a troupe was harder than climbing up to heaven.'[12]

The actor in China was essentially the product of Confucian society and the opprobrium he earned was the direct consequence of that society's double standards. A major reason for the public's inhibitions about the acting profession was its age-old association with sexual licence. The courtesan, the catamite and the theatre are an ancient triumvirate, but in China they were linked through a combination of circumstances stemming from the highly systematized segregation of women in normal society.

For centuries prostitutes were an integral part of the Chinese social structure. The tradition was that besides being sexual companions they were trained to entertain as poets, singers and musicians, becoming, so it seems, the forerunners of the actress. In general they were reputed to be blessed with a degree of cultivation denied the virtuous housewife isolated from the world and society. As there were no normal relations between young men and women or indeed the sexes generally by Confucian ethics, the 'sing-song' girl, as she is usually styled in English, offered a psychological escape from the tyranny of patriarchial households and the tensions they involved. The *demi-mondaine* became accepted in principle as the cultivated companion of scholars and gentlemen, creating a legend which was perpetuated in literature and on the stage and which shed its lustre over prostitution and the licenced quarters as the resort of the intelligentsia.

The history of the actress is a vexed question in China and it is difficult to form any detailed estimation from the ambivalent descriptions she has inspired. The theatre was never a field to which reputable Chinese scholars gave much attention and literary recorders of the stage have often been more solicitous about the avid taste of the Chinese for gossip rather than for information. The Chinese themselves most often quote the imperial palace during the period covering the seventh to ninth century AD as a starting point for acting history. The Emperor Ming Huang, whose reign covered the first half of the eighth century, started a training academy for both boys and women performers whose name, the Pear Garden, has passed into history as a term for the theatrical world in general. Although credited as the first theatre school, the emperor's academy was in fact only meant to train singers and dancers for the elaborate entertainments which went on in the pleasure-loving courts of those days. Other academies were founded in the capital for the same purpose and one of them is described as having a thousand trainees, all paid government salaries.[13] Another function of these institutions was to provide recruits for the imperial harem, which like those in other Asian courts of earlier times was maintained on an astonishing scale. To be an imperial concubine was also to be a trained entertainer and although such a woman was scarcely an actress in the accepted sense she provided a precedent of high origin for the combination of sexual attraction and artistic talent which became associated with the name ever afterwards.

During Sung times, which embraced a period from the tenth to twelfth centuries AD, we read of the continuance of the imperial training schools and of new developments in the field of public entertainment. The storyteller's art reached great heights and the puppet theatre, including the shadow show, became much patronized in this era. It was a time of commercial expansion and urban development and one scholar has recorded the existence of professional actors as entertainers of the town crowds. They were organized in small groups of five to seven in number, and were often members of the same family, so that women could participate without causing undue scandal. Whether they were actual performers or musicians is not clear but they indicate an early appearance of women on a public stage. These small groups toured the countryside, gave performances in the city theatres, and entertained the local bigwigs by demand. According to the records, the Sung capital of Kaifeng had fifty theatres, situated in segregated areas known as 'tile' districts, so called because the audiences brought together disappeared at random, like heaps of loosely arranged tiles which quickly fall apart. The theatres were described as fenced enclosures with a gateway covered by playbills and surmounted by streamers and flags. The entrance fee was two hundred coins presumably of small denomination, and the spectator had to climb a planked slope surmounted by a vantage point in the form of a bell tower, flanked on both sides by crowded galleries of spectators. These overlooked a pit, also jammed with spectators, standing before an open stage. The performances were characterized by buffoonery and seem to have been in the form of variety shows rather than straight plays.[14]

Theatre in the sense of a structured play form, with rules of composition and fixed role characterizations, made great strides forward during the thirteenth and fourteenth centuries, which the Chinese have always considered a vital formative period in their drama. The pleasure quarters provided both the setting and the actresses for many of these performances and continued to do so during the next three centuries, which were a time of immense theatrical developments and change. Stage performances of those days remained an intimate art, essentially based on song, music and controlled movement, requiring no elaborate settings. The traditional architectural styles of the larger houses, with galleries or rooms enclosing open courtyards, made an appropriate setting for what were often the private rather than the public entertainments of higher society. Sometimes a permanent stage was constructed but a large room or a courtyard were more often utilized as acting areas and it was not until later that public theatres staging a more literary form of drama began to appear. A banquet at a rich man's house, a social gathering in the brothel quarters, or a family anniversary, these marked the theatrical occasion for the educated classes and wealthier merchants.

A strong spirit of private patronage and amateurism has always infused the Chinese theatre, which has owed much to this factor. Many scholars and officials in the past beguiled their leisure-time with theatre, tried their hands at playwriting, trained their own troupes, and staged performances to which they invited their friends. Actors and actresses were often drawn from the ranks of their servants and slave girls. Professional actors were engaged to teach and lead these private troupes. Wealthy merchants also emulated these methods; besides satisfying their love of theatre and sensual pleasures, they gained great social prestige in their roles as cultural sponsors.

Typical of many educated theatre lovers of this period was the seventeenth-century poet and literary man, Li Yu, who having failed the government examinations lived by his writings and dramatic activities and depended on the patronage of high officials. He travelled widely and maintained a troupe of singing girls who performed in plays staged in the homes of the officials with whom he stayed as a literary guest. He earned a reputation as a talented producer, director and playwright and was said to have kept a household of forty people.[15] Another scholarly bohemian was Chang Tai,[16] also a seventeenth-century literary man, who came from a family noted for their extravagance in building elaborate houses and keeping troupes of actresses. Chang himself is recorded as having had a taste for 'pretty maids and pages, colourful clothes, good cookery, horses, lanterns, fireworks, drama, music, antiques, flowers and birds'. He was an accomplished lute player and a connoisseur of tea, in fact a typical specimen of the old-style Chinese hedonist, with whom the theatre was so often associated in many people's minds.

The history of Chinese theatre can be traced through a series of regional forms whose characteristics gave certain twists to the music and song which has been the basis of all theatre in China. The elaboration and fusion of such forms over long periods of time often created a definitive theatrical genre in a certain locality which made an impact far beyond its place of origin. This was what happened in Soochow in central China which became a dramatic centre of especial importance during the seventeenth and eighteenth centuries. It has been pointed out that Soochow's rise to artistic fame was economic in the first place; mercantile wealth encouraged artistic growth and patronage.[17] The town was situated in a rich rice- and tea-growing area, and being at a strategic point on the Grand Canal and within easy distance of a coastal port it was made an official transportation centre. Silk production gave it further commercial prestige. The prospects of patronage attracted poets and literary men from within a province that had always had its share of them. The result of these many circumstances was that the classical theatre attained one of its great periods in this area. Soochow actors and singing girls became known for their quality and style as well as being the arbiters of fashion.

The 'sing-song' girls who presided over the banquets of officials and scholars or entertained the merchants in the tea houses and wine shops became instrumental in spreading knowledge of the local theatrical style and creating a vogue. The merchants who travelled in and out of the city helped the process, while the waterways which connected the city were a ready means of taking actors, singing girls and boy apprentices to the capital, where the vogue spread, so helping to create a lyrical theatrical style which attained a wide following.

Another important body of merchant patrons of theatre in the eighteenth century were the salt merchants of Yangchow,[18] at that period a town of great economic importance housing the government's Salt Administration. It also occupied a strategic position on the Grand Canal, north of Soochow but in the same province. Its wealthy merchant class became some of the most ardent supporters of theatre; they ran their own troupes, gave public and private performances, and provided many actors with employment. Here again the pleasure quarters were the background for the same pattern of merchant wealth, cultural promotion and sensual indulgence.

Of equal importance to the talented prostitutes of the pleasure quarters were the catamites, whose prevalence and reputation in the Chinese theatrical world did more than anything else to earn disdain for the actor among the ordinary public. In China the complete segregation of women from ordinary life and the technical means taken to resolve this deficiency on the stage were responsible for a class of catamites who gained considerable notoriety as well as artistic acclaim. Pretty boys trained from an early age to simulate feminine mannerisms were often exploited or became exploiters. Although homosexuality was acknowledged in China, as elewhere in Asia, it was an offence punishable by flogging and studiously avoided in discussion by the ordinary public, who in any case assumed that actors, being social outcasts, indulged in every kind of immoral practice. All that mattered was to prevent their contaminating respectable society. In fact the catamites frequently moved in high society and there were many celebrated affairs in literary and official circles. A well known one involved the seventeenth-century poet Ch'en Wei-sung,[19] who though he failed to pass the government examinations was regarded so highly for his literary talent that he was given a post in the prestigious Hanlin Academy. He became enamoured of a talented boy actor in a troupe run by a friend of his family and the verses he composed to him have become famous in Chinese literature.

It was a fashion in the old days to have the boy actors who played female parts wait on the guests and serve wine at banquets, and this was still done in some circles in Peking until well into this century. Needless to say, not every boy actor was a sexual pervert but as training began about the age of seven it was a hard life, with all the attendant hazards for children separated from home and parents. There were no official training academies in our sense in old China and it was a common custom to sell boys as apprentices into private troupes run by former actors who often travelled the country looking for recruits. There are harrowing stories told of boys sold in this way and unquestionably there were many malpractices. Nevertheless, one should not forget that Dickensian England was scarcely a paradise for poor children, who were sold into trades and occupations in much the same way. There were plenty of just acting masters who treated their pupils well according to the standards of the day. Discipline was rigid and corporal punishment an accepted method of enforcing it, but it would be wrong to assume that every actor began life as a slave sold into bondage for immoral purposes. Parents who sold their children in this way usually did so out of dire economic straits and looked upon it as a means to get their family provided for. There were always those with ulterior motives, as well as boys who ran away and joined troupes for reasons of their own, but every actor had to be apprenticed to a troupe in childhood. It was the only method of training in the old days. Many of the more famous training troupes had no need to recruit youngsters, as there were always pupils to join their ranks. Professional acting became a hereditary vocation and theatrical families made sure their children went through the training mill. They had to if they were to survive in a highly competitive vocation hedged about with the most fearsome official restrictions. Any actor who did not thoroughly master his craft stood little chance of getting anywhere.

Besides the training troupes described there were a number of privately run schools which became active during the late nineteenth and early twentieth centuries. The last and most famous of these, the Fu Lien Ch'eng, closed its doors for good in Peking on the eve of the second world war. It had been active for forty years and some of the most talented Peking actors of this century were trained there. The actor Mei Lan-fang,[20] famous for his female roles, attended the school for a time in his childhood and has left a detailed description of its aims and organization in his memoirs. They are probably the most vivid account we are likely to have on the subject. Like all its kind the school was privately owned and was founded by a business man, an amateur musician and theatre lover, who took a professional actor as his partner. They began with half a dozen students and capital of 300 silver taels, the tael, a standard currency unit, being worth around thirty-four new pence or eighty American cents. The school changed hands in 1911 but the actor-partner carried on as general manager. During its four decades of activity the school trained seven hundred students, including costume and make-up specialists. Needless to say no girls were admitted.

A student joining the school could enter at any time once the consent of the owner was given. The parents were then asked to meet him with their son. If the would-be pupil was considered physically suitable and satisfactory references were provided, the parents left their child in the school's hands. After two months' probation a contract was drawn up and signed by the parents, as well as by a sponsor/guarantor in later times. The course lasted seven years and during that time the pupil was boarded, fed and clothed by the school, and could not withdraw of his own accord. If a student proved delinquent he was dismissed. The minimum/maximum admission age was between seven and twelve years. Every student had to take a full seven-year course. Performance was reviewed in the fifth year and if it was decided there was no future for a particular student as actor he was allowed to study as a theatre musician or costume and make-up assistant. The aim was to see that the student left the school at least accomplished in some aspect of the profession. There was no general education but the principal lectured them on moral principles and professional behaviour. Everyone was accorded the same treatment. There were two meals a day, steamed bread and tea for breakfast and a big bowl of rice and pork and cabbage or a similar accompanying dish for the evening meal. The students queued up five at a time with their bowls, and Muhammadan students got special food. Frugal living though it was, the principal supervised its quality. The teachers were entitled to two bowls of rice and four dishes. Twice a week the students were marched to the public baths. When the students went to bed a teacher stayed with them all night as supervisor and there was also a twice-nightly inspection by the principal. Students rose at seven in the morning and practised singing for three hours. If they were not required to go to the theatre they carried on with practice in other areas the whole day, which ended at 11.30, with a break for dinner. Learning was by practical experience as well as practice. Senior students performed in the school's own troupe which appeared regularly at the city theatres and was a major source of income for the school. Young professionals were also brought in from outside to act with the troupe. The professionals were always anxious to get experience and they also helped to tide over that difficult period in a Chinese theatre student's career when his voice broke.[21] Those students on call for the theatres, which opened at 12.30, were lined up for roll call, in formal dress, then marched to the theatre in a long file in descending order of height, a supervising teacher bringing up the rear. Arrived at the theatre they changed into costume, and when the theatres closed at six in the evening they were marched back to school in the same way. There was a second roll call before being dismissed for dinner, after which they studied again until 11.30. Most of the students in the school were from professional acting families. The teachers were on a visiting basis; some stayed to see a generation of pupils through, others were more short-lived, but all of them without exception were professionals actively engaged in the area of theatre which they taught.

In addition to schools like this there were the private teachers to whom most acting students went for more specialized knowledge once they had completed their basic training. The majority of children from acting families began their studies with private teachers and Mei has related his own routine at the age of nine. Each morning at five he was taken for a walk beneath the city wall to practice singing against its surface, a common method in former times for strengthening the lungs and voice control. After that, according to his narrative, his whole day except for short breaks was spent in work. In the morning he had a teacher for the words and melodies of famous plays. He stood by a table while the teacher sat beside him on a chair and beat out the time on the table with a wooden ruler which was also used to strike the erring pupil. Each phrase of the script had to be repeated between twenty and thirty times and at the end of each repetition the teacher took a copper coin from a pile standing on the table and placed it in a lacquer bowl. When each session had been completed in this way he put the coins back and started all over again. 'Sometimes,' Mei recalled, 'I was perfect after six or seven attempts but he still went on. Sometimes I was so tired that, although still singing, my eyes closed and I wanted to nod. He shook me and as though wakened from a dream I continued the struggle. His method was liberal for those days. If it had been any other teacher his ruler would already have cracked across my head.'[22] The old acting training was severe and hard on youngsters but to be the child of an acting family was to have few illusions about the necessity for work. It was get on or get out and for people denied status in normal society there were few places to go to outside their own ingrown profession, except perhaps the world of organized vice.

The type of theatre for which such arduous training was demanded reached a peak of expression in the nineteenth century and survived in principle, though with many modifications, until very recent times. It attained its greatest general popularity in the Peking style, which was only one of many regional genres and a synthesis of various local styles. China has had hundreds of different regional styles of theatre. A man from Peking, Soochow or Canton might well have countered any attempt to generalize about Chinese theatre by asking which Chinese theatre? Every area had its own versions, not necessarily musically pleasing and certainly not linguistically intelligible to the other. This being the case for the Chinese, how much more confusing for the foreigner confronted with the technical niceties of different dialects and local musical preferences. Nevertheless, whatever the regional variations, all Chinese theatre began with the same premise, a synthesis of music, speech and formalized movement realized through an elaborate system of commonly recognized acting conventions.

The Peking theatre gained its reputation partly because of a very talented body of actors who developed these conventions to a supreme pitch in the skilful presentation of something for everybody from the rich repertoire of the past. In 1935, Berthold Brecht had his first experience of Chinese acting when he saw the Peking actor, Mei Lan-fang, who played women's roles, give a demonstration before notabilities in a Moscow reception room. Speaking of the occasion in an article Brecht asked: 'What western actor of the old school could have demonstrated the elements of his art without special lighting and wearing a dinner jacket in an ordinary room filled with specialists? What about the sanctity of art, the mysteries of metamorphosis. . . .'[23] Western acting by these standards seemed hopelessly inadequate.

The Peking-style theatre was a popular entertainment despised by many intellectuals for its debasement of classical sources, although it was the successful adaptation of these which gave it strength and gained the affection of the public. It really owed its existence in the first place to the peripatetic nature of the theatrical profession. The melodic patterns of regional style were always important to inventiveness on the Chinese stage. When these patterns were carried to fresh areas by wandering performers they in turn became affected by local influences; dialect particularly aided change. Musical-narrative styles often ended up by being unrecognizable when compared to their originals. The Peking theatre was the product of two or three centuries of such cross-fusion. Its emergence as a popular form of entertainment really dates from the year 1790 when the eightieth birthday of the Emperor Ch'ien Lung was celebrated with elaborate pageantry and a spate of theatrical performances in Peking. New styles seen at that time retained their attraction for the theatre-going public of the capital which became the goal of actors from many different provinces. It was they who made the nineteenth-century theatre into an art which became a passion for its followers.

The Chinese theatregoer went to the theatre not to watch the play but to see and hear his favourite actors show their mettle, and show it they did. They declaimed, postured, struck attitudes and sang. Their techniques were marked by vigour and panache to which gesture, make-up and costume gave their own emphasis. A play came to life through the harmonious coordination of an entire constellation of technical means, every one of which was meticulously fitted into place through the rigorous perfection of its conventions.

The character roles of the traditional Chinese actor are divided into four main categories of male, female, painted face and comic roles. Within these are the further tight divisions of the bearded actor or mature man, the warrior, the patriarch, the official, the young male, hero and lover, the virtuous woman, the coquette, the matriarch and the clown. The clown again neatly compartments humanity in degrees of the ridiculous with his interpretation of the military dotard or the cunning peasant. Man and not his aspirations was the preoccupation of the Chinese stage. The greatest concession to fantasy was in the painted-face characters, whose bizarre make-up, colour symbolism and prescribed patterns portrayed generals, brigands or demons. Their vocal technique was marked by a tremendous range and volume. Everything about their grotesque figures and vocal bombast suggested might and power as they stamped and stormed about the stage, roaring their defiance, their eyes flickering in the mask-like frame of their many-hued make-up. Each role and role division had its prescribed costumes, make-up, gestures and forms of speech. The thoroughgoing generalisation of humanity did away with any necessity of elaborate settings. A table, a couple of chairs and an embroidered curtain were enough to delineate the world conjured up by the actor; virtue was virtue and evil evil whatever the time and period. One of the more typical bits of

business on the traditional Chinese stage was shooting the bolt
of an imaginary door, pushing back its two sections and stepping
over the threshold, all conjured up by the skilful pantomime
of the actor and defining time and place for the audience.
Behind that door might be found the virtuous wife whose
Confucian integrity sustained her through the interminable
absences of a husband who was either a warrior gone to the wars
or an official travelling to take the imperial examination. Her
wistful personality was interpreted through a vocal technique
characterized by a high, shrill falsetto which attained rippling
cadences of sound accompanied by graceful convolutions of the
long floating white silk cuffs attached to the sleeves of the
costume.

Or a swordsman was perhaps revealed clad in tight-fitting
black tunic, breeches, black satin flat-soled boots and a hat
like an outsize tam-o-shanter. A killer of tigers and a man of
the people, his scimitar was his constant companion used to
enforce a chivalrous code which Robin Hood might have
envied. His flashing blade seemed to leave a glittering trail of
light behind it as he leapt, parried and turned furious somersaults landing on his feet with the noiseless agility of a cat.
Yet this seemingly spontaneous outburst of violent movement
was superbly controlled with a pattern of gymnastic form which
would be repeated without change day after day. The admiring
audience waited for that moment when the actor sprang forward in a defiant pose that in effect said, 'Just watch me!' It
was the same thing in a more subdued way with the stage
interpretation of the scholar-official. His measured pace, caress-
ing of his beard and precise flick of silk sleeves became subtle
elements of a choreographic pattern emphasizing a crystalline
perfectionism as he expressed and re-expressed his sentiments
in song. In the words of Brecht, the masterly use of gesture
and movement in Chinese acting bore 'the hallmark of something rehearsed and rounded off, giving an impression of ease
and at the same time of difficulties which have been overcome'.

The music and dialogue of the traditional Peking theatre
were neither complicated nor deep and sprang quickly to the
minds of the ordinary public. The plays in general were drawn
from great historical novels such as *The Story of the Three
Kingdoms* or similar sources. Their subjects were familiar to

F

every member of the audience, who were in no doubt as to the character or motives of the personalities portrayed. More often than not, dramatists were anonymous or themselves actors. Few great literary names were associated with the plays of the Peking stage. The language of the plays was a special idiom which drew on the dialects of several different provinces for its euphony and sonority. Great use was made of the set phrases which were so plentiful in the Chinese literary language. Quotations came as second nature to the Chinese, for whom practically any situation could be evoked by some succinct phrase or couplet. The communal memory was stirred by these snippets from the classical language which through its imagery conveyed the most complex emotion in a surprisingly short sentence. It has been said that the language of the theatre was the single form through which Chinese thought became accessible to all the people.

Music on the stage was provided by an orchestra who sat in full view; it consisted of drum and castanets, played by the leaders, gongs, cymbals and two-stringed instruments. The first of these, the *hu-ch'in,* was the principal instrument of accompaniment for the singing. Every famous actor had his own hu-ch'in player. The shrill but supple rhythms of this instrument were offset by the softer plucking of the moon-guitar, whose swift syncopation formed a constant undercurrent of counter-melody. A strictly limited number of modes, whose standard patterns of slow beat, quick beat, reversed beat and so on covered the gamut of mood and emotion, resulted in short, well-formed tunes with an instantaneous impact. Every line and stanza was an entity which created a familiar response in the minds of the audience.

The first impression of any visitor to a traditional Chinese theatre was one of unbridled noise which assaulted the ear from every direction. The audience laughed and talked, vendors wandered to and fro selling melon seeds, peanuts and serving tea. Attendants hurled hot towels across the heads of the audience to be dexterously caught by their companions on the opposite side of the house. Everybody was obviously thoroughly enjoying themselves and the noise was so deafening that no one outside his own group knew what the rest were talking about, or even cared. The clash and clang of the brass percussion instruments on the stage was deafening and the last thing the actors seemed to be concerned with was the audience, or they with the actors, who came and went on the uncurtained stage as though they had simply been set in motion and would continue until they had run down.

The pulsating din and bustle seemed to reiterate that man the individual was irrelevant on the stage. Nevertheless there came that moment in every performance when the rhythm of the music changed. There was a hush as the lilt of some familiar air set heads nodding in time and fingers tapping out the beat on their knees. The actor circled the stage pouring out his story through song and gesture until the audience burst into staccato shouts of approval. Once again tradition had been honoured.

The group spirit of the Chinese expressed through the family system was very receptive to theatre as a demonstration of solidarity. Whether it accompanied the festivals which marked the community cycle, official banquets, family celebrations, the harvest home in the village temple or simply private junketings, a stage performance of one kind or another emphasized the close links theatre had with the daily life of the people. The merchant guilds were a particularly outstanding expression of this social cohesion. The principle by which everyone belonging to one trade or occupation became organized in a group was very old in China, but many of the important guilds in Peking dated their histories from the early seventeenth century when the Manchus conquered China and there was a need to re-group against alien influences. Guilds varied in size and strength according to the particular trade or occupation but every city had its own guilds. Every guild had its own patron deity or hero, a special protector of the group, usually a figure who had a seminal place in the history of the particular activity with which the guild was concerned. Great emphasis was laid on the worship of these patrons whose anniversaries were treated as special holidays on which there was invariably a feast and a theatrical performance. The Boot Guild in Peking in September 1918, for example, opened their expense sheet with the following preamble:

> To our God the Great Teacher and the God of Wealth we want to sacrifice to our God for the benefit of the Boot Guild so on the 15th day of the 9th month of the 7th year of the

Republic [1918] we will give a play in our temple and each must pay six hundred cash for incense fees. . . .

For the performance of the play they paid 90,400 copper coins.

Actors in south China on the patron saint day staged a special play whose theme was the birthday of the Goddess of Mercy. It was a ritual performance by the profession, not a public performance, and it began at eight in the morning and ended at noon. The play contained a scene which portrayed the monkey god and his armies and for this the acrobats from every theatrical troupe in the area took part in the spectacle. Nobody received any pay but everyone brought offerings and these were auctioned afterwards for the benefit of the guild. This was only one of the many guild customs which varied all over China.[24] The Peking actors formerly had their guild headquarters in a temple and worshipped a patron deity called Lao Lang, who was said to represent the Emperor Ming Huang, mentioned earlier as the first important patron of the theatre. Kuan Kung, the God of War, was also adopted as a protector by the acting profession as he was by many other vocations concerned with making money in public. By some inversion of reasoning, his powerful presence became the deterrent against evil forces affecting the welfare of the theatre. Small shrines to the patron deities were placed backstage in the theatres and it was common to see every actor pay his respects before going on. Kuan Kung was also a character in a famous cycle of warrior plays and the only deified hero who actually appeared on stage in plays written about him. A famous Shanghai actor who played this role for fourteen years in the old days refused to be photographed in his stage costume. When he entered the theatre he burned incense at the shrine and would not speak to anyone, a silence which was maintained in his dressing room where no one was allowed to see him apply his make-up.[25] Such was the ritual inspired by the impersonation of a sacred character.

The most important merchant guilds had their own halls, often elaborate premises with gardens, courtyards, banquet rooms and a stage. The Peking guilds were noted for the theatrical performances they sponsored at the New Year, either on their own premises or elsewhere. These performances customarily began at ten in the morning and finished at five in the afternoon. Many leading actors performed on the guild stages and the audiences were known for their high critical standards.

On New Year's Day in Peking the ordinary theatres opened at nine in the morning and closed at three in the afternoon. Audiences were thin, as most people were making the ritual visits to family which are customary on that day; moreover, as the actors had been up all night themselves for the ceremony of paying homage to the ancestors, they stood on the stage 'as though in the clouds', and were certainly not on top form. Nevertheless, every troupe of worth was compelled to go through this procedure, as it was a good omen for the new year ahead and also a form of advertisement for the troupe itself, so every actor had to be on stage. No salary was paid for this perform-ance but every actor received a red paper envelope containing a nominal sum in copper coinage as a sign of equality. The plays given on this day were all auspicious in content; death scenes, trials, anything calculated to introduce the wrong note at this season of rejoicing and renewal was barred.[26]

Once the New Year holiday was under way actors became frantically busy not only with public appearances but with private performances as well. These were a well-established feature of Chinese social life, much in evidence at this time of year, and an important source of employment for established actors, who were in great demand. In his memoirs, Mei Lan-fang has written that he used to give as many as three or four different performances a day at the height of the season, rushing from one to the other with no time to eat or rest.[27] The nature of Chinese theatrical technique made this kind of thing possible. An actor was trained to play a certain type of role and his training had fitted him to step into any play requiring such a role at a minute's notice. He needed no rehearsal. Performances for private patrons given in their residences, in restaurants[28] or in banquet halls were always the accompaniment to a feast and could be very elaborate affairs in the case of wealthy men. They might commemorate a wedding or an anniversary, or simply be the means of entertaining friends or business acquaintances. Whatever the occasion they were a most popular custom. That keen observer Robert Fortune has also left us a revealing account of one of these events in the early part of last century and it deserves quotation in full for its accuracy of detail and evocative atmosphere:

Whilst at Shanghae [Shanghai], I, with some other Europeans, had an invitiation to go to the house of a mandarin to see a theatrical performance or 'sing-song' and to dine with him in Chinese style afterwards. Sedan chairs were sent to take us to his house, where we were introduced to a number of his friends, and as the invariable custom is, tea was immediately handed round. Shortly afterwards a servant came with a tray full of warm wet towels not unlike those generally used in kitchens at home and presented one to each of us. At first we could not conjecture what these were but on looking at our Chinese friends we observed them rubbing their faces and hands with them and although not very agreeable to us we immediately did the same. I afterwards found that this was a common custom among the Chinese and I have often been much refreshed by it after a warm walk. In hot countries like China this plan is much better and more conducive to health than either washing or bathing in cold water.

While this was going on in the house the players were getting everything ready in a large room where the performance was to take place. In a little while one of them entered the room where we were, carrying in his hand several fine long ivory cards on which were written a number of the most popular plays of the day, any one of which the players were ready to perform at the command of our host and his friends. We were politely consulted on the subject which, as we did not know a single character of the language and had the greatest difficulty in understanding what was said to us, was not of much use. Having at last fixed upon a particular piece for the evening's entertainment we were all led into the theatre. The room was large and nearly square, having a platform at the upper end for the actors and the band and one of the sides being only separated from an open lane by a wooden railing so that the public might also have a view of the play. The centre of the room was completely filled with guests and from the roof hung a number of lanterns in Chinese style. As it was early in the afternoon when the play commenced the lanterns were not lighted and the piece went on in daylight, the Chinese actors not excluding it as we do in our theatres in England.

The play began with some pantomime-like feats such as we see in English theatres at Christmas. This was succeeded by something which appeared to be very pathetic, judging from the language and gesture of the performers. All were gone through in a kind of opera style, the actors singing their parts with false voices. The feats of tumbling which were now and then performed were extremely dextrous and clever and attracted our notice more than anything else, probably because they were best understood. The dresses of the actors were superb and must have cost a large sum of money. There were no females among them as it is not customary for them to act; but their places were supplied by men or boys chosen from among those who are most 'lady-looking', and so well were their appearance and dresses arranged that it would have required a practised eye to have detected the difference. The voices of the actors were not musical, at least to English ears, but the whole was in unison with the noisy gong and the wind instruments which are in common use among the Chinese. In fact noise seemed to be the thing which produced the greatest effect and we certainly had enough of it. I was struck by the various figures made by the actors on the stage, intended no doubt to represent something like those scenes or pictures which are so much studied in our theatres at home. A quadrant seems to be a great favourite and was constantly made by them in the different acts. They have no scenery to assist the delusion, only a simple screen which is sometimes used to represent a room out of which some actor is to make his appearance. Fencing is much practised and is perhaps the most curious part of their exhibitions. Each individual has two swords which he swings about his head in the wildest manner at the same time throwing his feet and legs about in a most fantastic way as if they had as much to do in the business as had the hands and arms. The exhibition or play lasted for three hours and then we left the theatre and returned into the other room. While we were there the servants were busily employed in rearranging the theatre which was now to be converted into a dining room.

The play was resumed again as soon as the dinner commenced and continued as briskly as ever. The 'lady actors' at intervals came down from the platform and supplied the guests with different kinds of wines. During the entertainment a piece of money was handed to each guest which they were desired to leave as a present for the actors at the conclusion of the piece. When this was given them the whole of the *corps dramatique* came round and each made a most polite bow of acknowledgement and withdrew. Still, however, the dinner ceremonial went on; hundreds of fresh dishes were brought in and as many in their turn removed. The Chinese guests were sometimes smoking, sometimes eating, just as it seemed good to them and uniformly praising everything which made its appearance on the table.[29]

Allowing for the typical reactions and prejudices of the foreigner ignorant about Chinese theatre this is an amazingly faithful picture of the procedure at a private performance in the house of a wealthy person. The choosing of the plays by the guests as described here was typical of this kind of show while the serving of wine by the boy actors of women's roles has been commented on earlier. Even the descriptions of the actors' performances, though elementary, can be recognized; the troupe hired for the occasion was obviously a first-class one.

Acting troupes in China always worked under the direction and control of a leader, himself an actor, who engaged each member of his troupe through contract. Troupes were peripatetic and covered a considerable territory in the provinces, often travelling by boat and by mule carts. The larger city troupes usually remained within the urban boundaries but even they moved about from theatre to theatre; no performances lasted more than two or three days in any one place. Troupes were disbanded and regrouped each year. A common practice was to break up each summer and band together in the autumn. Actors were re-engaged each time. Customs varied a little in different parts of the country but the general principles were always the same. Once a troupe was formed it remained an entity until the end of the tour. Actors changed their troupes according to circumstances and need, but once a troupe had built up a reputation the chief actors tended to remain together over long periods especially in the well-known city troupes.

All actors in China were paid on a fixed portion basis, that is to say the leader of the troupe paid each member a sum whose amount was in proportion to his acting importance. This practice remained in force until very recent times. Some Soochow troupes[30] started a custom at the beginning of the century whereby at the end of a six-months' engagement any profits were added to the actors' regular portions in proportionate percentage and if there was a loss deducted in the same way. Payment of the rank and file was generally meagre and that of supernumeraries little better than coolies. As balance against that, the leaders of troupes were responsible for the board and lodging of the actors while on tour. In Peking some of the old troupes ran dormitories for their actors.

One old Peking actor has described a beginner's employment problems at the end of last century:

Even after you had succeeded in joining a company, it was still impossible to make a living for you had to work without pay for six months. A new actor had to feed himself or perform on an empty stomach. For six months he didn't get a cent no matter in what straits his family were. He just had to tighten his belt so that his name might appear on the company's list. When actors like myself could go on as a carriage driver or a messenger we were already thankful. It was very hard to get a real part. After six months all we got was fifty per cent of the tips after each performance. An actor earning one string of cash,[31] slightly less than fifty cents a day, was already getting somewhere. To make two strings of cash a day you had to work hard for three years. This meant that actors who were not known had to perform and work at a trade at the same time, for they could not make a living by acting alone. I was a small tradesman myself. In 1900, the twenty-sixth year of Kuang Hsu, I joined the Tung Ching company. My daily pay was one string of cash but I dared not ask for more.[32]

A typical Peking theatre troupe in the early years of this century included, besides the leader and his actors, a business manager and a back-stage manager whose job it was to arrange the programmes and allot roles. In Peking an acting troupe was divided into male, female, painted face and young hero roles, and actors were engaged to take part within the various subdivisions of these main groups according to their qualifications and the needs of the troupe. Every troupe had to offer an extensive repertoire, including plays for special occasions or festivals. A high standard of acting was essential to play any of the principal roles and competition was very keen. Though the better-known actors led independent lives there was a large proportion of the less successful who shared communal kitchens in mean lodgings and whose existence was little better than a pauper's. When they grew old they were often in desperate straits and if they had no relatives or successful pupils to help them there was no one to give them a funeral when they died and that was the most dreaded fate for any Chinese. Often members of a troupe would make a collection so that the dead man could be buried in the common graveyard for actors maintained outside the city and kept up by the profession through its guild.

In the old days programmes were never announced in advance in the Peking theatres, and no actor was supposed to know what his role would be until the day of the performance, although it was usually possible with the right kind of persuasion to find out.[33] There were no printed programmes and the most that was vouchsafed was a little paper slip giving the titles of the plays. Programmes were changed without notice and it was the temperamental privilege of the better-known actors to cancel an appearance without warning. Even so, the audiences were well catered for in a city like Peking. There was always something going on and actors were certainly not in short supply. The larger companies performed almost continuously throughout the theatrical year and the better known theatres scarcely ever closed their doors unless for special reasons. Performances began in the morning and ended at sunset. No artificial lighting was used until well into the present century and evening perform- ances were forbidden by government edict because of possible disturbances and fire hazards.

The long history of open air performances in China, and the widely followed practice of performing in private houses, banquet halls, restaurants and the like, retarded the growth of a permanent style of theatre architecture. It is true there were the old temple stages, often built of stone, but their function was inseparable from religious ritual and they could scarcely be classed as purely secular and commercial in purpose. Permanent structures were the exception rather than the rule in former times and when they did exist were rather as an adjunct to another building or part of an amusement area. This last tradition was perpetuated in places like the Great World in Shanghai, laid out during the present century and imitated in Singapore. The mat-shed stage, a temporary structure of bamboo poles, planking, and rush mats for awnings, could almost be called the typical Chinese theatre. It has been used for centuries by itinerant troupes in villages, towns and at fairs, and it is still regarded as the most practical and functional method of serving the ephemeral needs of theatre. Erected over- night, and as quickly taken down, it might be a simple stage at the end of a city street or a roofed auditorium of matting and bamboo scaffolding capable of seating a thousand people.

It was not until well into the eighteenth century that theatres as permanent structures for public entertainment began to be seen in the cities to any appreciable extent. Peking, being the capital, had the first concentration, though once built these theatres underwent no further development in the city's conservative atmosphere. It was in Shanghai, a great port city much closer to western influence, that the newer kinds of theatre buildings were first seen in China. When the actor Mei Lan-fang was invited to Shanghai for the first time in 1913, the theatre where he appeared used stage footlights, and he has recorded his excitement at this phenomenon, at that time unknown in his native Peking.[34]

The oldest theatre[35] in Peking, said to date from the early eighteenth century, was only pulled down in the early 1950s to make way for a cinema. It was typical of a genre which lingered in the capital long after it had disappeared elsewhere. The close association of theatrical performance with eating, drinking and social occasions of every kind meant that when theatres were first built as permanent additions to city life, they were treated primarily as places where performance was incidental to catering for the gregarious habits of the people who went there to meet their friends, gossip, sip tea, crack melon seeds and generally indulge the uninhibited social instincts which were characteristic of the Chinese. This was only among the male population, let it be said; etiquette and prejudice forbade the attendance of women in such public places. Many of these early theatres were called tea houses, a name which has persisted into modern times, and the central portion of the ground floor of the auditorium was occupied by tables at which the guests sat facing each other and not the stage, the area being popularly known as 'the pond' to the audiences. A typical theatre of this kind was rectangular in design with an extensive galleried area on the second storey where the wealthier and more important members of the audience usually sat and in some cases were screened off from the vulgar gaze. Like theatres everywhere, those in China accommodated audiences according to the price they could pay, but there were areas in the galleries where only the privileged were allowed, and in later times, when women were finally tolerated, they were segregated in the gallery at the back of the theatre. The connoisseurs who were the dedicated theatregoers had wooden benches close to the stage on either side of it. The traditional Chinese stage was a square raised platform open on three sides and with a pillar at each corner supporting an ornate wooden canopy. Between the rear pillars of the stage there was a wooden wall with a doorway at the right and left as entry and exit, facing the audience. The doors were curtained with embroidered hangings, and a large embroidered satin hanging covered the rear wall in front of which the orchestra were seated. A low balustrade surrounded the stage; fixed to supports in the canopy above there was an iron bar used for acrobatics in the more spectacular plays.

The spectator did not pay for an admission ticket but for a small pot of tea which was served him by an usher when he entered the theatre. He was also given a cushion and a little paper slip with the names of the plays on it. From this he had a good inkling of what actors he was likely to see perform in the roles concerned and there was always a certain measure of pleasurable anticipation in not knowing who would finally appear. Ushers could be paid on the spot but many regular theatregoers ran accounts with them for they were important people and their word was law in the auditorium.[36] Peking theatregoers used to speak of going to listen to a play and of hearing an actor sing a drama. Where song and music were such an essential ingredient of the plays this was understandable, and there were always those moments in the theatre when a long and well-known passage of song occurred, when the fans would close their eyes and beat out the time with their hands while savouring the words. But it would be nonsense to suggest that there was nothing but singing on the old Peking stage, where the spectacular fighting scenes, the witty eroticism of the female impersonators, the earthy humour of the clowns, and, not least, the breath-taking feats of acrobatics and sword play, equally appealed to the audiences, whose noisy cries of 'hao, hao', 'good, oh very good', expressed their appreciation of a manysided art which had tremendous theatrical appeal. It used to be said in Peking, 'Actors are madmen, playgoers are fools', which is one way of defining the power of communication in the theatre.

The old theatres were badly lit, cold in winter, hot in summer, unbelievably noisy and vibrant with life. Authorities usually confined them to specific areas, and in Peking the Manchu government forbade any theatres to be built inside the walled areas of the city which housed the emperor's palaces and the

residences and offices of government. Most of the theatres therefore were crowded into an area outside one of the main gates of
the city, and here they traditionally remained close to a meat
market, a fish market, and with the licenced quarters not far
away.

The Manchus, who conquered China in 1644 and remained
in power until 1908, were in general permissive towards the
stage. Although their rule was characterized by a long series of
edicts and legislation designed to shackle the theatre, many members of the imperial family were unusually devoted followers.
Manchu society was surrounded with a web of rules and regulations devised to cover every aspect of living down to the last
button on their clothing. A great deal of the ritual devised to
uphold the power and dignity of conquerors, who had been
converted to Chinese customs rather than abrogating them, often
became cumbersome and discriminatory where it impinged on
the ordinary people's lives. The theatrical world was a particular
victim. A court order which caused them unnecessary suffering
was one dealing with state mourning when a member of the
imperial family died. Theatres were ordered to be closed, and in
the case of an emperor or empress a period of one hundred days
was decreed. This spelt financial disaster for theatre people in
general. The blackest time of all occurred in 1875 when the tenth
emperor died and his wife survived him by a matter of seventy-
four days. The double period of mourning which followed brought
bankruptcy to many in the theatre.

Others were penalized through such laws. In the autumn of
1689 the tutor of the grand secretary's son attended a convivial
party at which a play by a much admired dramatist and poet
was staged. As it happened to be a period of mourning for a
female member of the imperial family, authority was scandal-
ized and the tutor was dismissed from the imperial Academy
and forbidden to take further examinations for promotion. The
dramatist was similarly expelled from the Academy, yet a few
years later the offending play came to the attention of the
emperor, who admired it greatly and rewarded the author, a
comment on the paradox of theatre in high Chinese society.[37]

The court conducted its own bureau of theatrical affairs[38]
within the palace administration and many high personages
were closely involved with theatre and music in various ways.

It was even reported that the fifth Ch'ing emperor was the son of a Soochow actress who had entered court service, suggesting a more than usually close link of the Son of Heaven with a controversial segment of society.

The sixth Ch'ing emperor was a man especially known for his interest in theatre pageantry, and the celebrations given in honour of his own and his mother's birthdays during the course of his reign were noted for their elaborate theatrical displays. The festivities for his eightieth birthday in 1790 have gone down in theatre history because of the new acting styles that were introduced to the capital on this occasion.[39]

There were theatrical black sheep of the imperial family as well. The third son of the seventh Ch'ing emperor earned a reputation for his insolence, an interest in theatre and music, and a partiality for low company. He was finally reduced in rank and died in disgrace as the result of an affair concerning two young Soochow actors whom he kept imprisoned in his mansion.

Among all the imperial devotees of theatre, however, none was better known than the old empress dowager, the last effective ruler of the Ch'ing dynasty, who died in 1908. She was passionately fond of the theatre and regularly ordered Peking troupes up to the palace to entertain her. Practically every well-known Peking actor popular in the earlier decades of this century had memories of appearing at the palace.

A veteran of them all, an old comic role actor called Hsiao, in 1959 recorded that when he joined his first troupe in 1897 it was ordered to the palace twice a year. It was usual in the past for these occasions to be recorded in all actors' biographies as a mark of professional honour although according to old Hsiao such honours were hard earned. He recalled how one winter they were summoned to perform at the Winter Palace and set out at dawn on foot through the wind and snow as 'actors in those days were considered too low class to ride in carriages'. The performance began at noon and when the empress appeared they were all led out to kowtow before her. 'You might imagine that the backstage in the palace would be fairly roomy,' Hsiao has said, 'but in fact it was smaller than the average theatre. We dressed in the corridor and in mid-winter it was bitterly cold – when we ground a stick of the old-style ink in water it was soon frozen. Our head dresses were covered with ice ... there was only cold water to wash in ... we just put up with the discomfort only hoping that we wouldn't be summoned too often. On the stage we took great care not to make any mistakes for fear of some terrible penalty. We all breathed a great sigh of relief when this command performance was over, feeling as if we had been through purgatory as a punishment for our sins.'[40] It was a comment on a dying age of imperial patronage and the harshness of the ordinary actor's life.

In 1911, revolution broke out in China, the culmination of a long series of events in which a growing dissatisfaction with the old society reached a violent climax. It was compounded of many causes: the impact of western political, religious and economic ideas on the thinking of Chinese leaders and intellectuals concerned about their country's future, a long hidden resentment against a dynasty which had always been foreign to the Chinese, and above all the active presence of a growing younger generation educated by western methods. An important step had been the abolition of the old civil service examinations in 1905 and the substitution of a modern school system for the old Confucian style education.

China was officially declared a republic in 1912 and this was followed by a growing movement among the younger generation for the repudiation of the entire Confucian way of living with its family basis and emphasis on universal decorum. Yet the traditional obligations and attitudes remained peculiarly resilient and the customary social ties constantly reasserted themselves even among the young. Much of the sound and fury of national reform was offset by comparatively modest institutional changes; the fabric of the old civilization was still secure. There were many attempts to build round it but the disproportions remained.

The theatre was a mirror which at first only palely reflected the enthusiasms and ambivalence of the new age. The earliest sign of anything resembling a new theatre movement came from a group of Chinese students in Tokyo, an active centre of their revolutionary hopes. In 1907 they staged their own version of Dumas' *La Dame aux Camélias* in the local premises of the YMCA in order to raise money for a flood relief fund in China. A few months later they put on another play, a Chinese translation of Harriet Beecher Stowe's *Uncle Tom's Cabin*, whose theme of racial prejudice appealed to their current mood of protest against oppression. The religious sentiment of the original was eliminated and their version depicted a black victory over white troops and traders. In 1961 the author of the script, who had been an experienced actor of the traditional theatre's female roles in his youth, described the play as 'an attempt to alert the vigilance of our countrymen'.[41]

Whether the play had real theatrical merit apart from the melodrama of its nationalistic sentiments it is hard to say but it was successfully staged by a second Chinese group in Shanghai during the autumn of 1907. So began what has somewhat euphemistically been called the modern Chinese drama. Its sponsors were amateurs, untrained in western stage methods, often confused, but dedicated to their cause of social reform. A seminal point in the intellectual history of modern China was the May Fourth movement of 1919, so called after an outburst of patriotic protest by Peking students who were incensed by the Versailles Treaty concessions to the Japanese. The repercussions from it were in the first place literary and intellectual, resulting in a decisive protest against the old language and culture and a call for their complete reform. Among other things a deeper study of western drama was stimulated in the belief that it provided a potential weapon both as a medium for literary change and as an advocate of social reform.

Hu Shih, a dominating figure of the movement, a brilliant academic and one of the sponsors of language reform, at one point called for the relegation of 'useless survivals which remained intact', a reference to the acting style of the traditional theatre. He considered this should be abolished as 'the chorus, mask and formal aside had long ago been abolished on the western stage'. Progress in Chinese literature and drama, he suggested, could only come through more intimate contact with western writing and plays. Hu Shih and his fellow reformers wanted to make language a tool which could be used for realistic description, and to this end they minimized the old tradition of literary form. They succeeded in their language aims but ignored the true nature of theatre which cannot dispense with form. Their most significant effect on the drama was a more serious translation of western playwrights, among whom Ibsen received much attention.

During the early years of the republic the attempts to use western art forms were crudely imitative and nothing more. The lack of any true standards of critical appraisement, and the need of youth to be fashionably western at all costs, produced some odd results. A more level-headed approach to western arts developed as once more people began to go abroad for serious study. Nevertheless, there were many problems. The post 1911 period had enabled students and scholars to become acquainted with western art, literature and science, and there was a period of eager experiment and intellectual idealism, but this was fragmented by the political confusion and decentralization of China herself. Although the 1911 revolution brought great changes to the social system and created a climate for reform, it proved impossible to form a strong central government and eliminate unrest and corruption in the nation. The old inequalities persisted and the prejudices as well. One of the passionate questions to concern the new generation was the freedom of women, yet for years actresses continued to be boycotted in orthodox theatre circles both by the public and the teachers, nor could they enter the traditional schools, which remained a masculine preserve until 1930.

In April 1924 the Peking police authorities announced permission for men and women to sit together in theatre boxes (until then the sexes had remained strictly segregated in the Peking theatres). Even with this new ruling women were not supposed to occupy the stalls or orchestra, while for two or three years afterwards there were still one or two Peking theatres which refused to admit women at all, so deeply prejudiced was the ordinary public.[42] Even the early experiments with the new theatre were forced to rely on the old tradition of men taking women's parts, and it was not until the 1920s that prejudice was overcome to any real extent, and actresses, mostly girl students, were able to appear in the new plays.

The conflict of social values was reflected in many ways. As the mirror of revolution and change, artists, writers and the new theatre experimenters were faced with the problem of how to resolve creative integrity and adjust it to the problems of a new age. A broad issue was whether to discard Chinese tradition and follow the west unconditionally, whether to compromise between the two, or whether to remain simply and resolutely Chinese. The dilemma of adjustment between eastern and western creative methods has continued to dominate the arts in China and today has assumed new proportions.

For many people the chaos of their country, compounded by continuing civil war, political chicanery, Japanese military ambitions and the nagging resentment against continued western colonial domination, simplified the issue of the arts as purely ideological, and a leftist literary movement was born which had its repercussions in the theatre. There were undeniable causes to strengthen leftist viewpoints in the arts. The new intelligentsia in China were men and women who had studied abroad or received a western education but they were the urban minority. The majority of China's rural population could not read or write its own language, much less that of another country. Although Shanghai, Canton and Peking were the centres of new developments in art, literature and the theatre, and the seats of the progressive intellectual movements, these great cities represented an infinitesimal part of China. It was one thing for intellectuals knowing other cultures to adopt new methods in the arts, it was quite another thing to give these meaning to a less intellectually equipped class. In the theatre, for example, ordinary Chinese people brought up in the non-realistic traditions of their own stage had little in common with western-style dialogue expressing psychological conflicts remote from their own understanding and values. This was one reason why among many conflicting social issues the traditional theatre continued to be the most popular form of organized entertainment in the more sophisticated cities. Peking especially remained the jealous guardian of the older stage tradition and her citizens closely identified themselves with their theatre, boasting a connoisseurship which brooked no deviations from conservative traditions. However, the old theatre did not survive without adapting itself to the changing times. New training methods, the gradual acceptance of the actress, the introduction of electric lighting on the stage, the changed form of the stage itself in the western style theatres which sprang up, were all factors which gave a new look to the old theatre.

An influential step in theatre education was the founding of the Chinese Theatre Training Academy in Peking in 1930, the first of its kind to accept both boys and girls for traditional theatre training and to provide them with a general education at the same time as their professional study. Another innovation was the School of Experimental Theatre, founded at Shantung in 1934 to provide an ambitious four-year curriculum in studying traditional stage practice as a basis for developing a new theatre. Both these experiments were disrupted by the war.

The popularity of the traditional theatre during this period cannot be discussed without mention of the actor, Mei Lan-fang. His name became a household word during his lifetime and he occupied a unique place in Chinese society. The contribution he made towards carrying the old theatre forward into a new age cannot be overestimated. He introduced many innovations in stage practice. Not all his artistic experiments were successful but his contribution was a major one and he gave new dignity and respect to his profession. By his tours abroad, twice to Japan in 1919 and 1924, Hongkong in the same year, the United States in 1930 and Russia in 1935, he introduced a new note into international cultural relations. Paradoxically enough as a player of women's roles he did more than anyone to break down the prejudices against women in the theatre by agreeing to take actresses as his pupils and creating a new school of women performers.

The period covered by the events and trends described here was a time of transition in which the old constantly jostled the new and the new, in the form of western customs, clothing, methods of transport and styles of entertainment, increasingly impinged on city life and imperceptibly moulded the ways of the younger generation, who in their schools and universities were fast making a break with the old Chinese society. Women particularly had a long road to travel not only towards intellectual but also physical freedom. During the 1920s and 1930s many of the girls' schools in Shanghai, Tientsin and Peking, several of which were run by missionaries, included dancing as part of their physical training curricula. Folk dancing displays were staged, and Grecian rhythms and other kinds of movement to music were in vogue. The girls of a Shanghai training school in 1934 appeared wearing blouses, shorts and ankle socks as they emulated the leg prancings of the Broadway chorus girl. Shanghai also had its ballet teachers; there were several among the White Russian colony there. One was George Goncharoff from whom Margot Fonteyn had her first lessons.

In the 1920s ballroom dancing in the western style caught on in the westernized city of Shanghai and the 'sing-song' girl of the past rapidly yielded pride of place to the taxi dancer as jazz, the tango and the foxtrot lured the more sophisticated young members of Chinese society. The craze spread and became a thorn in the flesh of the government, who made constant attempts to put it down. In 1937 a ban on public dancing was imposed by the mayor of Nanking and in Shanghai the tax bureau was ordered to increase pressure on the dance hostesses and their public. Such measures continued sporadically through the years with only partial effect.

Among all the western influences marking this turbulent period none was more far-reaching, if perhaps less immediately apparent, than the impact of the cinema. The film not only revolutionized all ideas of entertainment for the crowd but confronted receptive young people with visual conceptions of ways of life and social relationships completely opposed to many of their own conservative principles. As a propagating force the cinema presented a challenge which was hotly opposed on repeated occasions for its immoral attitude towards sex, its degradation of eastern people, and its corrosion of traditional values. The government waged a continuous war with Hollywood. The careers of the new Chinese women film stars gave a different dimension to emancipation. The early Chinese film studios, for example, all ran training schools for their actresses. The earliest was active in 1924[43] at a time when it was still impossible for women to enter traditional theatre training schools.

The first screen actresses left no films of outstanding artistic merit, though their careers were often lived out in the glare of heady publicity, but they registered their own gain in breaking down prejudice against women in the theatre and public life generally. Pai Yang, one of the most talented of the early film stars, arrived in the screen studios from the Shanghai modern stage where she made a historic contribution.

Experiments with the new theatre were consummated in the 1930s by the meteoric rise of a young dramatist, Ts'ao Yü, whose play, *Thunderstorm,* raised hopes for a new era in the modern theatre. His psychological portrait of a Chinese family in moral decay owed a great deal to Eugene O'Neill, but for the first time it provided middle-class Chinese audiences with a theatrical experience within this genre which touched deep responses. A great deal of the play's success was certainly due to the China Travelling Dramatic Troupe which first staged it. This organization had been founded in 1934 and its aim was to establish modern drama on a financial basis which would enable it to hold its own with the traditional theatre which up to that time it had never done. The troupe functioned as a cooperative unit, its members received no pay but got board and lodging. If there was a full house everyone received $1 bonus, if there was a loss nothing. It was most frequently a loss in the early days. Any profit there might be was ploughed back for technical equipment and costumes. The usual arrangements were for 30 per cent of the takings to go to theatre management and the remainder to the troupe, who had to pay rent, lighting and publicity out of it. The troupe served as a training ground for several talented artists, including Pai Yang, and with her arrival the troupe's fortunes rose. Her performance in *Thunderstorm* broke all records for the company and they took $10,000 (silver) for a tour of seventeen performances. The outbreak of war in 1937 virtually ended the life of this first undertaking to make repertory theatre a part of the nation's cultural life, with no strings attached except insistence on high professional standards. It was a breaking-off point to which there has never been a way back.

The open conflict with Japan broke out in 1937 and this ended an age of experimental progress in the theatre. The government fled to western China and was followed there by most of the universities, training institutions and the greater portion of the literary and artistic world. There was a flurry of cultural activities under wartime conditions and the theatre was especially engaged. But in spite of the concentration of talents and a new public of a diversity previously unknown, the wartime theatre was inhibited by its commitment to the cause of propaganda and patriotic sentiment, while a vicious censorship stifled creative thinking. Political theatre with a different aim was encouraged at communist guerrilla headquarters in the north-east provinces of China where the peasants were being educated in the principles of proletarian revolution. In 1942 the communist leader Mao Tse-tung, in a series of talks at his Yenan headquarters, put on record his theories about art and literature. Briefly stated they affirmed that the validity of art rests on its devotion to a common political cause. Original talent is a fallacy. Art is for the Marxist-educated proletariat, and only through their idealistic self-representation is any art form acceptable in a communistic state. The proletariat and artists must both therefore be indoctrinated accordingly. In these talks Mao emphasized literature, a field in which he prided himself on his own knowledge and skill. Very little was said directly about theatre beyond a brief reference to village and army troupes.

Since Mao first formulated his principles in 1942 they have obsessed his thinking until today they have been imposed in such a way that art and society have been transformed on a gigantic scale in China. The process has gone on within a complex power struggle not easily fathomed by the outer world but it has been calculated, relentless and definitive.

When the communists seized power in 1949 the old government fled to Taiwan leaving behind them the greater part of China's literary and artistic celebrities, including the leading personalities of the theatre. Their attitude was one of hope tempered by desperation and mixed with trepidation, but after the social chaos and bitter privations of the postwar years, most people connected with the arts felt the situation could not get worse and were prepared to see what the new regime would do. They had not long to wait. A National Conference of Writers and Artists was called in the summer of 1949 and a galaxy of theatre people were invited to attend, ranging from Mei Lan-fang, the doyen of the traditional stage, to Ts'ao Yü, the presiding figure of the modern theatre. The convening committee introduced the cultural aims of the new government. Reform of the old drama was high on the list of priorities. This, it was stated, would not be done by administrative methods, as it was too popular with the people and their political consciousness had to be changed first. The reforms would be taken step by step through ideology to form.

Plans for a national federation of associations covering every field of art were drawn up. Regional unions were made responsible to a central authority in Peking, but were charged with responsibility for the dramatic activities in their own areas. Practically everyone with any reputation in their field was invited to join the federation if they had not been actively opposed to the party. Political orientation classes were set up for theatre personnel and a bureau of drama reform was established. The first organizational phase had begun. During the years that followed there were diverse activities in the world. The star system was abolished, although top actors in general remained relatively favoured people and were fêted and honoured for their artistic survival from a feudalistic past. Many of them were set to work teaching the younger generation. Local forms were revived and their old performers brought back into the limelight while the rank and file of the theatre profession, under state support, enjoyed a material security they had never known. A new discipline was evident in production and staging, research projects were set up and new training schools[44] founded including those for modern drama as well as dance and ballet. After its first face lifting the old style theatre seemed as firmly entrenched as ever. Whatever revolutionary ideas were afoot the old form was obviously not going to die a natural death. Foreign tours were organized and the traditional theatre acclaimed as never before by world audiences, for whom the ideological disputes and political power struggles which invested the theatre in China were largely a closed book.

In May 1956 a movement was launched under the title of the Hundred Flowers Campaign, designed to test opinion through the free expression of the nation. When a promise was given that those who spoke up would not be punished, there was a pent-up flood of denunciation from intellectual and artistic circles against the cultural tyranny of the regime, and their interference with the traditional theatre came in for much censure. A massive 'anti-rightist' campaign was launched in the following year but economic and political problems now overshadowed concern over cultural matters. By 1961, Mao's leadership was openly being challenged over the failure of his policies. The severity of the criticisms increased and by 1962 theatres everywhere were staging traditional style plays with historical plots, not only flouting his directives for reforming the old theatre but implicitly criticizing his leadership through their themes.

One in particular, called *Hai Jui Dismissed,* written by a Peking historian Wu Han, was destined to provoke the greatest controversy in the history of the party. The play dealt with a famous Chinese official of the sixteenth century who is remembered in history for openly criticizing the emperor's conduct as being detrimental to the people's interest. There was no doubt in the public's mind that the play was a criticism of Mao; it was a time-honoured method in China to get at the present through the past. There was equally no doubt in the mind of Mao. It is indicative of the power of the theatres in Chinese society that he used the play as the basis of a campaign which not only toppled his political enemies, but finally consummated his plans to reform the arts and led to the turbulent period which has now been dubbed the Cultural Revolution.

The mouthpiece and active agent of Mao in the tenacious campaign to subdue art and literature once and for all was his wife, Chiang Ch'ing. An assertive, self-assured, and according to many Chinese critics a personally vindictive person, she was a film actress of meagre ability in Shanghai during the 1930s.[45] After a somewhat chequered personal and professional life there, she left Shanghai as a member of a leftist-sponsored group to make government propaganda films at Wuhan on the outbreak of war in 1937. When she was passed over for good parts in favour of other actresses she decided to try her fortunes in the communist areas in the north-east where documentary films were being made. Though she made little progress in Yenan with her film career she managed to set her cap at Mao, still married to his second wife then sick in Moscow, became his mistress and eventually his officially acknowledged wife.

She emerged into the political limelight in the early 1960s when she set about reforming the Peking drama which she had studied in her early days, and which of all the old cultural forms had proved most unassailable to Mao's theories of reform. As one writer has put it : 'The Chinese people for two hundred years had followed and loved the known plots and known characters of the Peking opera with a zeal far surpassing that of an American baseball enthusiast or a British soccer fan.' It was a formidable task Mao's wife had undertaken for at the time it was reported that of the 3,000 theatrical companies in China, 2,800 were performing the traditional style theatre in one form or another. But the battle was joined and Mao's wife went to work indefatigably. In October 1965 the last traditional style play was performed in Peking with the complete silence of the press. On 10 November 1965, a Shanghai morning news-paper[46] published a highly critical article of the new historical play *Hai Jui Dismissed*. It was the first shot by Mao in an unprece-dented campaign which, fanned into furious criticism and debate, ended by destroying all those in high places who had defied Mao's authority and policies. In the spring of 1966 the Cultural Revolu-tion burst full upon the country and the Red Guards emerged from the schools and universities. A mounting campaign was driven home against the leading figures in literary and artistic circles. The theatre came under particularly heavy fire and many of its leading personalities were pilloried, there were reports of suicides and in the tumult and disturbances which racked the country until October 1967 the old style theatre was submerged as though it had never been.

The new Peking operas which now dominate the stage as a result of Chiang Ch'ing's campaigns and use of her political power, have contemporary 'revolutionary' themes and are costumed in ordinary style. The singing, acting and music are a compound of traditional techniques and western derivations.[47] Glittering, technically efficient, melodramatic and elementary in dramatic conflict, they portray a society where everybody is happy to sacrifice himself for the state. Their world is divided quite simply into pure heroes and unqualified villains and the main passion evoked is the love of Chairman Mao. In a society where the theatre must propagate dogma and teach a new way of life and thought, these pieces obviously serve a function which the old theatre with its stylized beauty of form and complete remoteness from reality could not encompass. Though to the western mind the elimination of the old stage art seems barbarous, the immense popularity of the new style plays with a younger generation, the product of two decades of Maoist teaching, sug-gests that the Chinese have indeed discarded their theatrical past.

5

JAPAN

Japanese culture was in early times greatly influenced by China whose civilization she emulated during the seventh and eighth centuries AD. Chinese court life then had its counterpart in Japan where painting, poetry and calligraphy became the new high culture and government followed Chinese administrative patterns. The borrowing from China led to indigenous modifications as the Japanese were temperamentally quite different from the Chinese. Chinese style government soon gave way to military power and initiative passed to a professional fighting class. Political supremacy was constantly in the balance through the armed clashes of rival clans. The warrior, or samurai, became the dominant figure in the society, obeying a personal code of honour enforced by his own sword. He gave his loyalty to a landed family or feudal chief and compelled respect through the cult of arms and martial austerities. The tenth and eleventh centuries saw continuing confrontations between powerful groups of these warriors. War and violence predominated in the land. By the thirteenth century the warrior class had consolidated their supreme power in a central military regime which effectively controlled the country, retaining the emperor as a puppet in the capital of Kyoto and his court a government only in name.

During the twelfth and thirteenth centuries there was a great upsurge of Buddhism in Japan and the monasteries, particularly those of the Zen sect, became links between the militant urban centres and the warriors who roamed the country. The monks themselves often took up arms, sharing in the aggressive spirit of the times and frequently becoming involved in the power struggles of the feudal chiefs. At the same time Buddhism exerted a great influence at an intellectual level and gave a new impetus to the arts. Zen Buddhism differed from other sects in its single-minded emphasis on sudden enlightenment and intuitive insight, aroused through both mental and physical disciplines. It was anti-clerical and stressed the individual rather than congregational participation. As a result it became particularly identified with the ethical code of the warrior for whose creed it provided a philosophical basis, advocating strength and mental alertness through austerity.

A second important factor in the religious trends of mediaeval Japan was the survival of the indigenous Shinto cult of the Sun Goddess. Shinto, or 'the way of the Gods', was based on a form of nature worship, a simple reverence in the presence of natural phenomena which were deified. It eventually became an organized religion with deep nationalistic overtones.

Religious developments particularly reflected how Japan, inhibited by the borrowed forms of Chinese culture, developed her own ways and means of expression although the Japanese never lost their admiration for Chinese sources. A kind of duality developed in consequence, and while court circles and others in the capital continued to cultivate distinctly Chinese arts, like poetry and painting, the warriors and townsmen of the provinces to a great extent cast off the influence of China. Urban growth and development in the provinces brought a much broader fusion of the Japanese and Chinese cultural outlook. This was particularly the case with dramatic expression. Themes were based on the stories and exploits of warrior heroes, and indigenous dance forms and poetic styles contributed a great deal to stage techniques. By the fourteenth and fifteenth centuries Japan had become culturally independent of China, and from then on, however closely related, they were two distinct civilizations.

By the end of the sixteenth century the many warring factions in Japan had been subdued under the power of a single warlord, Hideyoshi. He was succeeded by a man who had been his chief deputy in eastern Japan, Tokugawa Ieyasu, who crushed all rival opposition and founded a dynasty whose rulers held power under the name of Tokugawa until the middle of the nineteenth century. The capital was established at Edo, the present Tokyo, and this was made into a great fortified city with castle walls and wide moats, dominating the most strategic areas of central Japan. Three branches of the family were given control of three key areas and the remainder of the territory was divided into fiefs held by other loyal retainers. The holders of these territories were known as *daimyo* and were given autonomous control within their own area. In the north and west of Japan there were the 'outer' daimyo, men who only recognized the Tokugawa family after it had seized power. Their control was a perpetual problem for the central government and severe restrictions were applied to forestall any possibilities of revolt. Coastal building was restricted and rigidly controlled highways were maintained. Each provincial daimyo was compelled to maintain a residence in the capital where they spent alternate periods away from their own territories. Every time a daimyo returned home from Edo, he was compelled to leave his wife and sons behind as hostages. There were checkpoints on all the main highways leading from the capital where strict watch was kept for arms going eastward, women going westward, either of which would have indicated subversive intentions. A strong and efficient secret police system bolstered such precautions. The great pomp and ceremony with which the daimyo travelled to and from the capital inspired many themes in dance[1] and music and a number of plays took their plots from the rivalries and machinations of the daimyo.

Under the Tokugawa regime Japan became closed to the outer world and during the sixteenth and seventeenth centuries Japanese culture underwent many changes. The emperor and the court were left in seclusion at Kyoto, strictly supervised and providing a façade of imperial rule behind which the supreme military leader, the *shogun,* exerted real control from the new capital of Edo. The great warriors who united the country were themselves social nobodies, with scant liking for the refined qualities of the Chinese-inspired court culture, and there was a new kind of vigour and even vulgarity which infused the urban spirit of their times. The regime nevertheless adopted the social theories of Confucianism by creating four social classes,[2] the samurai-administrator, the farmer, the artisan and the merchant, the last lowest in the scale, following the Chinese precedent of decrying gain through non-productivity. The distinguishing mark of the first class was the privilege of wearing two swords; Confucian ethics and philosophy were officially encouraged for their emphasis on loyalty and stability and the proper relationships between the ruler and the ruled.

While the government patronized neo-Confucian doctrines, the older restraints also came to the fore. Shinto, the most ancient cult of the Japanese, became a patriotic rallying point for the less orthodox while the ethical code of the warrior, *bushido,* was given new emphasis as the result of Confucian principles of filial duty. A textbook on bushido dating from the sixteenth century[3] states that 'if anyone is incapable of carrying out filial duties to his parents from whom he is sprung, it is very unlikely that he will give loyal service to a lord, who is no relation, out of pure gratitude. When he enters a lord's service an unfilial son of this kind will be critical of any shortcomings of his master, and when he does not approve of anything he will throw off his allegiance and slip away at a critical moment or betray his lord by giving himself up to the enemy . . .'. This theme of loyalty with all its implications has been the basis for scores of plays on the traditional stage.

Enlarging on a further aspect of warrior ethics, the same treatise emphasizes that 'existence is impermanent as the dew of evening and the hoar frost of the morning and particularly uncertain is the life of the warrior, and if he thinks he can console himself with the idea of eternal service to his lord or unending devotion to his relatives, something may well happen to make him neglect his duty to his lord, and forget what he owes to his family. But if he determines simply to live for today and take no thought for the morrow, so that when he stands before his lord to receive his command he thinks of it as his last appearance and when he looks on the faces of his relatives he feels that he will never see them again, then will his duty and regard for both of them be completely sincere and his mind be in accord with the path of loyalty and filial duty.' Such emphasis on the impermanence of all things is as much Zen as Confucian in its implications, and the tone of this aspect of the warrior aesthetic was notably set by the stylized noh drama that particularly came to represent the intellectual taste of the samurai rulers.

The official world of bushido, neo-Confucianism and Chinese literary influences, was confronted with an irreligious urban culture of the ordinary people, whose uninhibited sensuality and spontaneous vigour stood in marked contrast to the decorum and restraint of ruling authority. The towns were filled with courtesans, geisha, actors and professional entertainers of all kinds, while new styles of popular music flourished. The government consistently opposed the more flagrant expressions of sexual licence and public behaviour by sumptuary regulations and a system of censorship. Throughout the whole period of the Tokugawa regime the theatre and the government were engaged in a constant running battle; bans, rules and regulations followed one after the other and the theatre community were kept strictly segregated.

The stratification of Japanese society according to Confucian tenets was enforced for nearly three hundred years. The ethical and social standards of Confucianism dictated the ordinary pattern of domestic life. Extended families were the rule, women were treated as inferiors and prevented from taking part in public life. Marriage was an arranged affair decided by the family elders, romantic love had no place in the scheme of things, and adultery was an offence punishable by death. Patriarchal control was supreme and filial piety the obsessive virtue. Society under these conditions was shorn of all initiative or freedom of action, conformism reigned. The rigid compartmenting of society created a universal sense of decorum and recognition by the individual of his proper place in the community. Japan remained extraordinarily stable under this system and there was negligible political dissent. The major disturbances were natural ones due to fire or earthquake. Fires were a perpetual hazard because of the prevalence of wood construction in buildings and some mighty conflagrations have been recorded in history. Fires and fire fighters provided material for a number of play themes and dance stories. There used to be a much quoted saying in Japan, less heard today, that the four major disasters of human existence were fire, thunder, earthquake and father.

The prolonged peace and stability which ensued under Tokugawa rule meant that internal trade and production developed rapidly and a prosperous merchant class became an increasingly important group on whom the warrior class became more dependent. Deprived of their profession under peaceful conditions, forbidden to work by the pride of their code, they often became the debtors of the socially despised merchants who controlled the nation's rice markets. Rice was the people's staple diet and the daimyos' fiefs were rated by the rice income, their salaries being reckoned in terms of rice. Some of the wealthiest rice wholesalers were those who dealt with the daimyos' storehouse keepers.[4] Commerical power brought social power to the merchants although this was not overtly recognized except perhaps in the gay life of the cities, where the licenced quarters, the theatre, the puppet show and new musical styles provided active evidence of the tastes and pleasure-loving natures of the wealthy city traders. Though their culture was essentially popular, a bourgeois manifestation, it reflected a degree of sensual refinement and artistic skill that was unique.

A proud impoverished warrior class and a disgruntled peasantry were both the sufferers from fluctuating rice prices which resulted from merchant speculation with the currency and towards the end of the eighteenth century there were increasing signs of social instability. As the Tokugawa regime began to show signs of weakness there were open indications of military opposition from the 'outer' daimyo who had never forgotten their historical rivalries. By the beginning of the nineteenth century the forces of change were making themselves increasingly felt. There was rising nationalism and an acceleration of unrest in the villages where economic changes and new market systems threatened the old smoothly working feudal system. The beginning of the end came in 1853 when American naval forces entered Japan and demanded trading facilities. Isolation from the outside world was ended and the country was split under the threat of foreign intrusion. Dissident samurai elements saw the chance to topple the regime. There was fighting, especially between Edo and factions in western Japan, but the new Tokugawa shogun who took office in 1867 voluntarily surrendered actual rule to the emperor at Kyoto, a young boy of fifteen in that year.

The period which followed the restoration of the emperor to the throne in 1868 was one in which a group of far-seeing, able young samurai, many from the formerly hostile western regions, saw the inevitability of western penetration and set about a programme of modernization. It was carried out on an astonishing scale, Japan enthusiastically turning to assimilating western ideas in a way that no other Asian country did. Railways, the telegraph and public utilities were developed, western style architecture was introduced, including new theatre buildings, and an industrial class came into being who adopted the food, clothing and customs of the west, all of which was reflected in the theatre both on the traditional stage and in the attempts to develop a new drama. A strong army and navy were built up to serve Japan's own ideas of expansion, following the example set by the western powers in their nineteenth-century drive for colonial possessions. By the first decade of the twentieth century Japan was well on the road to becoming one of the world's great industrial and military powers.

A strong militaristic spirit which emerged in the new Japan eventually overwhelmed more liberal tendencies with authoritarian and nationalistic ambitions. The determination to dominate China, whose politically divided territories had long been an area of Japanese interests, led to a war of attrition there. Stalemate in China and the outbreak of war in Europe tempted the Japanese to take advantage of the conflict among the western powers and, through China, to seize the rich colonially held territories of south-east Asia, thus strengthening the Japanese economy. Psychological as well as geographical and military miscalculations led to Japan's total defeat in 1945.

The resurgence of Japan since then as one of the most highly developed modern states has now ceased to astonish the world. Her technological and industrial skills reflect the magnitude of social change that has affected her people in profound ways. In the historically short period of barely a century Japan has provided her people with universal education of a rigorously high standard in which the accumulated knowledge of east and west becomes their intellectual right as members of an egalitarian society. A need to know more about the rest of the world on the grounds of self interest is found in every modern society. In Asia it has meant abandoning traditional cultural exclusiveness or else retaining it only for ceremonial effect – and Japan has been adroit in this adjustment. It is particularly the case with theatrical activity, which remains a living record of development from a feudal, authoritative and completely inward-looking society to a modern managerial state with a large and swiftly expanding prosperous middle class. It is always a revelation to find that in Tokyo the visitor on any one day of the theatrical season from November to June can be entertained with fourteenth-century noh drama, eighteenth-century kabuki, nineteenth-century transitional forms, the twentieth-century avant-garde, and a miscellany of revues, nude shows, political theatre and coffee-shop 'happenings'. There is no movement, style or experiment on the stages of Europe that does not find its counterpart in contemporary Japan.

One of the great landmarks in Japanese theatrical history was the rise of the noh theatre in the fourteenth century. Its development is inextricably linked with the name of two men, Kanami and Zeami, father and son, who brought the art to its mature form. Kanami was a professional actor who died in 1413 and trained his son from the age of six to follow in his footsteps. In 1374 the two were ordered to appear in a command performance at Kyoto before the young shogun, who was so impressed with the father and son team that he took them into his service. Zeami especially became a favourite of the young ruler and was often in his company. Kanami and Zeami were Buddhist names assumed on entering court service. Actors were men of humble birth but attachment to a temple community was one way of freeing themselves from the social stigma of their class.

The style of noh at that time was different from the later version which Zeami brought to perfection as a unified art. There were two main types of performance, called 'field music' and 'monkey music', names indicating a long history of fusions from court entertainments and folk performances dating back to 782 AD. In that year, as the result of changes in the administration of the imperial court, the schools of palace entertainers maintained by the emperor were disbanded and their members sent back to ordinary life where they became subject to labour service and taxation which they had escaped as court employees. Many of these footloose players sought new immunity by joining the great temples and shrines where they took over duties which included rites where elementary dramatic techniques were used to clarify the meanings of the sutras for the congregation. It was rather like the early miracle plays of mediaeval England where the important lesson of a Bible story was acted out to impress it on people's minds. As the disbanded court players became more firmly established they set out to boost their prowess with new ideas and the rituals became more theatrical and more secularized.

Greater attention to dramatic artistry also encouraged rivalry as the number of performers increased. They began to band together in groups in order to compete for the favours of the religious authorities who were their patrons. A kind of guild system developed and the performers became organized in what were called *za*.[5] At first used in connection with shrine protocol the name was later used to designate a district or village association responsible for certain shrine duties. Freer usage included artisans, craftsmen and finally performers who were not necessarily concerned with sacred matters at all. The performing groups, unlike the others, were retained on a purely business-like basis, being paid for their services. They were frequently granted monopolies by the temples employing them. Membership of these groups became limited and demanded a test of professional skill and aptitude. Records show that each za consisted of an upper group of adult players, a middle group and a third group of boys. New members paid a fee on joining and each appointment had to be sanctioned by the temple or shrine concerned. This kind of organization was a prototype for a great deal that later became common theatrical practice. The name za eventually passed into usage as a definition for a theatre, which was always a self-contained group of people in Japan, and it is still used in this way today, for example the Kabukiza in Tokyo.

Different provinces became noted for the skill of their theatrical troupes organized under this system and the talents of particular performers attracted the patronage of the wealthy lords. One regent who lived during the first quarter of the fourteenth century was said to have spent all his time watching the actors he brought from the capital. He has gone down among Japanese historians as a man who brought about the downfall of his line by his fondness for dog fighting and actors. He attached one actor to the household of each of his principal retainers and ordered them to be provided with fine clothes. He was not alone in his addiction and many a nobleman vied with his neighbour in lavishing favours on his stage favourites.

A common practice of the times was the organization of subscription performances, special open-air events whose purpose was to raise money from the public for repairing a shrine, building a new temple, or providing some kind of amenity. Great crowds paid to watch these performances, which usually lasted two or three days, a favourite site being a dry river bed with special stands and a stage erected for the occasion. The theatres for open-air performances were more like amphitheatres as we know them, with the stage placed in the centre of the arena. Two raised gangways led to the stage and connected it to areas off and sometimes to dressing rooms. Raised boxes on the perimeter of the auditorium were used by people of rank and were built in a circle. The most important members occupied the boxes directly facing the stage. An arena of this type commonly had a diameter of one hundred feet but was sometimes slightly more or a few feet less. The main body of the audience was seated on three sides of the stage, whose actual size remains unknown though it was more than ten feet wide. There were considerable modifications to these open-air theatres according to time and place. The arena for a subscription performance usually took about one month to construct, and noblemen and high temple dignitaries sometimes had their boxes furnished according to their own requirements. It was customary for such people to reserve several boxes, which were high priced and cost about thirty or forty times as much as the seats occupied by the general public in the area between the boxes and the stage. The audiences on these occasions were very different from the decorous spectators of a modern noh play and ate and drank in a boisterous atmosphere while watching the performers. These occasions provided relief from the repression of a daily existence where war, famine and sudden death were common hazards. The performances themselves varied a good deal in content and included such items as juggling, tumbling and stilt walking, as well as the song and dance which made up a great part of the plays and interludes.

This was the background to the art of Kanami and his son. When he attracted court favour at the age of forty Kanami had already made his name as a stage favourite of the public. He was a thoroughly seasoned and hard-bitten actor, skilled in all branches of his craft including music and play composition He was an innovator who did much to add structural changes to

noh performance by his adaptation of a popular song form
consisting of a chanted narrative in which the beat of the vocal
rhythmic pattern was emphasized at the expense of the words.
It had been performed by women, who once took part in the
great temple processions but who in Kanami's day had become
popular entertainers with little social standing. Their vocal
rendering was accompanied by stamping or turning in accentuation of the rhythms.[6] By experimenting with forms like this
Kanami gave a new quality to noh techniques. The materials
for his plays, as with other dramatic composers, were taken from
songs, legends and poems already in existence as well as from
the epics familiar to everyone through the performance of blind
ballad singers who travelled the countryside. Kanami had a
masterly command of his media enabling him to make a judicious
selection of material suitable for new musical and choreographic
effects. His son, Zeami, carried the ideas of his father to an
ultimate pitch in his own compositions, which have become
the great plays of the repertoire. He sought for the quietism,
refinement and understatement characteristic of the noh as it is
seen today. Zeami's work in the theatre resulted in a restrained
but powerful style of expression whose appeal to the popular
audience diminished as it increased for the samurai class. Under
their patronage the crowds' taste ceased to matter. Before he died
Zeami incorporated all the knowledge derived from his father
in a secret manual called *The Book of Handing on the Flowers*.
Like many such works it was intended to preserve professional
secrets enabling a son or disciple next in line to continue the
family tradition. Zeami's son in fact died and to his great grief
he was left without a successor. His manual only came to light
in 1908 when it revolutionized all previous studies on the
subject.

Noh drama is impregnated by Zen Buddhist concepts, with
their emphasis on allusion and a concern to escape from the
binding realities of time and place. A play aims to catch the
mood of a fleeting moment by complete rejection of realism
and a subtle fusion of technical resources. Although the border-
line between religious introspection, ritual and dramatic effect
is nebulous, it is possible to be too precious about the noh; it
was from the beginning the creation of actors, and highly professional ones at that.

The protection and patronage of the ruling classes after Zeami's day gradually placed the noh theatre behind a social barrier. The status of the actors was raised and they were treated as members of the samurai class. Heads of the different schools of performance were elected and hereditary succession was mandatory. The noh theatre became a reflection of the feudal system in miniature. Noblemen retained their own troupes, whose members were bound by the rigid etiquette of their masters, but who none the less lived well. In 1618 four official schools of noh were recognized and a fifth added in later years. These schools still exist today. Orders were issued to every feudal lord rated at more than ten thousand *koku* of rice per annum to pay one koku as support for the noh actors. Rice was the official means of payment in those days and a koku represented approximately 180 litres by present western measurements. In this way national support was provided for the noh stage. During the early part of the Tokugawa era actors only performed in the presence of their masters and this custom was strictly enforced, but towards the end of the seventeenth century rules were relaxed a little and subscription performances for which permission had to be given by the local feudal lord were sometimes staged. With the declining power of the regime in the early nineteenth century such performances became more frequent.

The last command noh performance for the inauguration of a new shogun was held in 1858. Ten years later, when the emperor was restored to the throne and the old military rule had collapsed, the allowances of the actors came to an end. A class of artists who for centuries had depended on government support faced a bleak and uncertain future. By proclamation they were given the option to follow the old regime into exile, to appeal to the new imperial court for protection, or simply to return to their home towns. Confusion reigned and actors sought to find other occupations.

In 1871 a roving ambassador called Iwakura touring Europe and America saw a great deal of western opera and his experiences inspired him to work for a revival of noh on his return to Japan. With two members of his staff he contacted noh actors and the upshot was that in April 1876 performances were arranged at Iwakura's private residence for the emperor and members of the imperial family over a period of three days.

It set a precedent for whenever the emperor in future visited the houses of nobility or men of state.

In 1878, as an act of filial piety to the empress dowager, the emperor had a noh stage built within his Aoyama Palace and in June of that year the leaders of the different noh groups were given official appointments and 3,000 yen each to purchase costumes. The future began to look more reassuring. When the former American president, General Grant, visited Japan in 1879 a performance was staged for him in Iwakura's residence and the American was so impressed that he lavished high praise on it and urged preservation of the art. In March 1881 a noh theatre was opened in a Tokyo park, supported by forty-eight members of noble families who named themselves the Noh Society. The first performance was given before the emperor and plans were discussed for making the society open to the public but these lagged for lack of sufficient means to maintain the project.

In June 1894 the visit of a famous New York opera star, Minnie Hauk, to Tokyo helped to stir new interest. The soprano who had performed all over Europe visited Japan two years before her retirement. She was invited with her husband and the German minister to attend a noh performance. The singer was genuinely impressed and showed an instinctive appreciation of form. She expressed this appreciation in writing after her return to America, and coming from such a knowledgeable artist her words were listened to with new respect. The praise of such foreign critics encouraged new efforts.[7] The general public, however, was still somewhat out of its depth with noh because of a long alienation from its austere and controlled style. In July 1896 a Noh Association was formed and the general public was invited to enrol. Joint performances were planned by the leaders of the five main schools. There was an audience of six hundred on the first day, a good omen, and the beginning of continuing interest and support from the public.

The noh drama in its present-day form remains an art of the connoisseur, a highly polished performance of consummate attainment, the end product of a long intermingling of popular entertainments and ancient ritual forms. Technically speaking a noh play is a script for performance of both singing and dancing. It is devised with arranged sequences of prose narrative

– intonation would be a nearer description – sung solo passages and choral pieces. The singing style of noh has a special sonority that has an affinity with Buddhist chanting and the verses are mostly composed in a regular metre. The language used on the stage is a mediaeval dialect containing many archaic verb forms; and because Japanese is a language of countless homonyms there is great emphasis on aural nuances, puns and plays on words. A play is structured round an introduction, exposition and climax, and within this pattern it is usual to arrange five sequences in a two-act framework. An interlude between the two acts usually consists of a completely independent comic piece or dance display. Generally speaking a play is a piece for two principal actors, often compared to protagonist and deuteragonist. Both have their own techniques and the actors who play them specialize in those roles. The first actor always wears a mask, the second actor never does. There are subsidiary roles to accompany one or other of the main roles and child actors on occasion are necessary and important. The leading actor is both singer and dancer and it is around his characterization that a play is developed.

A dance is the dominating feature of most plays and the core of the exposition through which the principal character is shown in climax. There are different dance forms for different kinds of characters but each dance is divided into three or five sequences with intricate, highly conventionalized gestures and posturing. There is absolutely no concession to naturalism and representational movements such as weeping are the quintessence of formalism. Many of these gestures are highly reminiscent of Chinese stage forms and perhaps point to a common ancestry. A typical feature of noh dancing is the sliding step used by the actors, who move about the stage without raising their heels, lifting the toes only and keeping the feet parallel and together. Another characteristic is the stamping, in which the knee is lifted waist high and the foot brought down squarely on the ground with controlled precision. Here there are seeming connections with Indian dance forms. In some of the demon and warrior plays the actor carries out gigantic leaps, again precisely controlled.

The maximum number of musicians in a noh play is four, one flute player and three drummers, whose different types of instrument have their own time-rhythm function. The throaty cries emitted by the drummers before and during a performance, which puzzle many people at first hearing, are a practical device for marking time between the drum beats as well as adding their own effect to the sound patterns. Besides the musicians there is a chorus of between eight and twelve who chant the words to accompany the dances, narrate the opening scene, and comment impersonally on events within the play, often setting up a question-and-answer theme. The chorus take no part in the action but occupy a special area at the right of the stage to the audience. The musicians sit at the rear of the stage behind the performers. Both musicians and chorus wear traditional formal costume and move and sit with ritualistic solemnity and control.

The stage itself is essentially a dance platform of seasoned, highly polished timber, approximately twenty feet square and about two and a half feet in height. It is canopied even though it is indoors and is supported by four square pillars about fifteen feet high. Each pillar has a special name relative to its stage function. A formalized painting of a pine tree is always found on the rear wall of the stage. The stage itself protrudes into the auditorium, being open on three sides. To the left of the audience it is connected to the green room by a covered bridge-way, the entrance to which is concealed by a heavy satin striped curtain. The bridgeway is flanked by three pine saplings which serve as markers for the actors on the bridgeway. When the actors are due to make their entry, the curtain is flung upwards from the ground with dramatic suddenness.

Costumes for most of the women characters, always played by men, are made of richly embroidered silk and have a unique bulk which adds a sculptural quality to stage compositions. Class distinction, individual character and the idiosyncrasies of everyday life are not the concern of the noh. The characters are not living personalities but represent a symbolical transcending of time and space; they are the agents of a momentary vision, and in the case of the women's roles there is a sexual impersonality different from the more sensory impact of either the kabuki or the puppet theatres. Noh presents the supreme example of the disciplined actor who is completely anonymous within the form, and for this the masks worn in the principal roles are a vital contributory factor.

These are the bare technical bones of an ancient theatre that tenaciously continues in contemporary Japan and is performed regularly on about a score of special stages in Tokyo and Kyoto and a few other large cities. Its chief supporters are among devoted amateurs who organize themselves into noh clubs and are to be found at all the performances. These take place mainly at weekends, continuing throughout the year except for July and August which are off-season for all theatre in Japan. Many amateurs take up noh singing as a pastime and the universities have their own bands of devotees. From time to time more spectacular outdoor performances are arranged in honour of some special occasion and the noh remains a cultural show-piece, a 'national treasure' which still engenders chauvinistic pride. It is essentially an intimate and a minority theatre, completely outside the ken of a pop generation and ignored by the majority of the new middle class. It persists, nevertheless, and there is nothing to indicate that it will disappear yet.

Like other Asian countries Japan has had a long history of puppet theatre but in her case the genre attained such an elaborate form that it rivalled the legitimate stage in its attraction for the public. Puppetry of a primitive type is mentioned in tenth-century records and from then on there are numerous literary references to the art. It is sufficient to say here that the great era of puppetry in Japan developed as a result of a new style of musical narration, whose particular strength and quality derived from the ballad recitatives of blind muscians. They wandered the countryside reciting the epic tales of the great mediaeval clan feuds. As accompaniment they used a pear-shaped lute, an instrument also found in ancient India and China. The abandonment of this for a new three-stringed instrument, the *samisen*, of Chinese origin, helped to develop a more expressive type of balladry that in turn provided a new scope for puppetry.

During the seventeenth century the innovations of a number of musicians and puppeteers gave the puppet theatre completely new dimensions. The puppets themselves gradually changed until by the eighteenth century they had become intricately articulated figures capable of a wide range of expression, from violent passion to the most tender emotions. A team of three performers, comprising a narrator, a samisen player and a puppeteer, were the mainstay of what the Japanese themselves called the 'doll theatre'. A turning point in puppet history was the opening of a new theatre, the Takemoto-za, at Osaka in 1684. The narrator of this new group, which had broken away from a Kyoto puppet theatre, was a man called Gidayu whose particular vocal talents put all his rivals in the shade. When four years later he invited Chikamatsu, a well-known kabuki playwright, to collaborate with him it was the beginning of a partnership that ushered in an era of glorious achievements for the puppet stage, whose name was for ever afterwards to be associated with the town of Osaka.

Gidayu and Chikamatsu collaborated until 1705, when they presented a play called *The Love Suicides of Sonezaki,* which was an overnight success and recouped all previous losses for the theatre. It was the first of a new series of domestic tragedies which gave an accurate picture of bourgeois life in the Tokugawa era. The plot of the play is stark; the hero, clerk to a merchant, is cheated out of all his money by an acquaintance. Unable to bear the thought of losing his paramour, a woman of the licenced quarters, he commits suicide with her. After the success of this play, Gidayu bowed out of theatre management, though he still continued to perform. He had become a venerable figure of puppet recitative who was awarded honorary rank by the court. His name has passed into usage as the definition of the musical genre he perfected. During his day there were notable changes in puppet technique; in the famous suicide play, for instance, the puppeteers appeared in view of the audience for the first time. Towards the end of his career Gidayu had a rival, a former pupil, who started his own theatre in the same street as his master. In Tokugawa Japan a theatre was a business organization that competed for the custom of the public by producing plays for profit. The playwright was the man whose skill and cunning determined the economic success of a production. Box office appeal did not jeopardize artistic ideals. Competition of the kind just described in fact stimulated Chikamatsu to some of his best work.

Until his death in 1725 Chikamatsu continued writing for Gidayu's successor and during that time he produced more of his domestic tragedies, many of them written within a few weeks of the events on which they were based. This in itself was a concession to sensationalism that might have been disastrous with a less skilful writer than Chikamatsu, who made 'hot news' serve a double function in its appeal to the crowd and as a spur to his new style of dramatic invention.

The nature of the plays made them particularly tempting to actors and in 1719 Danjuro the second played the part of Chikamatsu's love-lorn clerk in a kabuki version of the successful puppet play. It was one of many such future borrowings from Chikamatsu's domestic tragedies which gave the kabuki theatre a new ascendancy.

Tradesmen, shopkeepers and prostitutes seem unpromising material by the classic conceptions of western tragedy, and plays like the one just described reduced a Japanese audience to tearful emotion rather than inducing sentiments on the grand scale, but Chikamatsu was a master of the dramatic moment and pushed it home with cunning insight. The lurid materials of adultery, elopement and suicide, based on real life events, were transmuted into something more than sentimentality. Puppet manipulation, and the musical elements of narration and samisen playing, are interlocking elements which cannot be separated from the text of a play. It was Chikamatsu's instinct for these relationships that made his work so credible to his audiences. In the domestic tragedies the puppet's movements are more restrained than in historical plays, where emphasis on visual spectacle required bravado. In his domestic tragedies Chikamatsu came close to creating a new theatre within the limits of his audiences' receptivity. By western standards these plays seem highly formalized but this is partly because Japanese gesture and behaviour in everyday life were very formal. The etiquette required of the different classes of society induced restrained surface patterns of human behaviour in emotional situations. Displays of personal feeling and sexual passion seemingly lacked ardour only because the Japanese did not display emotion in public our way. The plays were steeped in an atmosphere of reality and were plausible enough to the townsmen for whom they were written. Chikamatsu had nothing revolutionary to say; his bourgeois characters could make decisions and query their fate, but there was no reprieve from the inevitable law of society. It was the uncompromising reality with which the highly charged emotional problems of Confucian

dominated marital-sexual relationships were stated that fascinated the Osaka merchants and shopkeepers. To see their own
psychological problems held up to dramatic commentary was
a startling experience after a long fare of legend and fantasy.

Osaka merchants, unlike those of Tokyo, were not the special
providers to samurai society, or retailers for the ordinary
consumer, they were wholesalers and brokers dealing in the
needs of the whole country, rice, oil and cotton. Osaka was the
commercial heart of the nation. Where the Tokyo merchants
made vast profits through their liaison with the purchas-
ing officials of the government, the Osaka merchants amassed
small profits over a long period. They were extremely prudent
but at the same time they developed a commercial code in which
a merchant's word became as good as his bond and even
promissory notes were issued without security. This element of
trust gave its own cohesion to society and a sense of righteous-
ness whose betrayal was the more heinous for its disregard of the
community.

In merchant society, apprentices lived within the master's
household and were an extension of the family, although clear
distinctions were made between their social status and that of
their employers. Women could not escape from the framework of
feudal society but business ability was respected and the Osaka
merchant's wife often wielded power in the home and controlled
the men indirectly. If an elder son had no commerical ability
it was often the custom to select an able employee and adopt
him into the family as husband to the daughter, and this sometimes added to her wifely power.

If the industrious apprentice was rewarded with the hand of
his employee's daughter, the idle apprentice was sometimes
tempted to make love to her. Flouting of Confucian sexual
decorum brought supreme penalties for the culprits and to
cross parental wishes in the matter of marriage had disastrous
implications in the careful Osaka merchant community.
Adultery and elopement were punishable by death and an unhappy pair frequently took matters into their own hands by
committing suicide, knowing there was no redress for their
defiance of the social code. The prodigal sons and profligate
employees of the puppet stage, troubled by debt, filial obligations and hopeless love affairs in the licenced quarters, were an

expression of the psychological undercurrents of this environment.

The licenced quarters, which provided a running theme for both puppet and kabuki plays, were first established by the government in 1589, although prostitution had flourished independently since earliest times. These quarters were at first regarded as a catalyst and a diversion in a society of warriors who after centuries of fighting might still provide problems for an established regime. The great quarters of Kyoto, Osaka and Tokyo, so often portrayed on the stage, developed elaborate hierarchies with their own ramifications of protocol and obligations. They served a world of venal pleasures and their affairs were conducted with decorum and hard-headed efficiency amid an atmosphere of elegance and sensual refinement. Presiding over the quarters in the large cities were the famous courtesans, time and time again portrayed on the stage as women of great spirit, generosity of character and artistic talent. They were the aristocrats of their enclosed world who dispensed their favours as they chose. Beneath them came a galaxy of other women whose specific ranking and qualifications defined their position in the scale.

The licenced quarters were patronized by a wide public and served as a social centre and outlet for male conviviality without offending public opinion. In the society served by these quarters few men spent their leisure hours at home, especially when, as so often was the case, the home was their place of employment and marriage was purely an extension of the obligations to the family business. Though the authorities condoned the existence of the licenced quarters and of course drew revenue from them they were regarded in rather the same way as the theatres, an unavoidable nuisance to be kept under constant surveillance. There were good political and economic reasons for not suppressing either of them, one being that they provided a listening post for the government's police spies. The conflict between personal emotions and obligations to society, which these circumstances aroused in a particularly obvious way, afforded Chikamatsu material for some of his most poetic writing. Tradesmen and prostitutes were tawdry enough figures in everyday life but through them Chikamatsu was enabled to catch ordinary humanity in its high moment of dramatic revelation.

Technical innovations during the eighteenth century made the puppet theatre a continuing attraction for the public. In 1734 plays were staged for the first time using three manipulators, a convention that has persisted since and lends the Japanese puppet show its unique appeal. By this means it became possible to produce greater flexibility of movement and fidelity to life. The puppets could breathe, express all kinds of complex emotions and move their bodies generally in a most convincing way. Yet the presence of three puppeteers in full view of the audience seems like a direct contradiction of the reality it sought to create. It was the contradiction that intensified dramatic communication for the Japanese. In the fusion of movement the mind, concentrating between puppet and human, became intensely aware of unreality as the agent of the most immediate reality. Advances in staging the plays, and a talented group of writers who carried on the traditions of Chikamatsu, kept the doll theatre abreast of the kabuki stage, even though the latter entered a new period of popularity which attained fever height.

Towards the end of the eighteenth century a puppeteer called Bunrakuken, from Awaji Island in Osaka Bay, set up his theatre in Osaka where he had a growing success and laid the foundations for a new phase in puppet history. His descendants carried on his traditions and in 1872 moved the theatre to a new site, as the result of a government scheme to assist planning by re-locating theatre people on loaned land. The new theatre took the name of Bunraku-za, and *bunraku,* a shortened version of the family name of the old Awaji puppeteer, has been used by the Japanese ever since to designate their puppet theatre.

In the last years of the nineteenth century a tremendous vogue for the amateur study of puppet balladry arose in Osaka, a vogue paralleled in some ways by the passion for Chinese theatrical singing among Peking amateurs in the same period. There were hundreds of clubs formed in Osaka and this contributed in no small measure to a minor renaissance of the art. Osaka became nicknamed the city of puppet balladry, and it was said that it was impossible to walk down any street in the city without hearing the sound of recitals.

Early in the present century the bunraku theatre ran into financial difficulties; the director speculated unwisely and his son was incapable of carrying on the tradition. The theatre was bought out by two theatrical impresarios, Shirai and Otani, and in March 1909, the bunraku was taken over lock, stock and barrel by the Shochiku Company who continued to run it for the next four decades. Today the Shochiku Company is a monster organization which controls major theatre interests, including the Kabuki, throughout Japan, and has only recently surrendered control of the bunraku which has become little patronized by the Japanese. During the last half century the puppet theatre has dwindled in popularity, not least in its home town of Osaka where it plays to sparse houses in the fine new theatre built for it in 1956. Outside interest and foreign tours, combined with government recognition of the puppet theatre as a 'national treasure', have brought it a respite but the bunraku has become a superbly anachronistic entertainment, totally incomprehensible to a younger generation, and its survival seems precarious.

In the bunraku theatre as it is performed today each puppet, the largest of which runs to about four feet in height, is operated by three men. The leading puppeteer supports the trunk of the puppet with his left hand while his right operates the puppet's right hand, another man looks after the puppet's left hand and a third takes care of the feet. It is said that it takes ten years for each member of the team to learn the elements of his particular function and thirty years in all to become a leading puppeteer. The trio move around the stage with a fluid ease that makes it seem at times as though they are simply carried along by the puppet instead of the other way round.

The western observer is at first worried by the fact that the puppeteers are always clearly visible to the audience from the waist up, but after watching the plays for any length of time the convention is soon accepted. There are specific dress conventions for the puppeteers, the leader wearing full ceremonial costume with stiff brocade shoulder pieces and with his head uncovered, a description which also applies to the narrator and samisen player. The other two puppeteers wear black cotton hooded robes with a gauze visor through which they can see but not be seen and the inconspicuous nature of their appearance adds one more dimension to the effect of unreality conjuring up reality. After an initial period of adjustment these impassive figures and the economy of their gestures merge with the dynamic action of the puppets, the measured but emotional phrases of the narrator, and the sharp twang of the samisen. The impact is total and the coordination remarkable.

There are rigidly prescribed gesture and movement categories for the different characters and for each play. These are hallowed by tradition down to the least detail of raising a hand or fluttering an eyelid. Technique can be broadly divided into human gesture and its effects, and those movements which are not so much replicas of human action as the means to perform superhuman feats in space. The heads of the puppets, which have been classed as works of art in their own right, are made in various character categories, although the head of an individual character in a play is immediately recognizable to the theatregoer.

The stage of the modern puppet theatre is thirty-six feet wide, twenty-five feet in depth and fifteen feet high, and demands an astonishingly precise control of space by the performers, who often work at two and even three levels at once. The narrator sits to the right of the stage area from the audience and performs on a raised dais with a script before him on a lectern, while next to him sits the samisen player. The narrator projects the voices of the characters on stage as well as providing information on time, place and circumstance and the inner workings of people's minds. The vocal technique of the narrator covers an enormous range of pitch and intensity. His performance is an emotional *tour de force,* his voice, expression and contortions turning him into the *alter ego* of the puppet whose lines he mouths. The samisen player is entirely functional. He controls the timing like a conductor and cues both the narrator and the puppets on the stage. His string articulation is clear-cut and his powerful underscoring of voice and movement at no time falters.

The most important part of the repertoire is drawn from the plays of Chikamatsu and his successors, and there have been few additions in later times. A play called *The Miracle at the Tsubosaka Temple,* written in 1879, is one of the most recent in traditional style. There have been several attempts to introduce modern materials, including versions of *Madame Butterfly* and *Macbeth,* but none of them has survived. It is as though

Above: Ichikawa Sansho, who was given the courtesy title of Danjuro the tenth, in a photograph taken in 1952 showing him wearing the traditional ceremonial costume of the Ichikawa family

Right: The last of the Danjuros, 'flower of the kabuki', the late Ichikawa Danjuro the eleventh. In this photograph taken in 1953, when he was still known under the title of Ichikawa Ebizo the ninth, he is shown in the role of Sukeroku, a swaggering young hero of the gay quarters, first played by Danjuro the second in 1713

Left: Prince Tedjakusuma of Jogjakarta, Indonesia, who was the first man authorised by the Sultan to teach the Court dance to commoners; the Prince, now in his nineties, opened his own school in 1918 and it is still active today

Above: The grandson of Prince Tedjakusuma performing the opening salutation of the Javanese Court dance

Contemporary popular theatre in India: the setting for a Tamil historical
play performed by the T.K.S. Company, Madras 1964

A contemporary Japanese stage setting showing the strong influence of
kabuki stage methods: a scene from the play *Furo* by Junji Kinoshita

An old Chinese stage in a temple courtyard

Chinese women in the theatre sixty years ago, seen in their segregated gallery seats at the rear of the auditorium

Left: The yagura or drum turret on the roof of an early nineteenth-century kabuki theatre, the Kanamuruza, Kotahira, Shikoku Province: in the old days it was the custom to beat a drum to call the audience to the show

Below: The drum tower of the Kanamaruza

The interior of the Kanamaruza

A milestone in the history of the modern Japanese theatre: a scene from
Twilight Crane by Junji Kinoshita

A heroine of the contemporary Chinese stage: a character from the play
Red Detachment of Women showing the strong influence of Russian ballet
technique

this old theatre is incapable of absorbing new forms and remains as the lingering survival of an era.

The puppet theatre enjoyed a parallel rise to popularity at more or less the same time as the kabuki theatre; both forms developed in the early seventeenth century and remained rivals for public favour over a considerable period of time. The origins of the kabuki are said to have been the song-dance entertainments given by groups of courtesans around Kyoto at the turn of the sixteenth century. O Kuni, a professional shrine dancer, introduced a new dimension into these entertainments in 1603 when she attracted the attention of the crowd with her own interpretations of shrine dancing. The followers who capitalized on her innovations became too blatant in combining them with solicitation, and the government thereupon published a decree banishing all women from the stage in the interests of public order. It was the first shot in a battle which continued to be waged between the government and the entertainment world for the next two and a half centuries. The disappearance of women from the stage was quickly countered with their replacement by catamites but in 1652 they too came under a ban because of the disturbance their presence provoked. Boys were replaced by men who were compelled to shave off the front of their hair so as to obviate personal appeal and provide a distinguishing mark. This ugly bald patch was eventually covered with a purple silk patch which finally became a distinguishing feature of the theatrical wig used by actors who played female roles and it is still preserved as a decorative feature in this way today.

The *onnagata* or female impersonator now became established, and was to contribute more than any other factor to the early development of the kabuki as a theatrical form. Greater concentration on the acting process became necessary and the juggling with reality and unreality so characteristic of kabuki acting was given a new motive. The playing of women's roles by men on the Asian stage, and particularly the Chinese and Japanese stages, created many paradoxes. The female impersonator, in the first place, became an essential if the theatre was to survive without actresses. The use of boys or feminine young men as a substitute for women was certainly not new in the history of the theatre nor was the association of this practice with paederasty. In Japan the acceptance of the catamite as a

rival to the courtesan was to be expected. Paradox created
paradox. On the one hand realism in costume, personal appearance and make-up was emphasized to the extent that a man
was indistinguishable from a woman. There is the story which
has become something of a chestnut in kabuki histories of an
eighteenth-century actor, famed for women's roles, having his
bottom pinched by another actor who mistook him for an attrac-
tive member of the audience. The implication that sexual
verisimilitude is identical with character transmutation raises
many questions in the western critical mind. For onnagata acting in the end has nothing to do with the outward trappings of
stage performance. These are a visual symbol beyond which the
credibility of the audience is transported into a state of imaginative acceptance that has little to do with verisimilitude.

Berthold Brecht's comments quoted in the previous chapter
emphasize the distance between the real nature of acting conventions and naturalistic imitation, and could be applied to the
kabuki actor no less than to the Chinese. In a treatise called
The Words of Ayame,[8] an eighteenth-century playwright and
actor set down for posterity the secret instructions to his pupils
of one of the most famous early players of women's roles,
Yoshizawa Ayame, who died in 1719. It is not only an illuminating commentary on the nature of the art of female impersonation, but illustrative of the conflicting attitudes which have
surrounded it. Ayame began life as a catamite in the pleasure
quarters of Osaka and under influential patronage rose to
become an artist respected for his integrity towards his craft.
His words have been quoted and re-quoted as the golden rules
of the female impersonator's art. In one section of the work
it is recorded that the master stipulated that an actor playing
women's roles who was himself married should blush if he heard
anyone talking about his wife. The actor, in other words, was
expected to play his role offstage as well, and in fact it became
the practice for onnagata actors to wear the clothing of their
stage sex in ordinary life. Daily habit thus made the correct
postures for wearing women's clothing an automatic reality
for the actor. Transvestism and acting nevertheless are two
different things. Even handsome young men age and no actor
who played women's roles without any talent could have survived
on the stage through outward appearance alone.

The greatest Japanese onnagata actors of the present century have been exceptionally unfeminine in their personal appearance to the point of being downright ugly. Anyone meeting an onnagata actor face to face backstage for the first time is usually surprised. The wrinkles of a middle-aged or even elderly man beneath a thick chalk-like make-up and the gap of a seemingly toothless mouth are not exactly indicative of feminine appeal. It was the custom of all married women before 1868 to blacken their teeth and shave their eyebrows, the relics of some ancient puberty rite that became a universal fashion and has been perpetuated in the kabuki actor's make-up. The grotesque appearance of such make-up is immediately forgotten when the skilful actor is seen on the stage, where skill and cunning in extracting the substance of femininity are displayed through the sheer power of acting based on conventions which have been handed on from one generation to the next. For an hour or so the movements of a portly middle-aged actor are transformed into the graceful elegance of a court lady or the shy delicacy of a young girl. The kabuki actor, in the words used by Brecht to describe the Chinese actor, 'limits himself from the start to quoting the character played, but with what art he does it.'[9] In effect he says to his audience, here is an interesting character, now watch how perfectly I can act it for you, as my father did and my grandfather before him.

The kabuki is beyond everything else a vehicle for virtuoso acting, and in this sense it is unlike the puppet theatre which has been its close partner. The puppet theatre also has its virtuoso performers, but they could not function without a recited literary text. The actor is the reason for everything in the kabuki theatre and it is the vibrant rapport he generates between stage and audience that can turn bathos and melodrama into an assault on the unconscious. The emotional fire sparked in the old-time theatregoer was the fiercer because of his complete identification with the actor's techniques. The actor was the very heart of the kabuki, the idol of the town, though the authorities took a less idealistic view and treated him as a social outcast, a status he shared with all those who in official eyes had a monopoly of 'unclean' occupations. They had no civil rights but were governed by their own customs and leaders who were officially appointed by the government as spokesmen for their groups. They were obliged to wear distinctive dress, forbidden social intercourse with people of other classes, and could only marry their own kind.

A celebrated scandal which rocked Tokyo in the year 1714 indicates how severely the authorities viewed any flouting of the laws which human nature nonetheless defied. At that time there was an actor called Ikushima Shingoro, noted for his love scenes, and reportedly so handsome that the women of the town were wild about him. One of his admirers was Ejima, a high-ranking member on the staff of the women's quarters in the shogun's castle. Returning from an official pilgrimage one day with her entourage she slipped into the Yamamura-za, one of the four big theatres licenced by the authorities. When the play ended she invited Shingoro into her box to drink with her party. News of the event got back to the castle and a full investigation was ordered. Everyone implicated in the affair was severely punished, some with the death penalty. Ejima was placed in close custody and the actor was banished to an island for eighteen years, being pardoned only one year before his death. The theatre world was hard hit; the Yamamura-za, one of the most popular theatres in the town was closed, the building demolished and all its assets confiscated. For the next one hundred and fifty years Tokyo was allowed to have only three theatres instead of four.

The government used every possible means for bolstering its meticulous system of class distinction in daily life. One example was the type of clothing people were compelled to wear as a mark of social standing. Both quality and style of garments were laid down in published regulations. These varied to some extent in the different provinces but in general silk and the use of colours like red and purple were forbidden to commoners, also the use of elaborate patterns. Ordinary people of whatever age or sex were made to use materials of dark blue, grey or orange in their everyday dress, the one concession being that material could be plain or striped. It was almost a caste uniform. People found ways of getting round the rules, particularly the wealthy merchant classes, but clothing generally followed simple styles. In the theatre, rich silk and brocade costumes were characteristic of the noh stage, but in kabuki it was different and the townsmen were forbidden to use such expensive materials. In

1636, for example, the manager and leading actor of a Tokyo theatre were jailed for using costumes considered too luxurious. A decree of the same year allowed actors to wear clothes of un-bleached silk and cotton when they were off-stage while refined silk was also permitted for professional use. Purple and crimson linings, cloth dyed to order and embroidery were forbidden, as was silk crêpe for stage curtains, only cotton or ordinary silk being allowed. Articles of elaborate workmanship were prohib-ited on the stage and theatre managers were required to swear on oath against their infringement of regulations. In spite of this, actors were periodically imprisoned for thirty days for disobeying costume requirements. Actors were not permitted to leave the theatre quarters and were required to live in its close neighbourhood, though not in dwellings occupied by people other than their own profession. It was equally a penalty for other people to live in houses frequented by actors. Records show that these rules were often broken when actors were called out to entertain at private parties. There were constant arrests and imprisonment or banishment of people for straying beyond the limits. The theatres themselves were restricted in number and confined to special areas. In Tokyo they were moved into three designated areas in the mid-seventeenth century and there they remained for the next two hundred years. Four large theatres were licenced but one of these was pulled down as previously described. Eight other smaller places of entertainment were sanctioned, plus the stages in various shrines and temples where the authorities allowed performances upon special application. In 1694 a ruling was laid down that the numbers of actors in the troupes of the large theatres should be limited to twenty, with ten apprentice actors.

Theatre buildings were made of wood and therefore very vulnerable to fires. There were many outbreaks. The kabuki stage was originally modelled on the noh prototype of a square, roofed platform enclosed by four pillars and connected by a runway to the backstage area. This basic form was developed through different stages but the most notable feature of all was the development of the short noh runway, connected obliquely to the stage, into a longer version which ran right through the auditorium left of the audience and connected the front of the stage to a small room in the rear of the theatre,

popularly known as the 'hen coop'. In later times a subsidiary
runway was added at the opposite side of the house but today
this is only temporarily constructed for special plays, the original
single runway known as the 'flower way' or *hana michi* being a
permanent structure. The introduction of this feature in the
theatre had a profound and lasting influence on the development of acting style. Actors can dance, pose, and make entries
and exits on the runway carrying the action of the play out
into the audience. It has become one of the most hypnotizing
theatrical devices of all time. The tension in the audience as
the actors pass along the runway at the level of the spectators
heads has to be experienced to be fully realized. The posturing
and larger than life techniques so characteristic of kabuki were
given great impetus by this device.

The noh-style stage with a roof was retained even when the
theatre became a covered auditorium in place of a bamboo
stockade. Towards the end of the eighteenth century the noh-
inspired stage gave way to a form that eventually became a
rectangular frame structure though still using the runway
through the audience. The centre of the auditorium and the
portions on either side of the two runways were at first open
areas in which the audience sat jam packed on rush matting;
eventually they became divided into a chequerboard pattern of
small penlike compartments in which the audience sat and
entered from catwalks. Three tiers of boxes ran the whole length
of the auditorium at either side, the top tier having a canopy.
The flat plaster ceiling of the auditorium was supported by
trestle beams whose pillar supports ran down through the box
tiers and the ceiling area was marked out in a pattern of squares
by the timbers. There were variations in the different theatres
but this was the general form of a typical kabuki theatre. Backstage a three-storied complex of rooms and offices were arranged
according to the hierarchy. At the entrance were the bathrooms
for the actors and the stage-hands' quarters. On the first floor
were the musicians' rooms and those for the playwrights, the
manager and the small properties department. On the second
floor were the female impersonators' rooms and on the third
floor those of the leader of the troupe, the remaining actors and
the rehearsal room.

Sophisticated stage machinery and the use of a curtain were

early features of the kabuki theatre. The revolving stage was introduced in 1758 and thereafter became a permanent fixture in all large theatres. It was worked from below by a sweating gang who pushed it round as though turning a gigantic capstan. These unseen toilers in what was nicknamed 'hell' in theatre slang were given applause for some particularly effective manipulation. In 1842 a double revolving stage was introduced, the outer circumference of which revolved independently of the rest. The use of traps on the runway and the stage were other features incorporated to create more spectacular effects. There was no heating or lighting in the old theatres, nor toilets, and the only ventilation was by means of slatted windows at the side of the theatre. The auditorium presented a noisy bustling scene of uninhibited enthusiasm and adulation on the part of the fans. Each actor had a 'shop name', a professional nickname which was used only within his family, and it was the custom of the fans to shout these names aloud on the entry of their favourites or for some particularly effective piece of acting. Stock phrases like 'I'm defeated' or 'I'm jealous' were another way of expressing approbation. The front of a theatre was gaily decorated with lanterns, long banners on bamboo poles and signboards depicting scenes from the current programmes. Situated as they were in the middle of the pleasure quarters, the theatres were invariably surrounded by tea houses where the audience could rest, dine or bathe in the intervals, as well as make assignations with actors and courtesans.

The theatre was at its gayest at festival time. A most important occasion was the 'face showing' performance in the eleventh lunar month. Actors were engaged in the tenth month for the next theatrical year. The face showing was intended as publicity for the season that lay ahead. Performances lasted from dawn to dusk, and programmes were changed every two months, though this later became one month, a custom which prevails today. Programmes followed a strictly defined order of precedence in the plays performed. These again were designed to be given at certain seasons and what was right for the spring was not necessarily acceptable for the winter season. There was a considerable amount of flexibility and change in this kind of thing through the years but one thing that remained constant was the need to provide material to bring out a famous actor's particular talents.

Playwrights were resident employees of a theatre and worked in a team with a master craftsman at the head. He was the chief adviser to the management and planned the plays according to the needs and fashions of the day. Of equal status was the guest writer, who might be asked to write a particular play to order but whose function was purely literary. Beneath these two and working under their direction were the second and third playwrights who were like journeyman writers. Beneath them again were the men responsible for technicalities in a play, who acted as prompters and wrote out the scripts in legible calligraphy. No one but the leading actor was allowed to see the finished script. The chief playwright read it out to the assembled company so that each actor understood the nature of his role. Effective reading was another of the playwright's required qualifications. The piecemeal construction of plays indicates why it is possible for excerpts to be preserved when the play as a whole has long since been forgotten. Plays were written for audiences who spent a whole day at the theatre and in consequence expected a run for their money. The playwrights had to take into account seasonal events, as well as local characteristics and tastes, which might vary a good deal. Plays constructed according to this system were known in the profession as dream plays, meaning to say that the character parts were not real and only came to life when the actor appeared on the stage. The play was merely the spark for the fireworks of performance which set the crowd roaring their approval. Although the authorities despised the actor, he was worshipped by the ordinary public, who followed his professional progress, his achievements and his private life with all the assiduity of the modern film fan. Every New Year almanacs were published grading actors' performances and form was eagerly studied by the theatre *habitués*. Little books were printed with extracts from plays made famous by some actor and the young bloods recited them aloud going to and from the theatre.

Just as Osaka was symbolic of the puppet theatre so Tokyo recalled to mind the bombast, vigour and magnetism of the kabuki. Before it became the political capital in 1603 the town was insignificant and did not develop an indigenous cultural character for another hundred years. By then artisans, trades-men, merchants and the inevitable entertainers and performers they attracted had begun to move away from the austerity and even crudity of the warrior's way of life. At first the new capital was dependent on the products of Kyoto and Osaka but after this period of assimilation the balance was changed and Tokyo began to take on her own cultural character as the merchant class prospered. The samurai regarded the merchants with little more than toleration but by the middle of the eighteenth century changing economic and social factors brought them new power. Though the samurai governed, it was the merchants' money that kept the wheels of administration turning.

The Tokyo merchants were quite different in character from their Osaka counterparts. Namiki Gohei, the late eighteenth-century kabuki playwright, warned his disciples that plays for Tokyo audiences had to be robust and forceful with plenty of fighting. Osaka audiences were less hot-headed and more prudent, he said, and an emphasis on duty and obligation was the important ingredient for their plays.

Samurai methods to some extent rubbed off on the ordinary Tokyo citizens and they became noted for their brusque wit and love of style. The apogee of their culture was their theatre, whose spirit and that of the city itself was epitomized in the celebrated Danjuro family, a magical name in the kabuki world and one which has been perpetuated through eleven generations of actors. The first Danjuro was born in 1660 and died in 1704. As a stagestruck boy of thirteen he decided to become an actor and today he is venerated as one of the father figures of the kabuki. He developed and perfected the technique called *aragoto*, 'ruffian stuff', whose bravura and stamping are punctu-ated by *mie*, climactic passages in which an actor works himself up to a tremendous emotional pitch with bold gestures, grimaces and squinting eyes, as he pauses in a defiant stance and for a vibrant moment imposes himself on his audience. According to legend, the pounding on the stage of the first Danjuro was so ferocious that it drew a strong complaint from a local china merchant. Apocryphal as the story may be, it sets the tone of a virile tradition which earned for the Danjuro family the ringing title of Flower of the Kabuki.

In April 1962, the persimmon, green and black striped curtain of the Tokyo Kabuki-za was drawn aside to reveal a unique ceremony. The great stage, seventy-eight feet wide, was filled with one hundred and fifty actors seated in rows and wearing the ceremonial dress and hair style of the Tokugawa era. Their heads were respectfully lowered towards the audience. As they raised them in unison the actor in the centre of the group was greeted with shouts and cries from every corner of the house. The last of the Danjuro line had succeeded to the title of Ichikawa Danjuro the Eleventh. It was the fulfilment of a long cherished hope in the kabuki world which had been without a Danjuro since the ninth holder of the title died in 1903, the tenth holder of the title being merely an honorary figure.

Danjuro the ninth steered the kabuki through a critical period. When the Tokugawa government collapsed and power passed to men who were fired with ideas of modern reform, it seemed that the kabuki might disappear. Danjuro devoted his life to giving dignity and standing to the old theatre under the new regime. He was asked to perform before the emperor in April 1887, the first time that the imperial family had seen kabuki. The play presented was *The Subscription Scroll*, adapted directly from the noh repertoire by Danjuro the Seventh in 1840. It is said that when this distinguished kabuki actor went to borrow the costumes he required for his pioneer production, he virtually had to prostrate himself before the noh wardrobe master, so great was the social gulf between the two theatres. The appearance of the ninth Danjuro before the emperor, therefore, was an unprecedented event and one which gave a new aura to the kabuki. Throughout his career Danjuro the Ninth defied convention and experimented for long periods with realistic speech, gesture and expression on the stage. He was always trying new methods in the spirit of the times, but he was no iconoclast and though many of his experiments failed and he met severe criticism, in the long run he was judged one of the great traditional actors. His death in 1903 left a feeling of irreparable loss in the theatre world for he had left no successor. The actor who had been schooled for the task died in 1897 to the great grief of Danjuro. He is reported to have said 'this is a great blow, had Shinzo lived my principles for reforming the theatre might have been handed on after my death'.[10] For the Japanese actor there was only ever one man who was the right person to carry on his name, whether it was his own son, an adopted son or a talented pupil. A successor is singled out for his abilities quite early and is carefully schooled and supervized by the senior actor. It is the hope of every great actor to be able to perpetuate his artistic self in this way. The new successor takes the same name, only the generation numeral being different. It is then his duty to preserve the repertoire and acting standards of the line and to pass them on in his turn.

The lack of a Danjuro took something from the lustre of the kabuki all through the first half of the twentieth century. Changing times and the dwindling company of actors of the old calibre began to make it seem as though the name had disappeared for good, and with the war the existence of the kabuki was further threatened. But in fact the postwar years saw a successful revival and there were even thoughts of a new Danjuro again. Sansho, the son-in-law of Danjuro the Ninth, had adopted a young actor called Ebizo, with the idea of preparing a successor to the great family title. Sansho himself was rather an exception in orthodox theatre circles. He owed his position in the first place entirely to his marriage connections and he was really a kind of administrator in the family, a guardian of their interests and history. He made his first stage appearance in 1903 but his rare presence on the stage was regarded as merely a courtesy routine by the profession. After the war he worked hard on behalf of the theatre and in view of the nature of the times and his guardianship of the succession rights it was decided to reward him shortly before his death in 1953 with an honorary succession to the title Danjuro the Tenth and so put the name in family circulation once again. After his death it was a matter of waiting for the opportune moment to place a true Danjuro on the stage again after sixty years.

By the early 1960s the kabuki was facing a depression in spite of its foreign tours. Since the war it has rapidly lost appeal for a younger generation. There had been awakened interest in some of the universities in the form of kabuki clubs, and the Ministry of Education made it possible for school children to visit the traditional theatre at reduced rates, but these were drops in the ocean in view of the lack of a regular public. For one thing, the traditional style performance, consisting of a five-hour programme from eleven in the morning to four in the afternoon, and an evening show from five to ten with a different bill, presented problems to a public faced with all the stresses of modern industrial civilization. A theatregoer had to spend more than twelve hours in the theatre if he wanted to see the complete performance and even if he staggered this over two days such a leisurely pace was far removed from the normal working day, or the pocket, of most ordinary citizens. Moreover, the spread of television kept far more people at home for their entertainment. The theatre could no longer rely on a regular clientele of seasoned playgoers. It depended on group bookings of the kind which might entail a bank renting the theatre for an annual outing of all its branch employees, or at least a whole block of seats reserved for a party up from the country to see the sights.

Because of its costs, capitalistic control and feudalistic content, the kabuki was under constant attack from the younger intellectuals, both those within the theatre and those outside it. In view of all these mounting problems the kabuki authorities welcomed the opportunity to create a new Danjuro and make a bid to recapture a little of their former lustre. The event was preceded by a tremendous publicity campaign in which the modern media of radio and television were utilized to the full. Ebizo had always been regarded as the ideal handsome young actor and this was an added advantage. He himself spent six months preparing for the great event and took part in several religious ceremonies held to honour the memory of his distinguished predecessors. The succession ceremony more than justified people's hopes; it was a resounding success and during the two months that the ceremony was staged as a spectacle in the normal course of the performances audiences numbering two hundred and fifty thousand paid for tickets. It seemed that there was still magic in the Danjuro name, modern publicity methods notwithstanding. The triumph was to be short-lived, for in 1965 the new Danjuro died prematurely of cancer and the news was received with emotion and despair in traditional theatre circles.

Kabuki is a costly spectacle to run and since the second world war it has depended on the great combines to keep it going; the result is that it has not escaped the kind of commercialization that show business imposes. Gone for good are the days when a poor student could for a few yen climb up to the theatre gallery, there to shout excited approbation of his favourites on the stage far below. Gone also are the standards of appreciation which made such occasions a glorious necessity in life. Company anniversary parties are now a mainstay of the box office and the business executive has replaced the shopkeeper in his seat beside the 'flower way'. State recognition through a national theatre has today assured the kabuki an honoured place as a cultural asset, and tours in America and Europe have indicated a considerable western interest. Yet in many ways the phenomenon of kabuki is an artificial one in these times. It survives through a combination of circumstances which have little bearing on its original basis of support, the interest of the ordinary Japanese people. It is now a prestige attraction whose high prices are beyond the purse of the commoner even if he wished to go to the kabuki. It is much simpler for him to sit before his television set at home where entertainment is free.

Like the old-style playgoer also, the kabuki actor belongs to a vanishing society. Where he once evoked the inimitable response of the crowd he is much more likely to earn the admiration of the western visitor today. This is not to say that he is about to disappear, but film and television more and more often lure him away from the stage. It is true that there are still many actors whose roots are in a traditional past and who have their successors. Their fate will depend on a public completely different from that of even twenty years ago and who are now entering on a final phase of the cultural metamorphosis that commenced in the late nineteenth century.

After the political transformation of 1868, Japan was seized by a great fever of reform through learning from the west. Reform was a watchword heard everywhere. At the opening of a new theatre in 1884, Danjuro the Ninth summed up the spirit of the times with the statement, 'The theatre was once pure entertainment. Its influence today is not small, however, since it praises good and chastizes evil through "living history", reproducing the manners and emotions of yesterday and today. It is right that in civilized countries the theatre should be considered a means of education. . . .'[11]

The attitude expressed here forecast a division of opinion

which has characterized all serious experiment in the modern Japanese theatre ever since, where the balance has swung between didactism and art. Political didactism was given its first airing in the theatre during the 1880s when a group of young men took up the cause of a liberal people's rights movement in opposition to the government party. They were more swashbucklers than actors and had no clearcut political policy of their own and little sense of social mission. One of their number decided that there could be a new theatre through adapting kabuki concepts of realism to social themes. The result of these early experiments was that political theatre for itself disappeared, as people who were much more interested in the art of acting took over. New groups emerged who began staging genre plays dealing with the current topics of the day and in turn these attracted a greater amount of professionalism among the participants. From these beginnings emerged what is today called the *shimpa* or 'New School' style of theatre. It is a kind of halfway house between the kabuki and the western play, a popular melodrama portraying the social customs of a period and still closely influenced by kabuki stage methods. It has retained its own following and has always been a better box office draw than the true modern theatre movement called *shingeki*.

It is symptomatic of the shimpa that one of the most popular partnerships on its stage until the early 1960s was an actor famed for playing women's roles in the traditional style, Hanayagi Shotaro, a favourite of shimpa fans, and Mizutani Yaeko, a talented and versatile actress equally beloved by the shimpa audiences. Until the death of Hanayagi, this pair of artists were popular for their stage roles as lovers, with Hanayagi as a handsome young man and Mizutani Yaeko as the beautiful geisha of tradition. Such themes of unfulfilled love and the invariable unhappy ending were a characteristic aspect of the shimpa repertoire. The audiences never tired of seeing artists like these two portraying the *demi-monde* society of another age. Newer plays are set in more recent times and tend to be less sentimental and maudlin than the repertoire of the past. Light satire, social comedies and domestic themes have replaced some of the old melodrama. While it continues with one foot firmly planted in the past, the shimpa at the same time appeals to the sentiments of ordinary contemporary people who are not interested in anything that goes too far above their heads. Shimpa makes no intellectual demands nor seeks ideological commitment, it is bent only on satisfying the tastes of the average audience in search of entertainment.

The first uncertain steps in training actors for an independent modern theatre free of all ties with the past were taken in 1909 with the publication of the bye-laws of a group called The Literary Society. It was under the direction of Tsubouchi Shoyo,[12] of Waseda University in Tokyo, the first great translator of Shakespeare into Japanese and a towering figure of the early modern theatre movement. The Literary Society was originally planned for a broad literary movement to be developed in the university, but it was superseded by a research centre for theatre development retaining the same name. Tsubouchi took full charge and gave land for a building. Twenty-five students were enrolled in the first class which was held in the director's residence until the building was ready. Tsubouchi's aim was to train actors who had no previous experience in the theatre. In this way he considered a real break could be made with the conventions of the old theatre and the cultural level of its personnel improved. The first two years were devoted to general education and the courses included applied psychology, English, elocution, aesthetics and art history, in addition to acting techniques. Entrance fee to the course was three yen and a monthly tuition fee of the same amount was charged. There was no thought of a money-making venture in the first place, but the work of the group attracted such attention that they were invited to stage *Hamlet* at the new Imperial Theatre in May 1911. A fee of 2,000 yen was offered, an unheard of sum for such a venture.

The Imperial Theatre had opened its doors in March of that year. It had been built by a joint stock company founded in 1906 in rivalry to the traditional theatres of the period and was intended to break away completely from the old style kabuki building and to provide a national theatre on modern western lines. The imposing white building in French renaissance style created a sensation in its day, although in later years it came under heavy criticism as being unsuitable for kabuki, particularly its defective 'flower way'. It became most famous for its sponsorship of visiting foreign artists and for many of an older generation it is linked with memories of performers like the Peking actor, Mei Lan-fang, or the Russian ballerina Pavlova. It was torn down in 1964 to make way for a new and more spectacular structure. In 1911, however, the Imperial Theatre was a startling innovation with its foreign style auditorium, foyers and seating arrangements. The old-time practice whereby tea houses adjoining the theatre served as ticket offices was done away with, printed programmes were distributed free of charge and smoking and eating in the theatre itself were prohibited. There was both consternation and criticism in the world of traditional kabuki theatre management, but the Imperial was a signpost to the future for many people. It became the centre for the modern theatre productions, of which the Literary Society's *Hamlet* was the forerunner. In November of the same year they presented Ibsen's *A Doll's House*. Ibsen was widely read and widely imitated in Japan at the beginning of the century and there was scarcely a new playwright who did not take a leaf out of the great Norwegian's book. His talent for creating in his plays recognizable human beings who probed current social problems through the medium of everyday speech stirred wide reactions among the new intellectuals.

Ophelia and Nora in these two epoch-making productions were played by an actress called Matsuo Sumako, a country girl of great personality who was admitted to Tsubouchi's theatre training group through the personal efforts of her husband. Though no beauty, she had tremendous character and from being practically illiterate she made such swift progress in her studies that she was early singled out and cast for both leading roles at the Imperial performances. They brought her immediate fame and marked the beginning of the stormy career of Japan's first modern actress.

Tsubouchi treated any breach of personal integrity by members of the group with great severity and insisted on the resignation of anyone who became involved in improper love affairs. Matters were complicated, therefore, when he discovered that his leading actress and his favourite disciple and actor, Shimamura Hogetsu, were involved in a violent affair. The upshot was that the two resigned in May 1913; the event became sensational news in the press and a *cause célèbre* of the day. It was the end of The Literary Society, which was disbanded in July 1913 after six performances of *Julius Caesar* at the Imperial. The two lovers remained together and Hogetsu organized his own troupe in which Sumako played the leading roles. She revived her role as Nora, and among other plays starred in Wilde's *Salome* and Tolstoy's *Resurrection*. A sentimental melody composed for her in the last play, 'Katusha's Song', became a 'hit'. The new company had a great success in its aim to take 'theatre to the masses'. Tolstoy's *Resurrection* went on tour to Formosa, Korea, Manchuria and Vladivostok. Sumako won great fame though her temperament became proverbial in the company. Nevertheless, there was some criticism of the troupe's constant playing to the gallery. Before he could answer his critics Hogetsu died of pneumonia in 1918. Sumako took control of the company but she never recovered from the shock of his death and two months later committed suicide.[13]

Contemporary with The Literary Society was a group known as Free Theatre. In its bye-laws, published in February 1909, its purpose was defined as 'to give an honest trial to plays appropriate for the new age and to open the way for new plays and the new theatre'. Its leading lights were Sadanji, a young kabuki actor of progressive ideas who had studied western drama in Europe, and Osanai Kaoru. Theirs was the first attempt to create a group directly influenced by contemporary European ideas. Osanai himself visited Europe in 1913 and came back with notes on the productions of Stanislavsky and Reinhardt which had proved a revelation to him and led to further experiment with productions.

The Free Theatre movement was an incentive to the rise of other groups and after 1913 there ensued a period of energetic production of one play after another from the western repertoire. It was a period of trial and error marked by a common eclecticism and a concern for the literary quality and artistic nature of theatre rather than the commercial possibilities of the well-made play.

His work in the Free Theatre led Osanai on to found his own Little Theatre at Tsukiji on the eastern side of Tokyo. It seated only five hundred people but its importance far outweighed its size for it meant that a legitimate contemporary

H

drama had its own theatre for the first time and the way was clear for intensive training and experiment. Though the history of this Little Theatre was one of constant economic problems, by the time it was dissolved on the death of the founder in 1929 it had staged ninety-five productions by western dramatists, including Ibsen, Strindberg, Hauptmann and Chekov, followed by names like Pirandello, Capek, Shaw, Yeats and Roland. In addition, twenty-six plays by Japanese writers were put on. Osanai's long-term plan for training amateurs thoroughly in European methods to bring about a new tradition of acting began to show constructive results during this period. Today there are few veteran actors in the modern theatre who were not at one time connected with the famous Little Theatre of Tsukiji.

The shingeki, or modern drama, in spite of such experiments remained the ugly duckling of the Japanese theatre. The movement in any case had been led from the beginning by a comparatively small group of people who wanted access to the new knowledge and thinking of the western world. The plays that were put on were mostly beyond the comprehension, much less the appreciation of the ordinary public, and even the new Japanese plays were in many ways alien to traditional thinking. Identification with the modern drama brought little but poverty and political persecution for its most dedicated followers.

The Little Theatre became active during a period of political unrest. An economic recession, police repression of labour unions and the mounting tide of militarism all helped to create a leftist movement among the intellectuals. With the death of Osanai in 1929 the Little Theatre group split into two factions, one of which took an outright stand for a leftist proletarian theatre concerned only with its political message, while the remaining group adhered to its search for a better art theatre. A new group, The Japan Proletarian Theatre Federation, now dominated the modern drama scene and some of the important productions of this period were Gorky's *Mother,* Tretakov's *Roar China* and Remarque's *All Quiet on the Western Front.* After 1930, scripts and performances became subject to increasing censorship and bans, theatre people were arrested, and even those who attended performances were subject to police interrogation. The Japanese conquest of Manchuria in 1931 was a signal for the emergence into the open of the fanatical nationalistic and anti-liberal policies of the militarists in power and there was overt hostility towards free intellectual expression. The witch hunt began and the modern theatre was an early victim. The Proletarian Theatre Federation was forcibly disbanded and other liberal groups were compelled to confine themselves to social drama aimed at the conventional middle-class traditionally-minded audience. In 1940, out of three modern theatre troupes which had been allowed to carry on two were ordered to be closed down and many of their personnel were arrested. The remaining troupe that survived the war period was made to take to the road giving performances for factories. It had to abandon its high artistic ideals. The period from 1940 to 1945, therefore, is a completely barren one in the annals of the modern Japanese theatre.

Soon after the war ended, the dispersed modern theatre groups combined to stage Chekov's *The Cherry Orchard*, a play that has always interested the Japanese. Because of the American Occupation authorities' distrust of the feudalistic spirit of the traditional theatre, the shingeki, or modern theatre, was viewed with rather more favourable eyes and enjoyed something of a comeback. Its brief reign was soon broken by the revitalization of the traditional theatre against whose powerful advantages it was compelled to struggle. The kabuki, with its spectacular acting, brilliant staging and financial backing was soon drawing full houses again, the noh showed renewed activity and received a growing interest among the public, while the shimpa exerted as great an appeal as ever for its sentimental followers. The rise of the Japanese film industry to the front rank of international achievement and the arrival of television were factors which to some extent created a greater flexibility and interchange between the old and new theatres, although at the same time they undermined the position of the shingeki, always precarious as a public entertainment.

In the ten years between 1946 and 1956 there were more than forty modern theatre groups active in Tokyo but of these only three maintained any consistent standing as professional troupes qualified to stage an average of five regular performances a year. Each production averaged a run of twenty to thirty performances and attracted audiences of from between 12,000 to

20,000 people. In 1953 a production of Ibsen's *Enemy of the People* ran for twenty-eight performances and required a budget of Yen 935,000 to cover expenses and hire of a theatre, this last one of the most devastating problems of the modern theatre movement, which relies chiefly on rented halls. The tickets for this performance cost Y200 of which Y133 only was net income, the remainder being tax. Even though the troupe drew its audience of 12,000 the balance remaining after all expenses had been met was not enough to pay the salaries of the actors and stage personnel. This may be taken as a fairly average state of affairs. Actors today are more and more compelled to seek work in the films and television in order to live and to keep their troupes going. In the ten-year period named, the various groups staged a total of 460 plays of which 196 were translated from western dramatists. By far the most popular among these were *A Streetcar Named Desire* and *Death of a Salesman,* both tremendous successes which played to some of the biggest houses known in the history of the modern theatre.

A Japanese critic attributed their success to the fact that the themes awoke response in the minds of the ordinary public.[14] Although the professional salesman is not a common figure in Japan, the situation of a hard-pressed father placing all his hopes on the future of a son strikes a very common chord. The regional characteristics of the American south given expression in *A Streetcar Named Desire* are also alien to the Japanese but the weakness and frailty of women is for them a long familiar theme. Apart from this, the innate theatricality of such plays was a new departure from the literary classics which had customarily been the major part of the shingeki repertoire.

A milestone in the history of modern Japanese playwriting was the production during this period of the play *Twilight Crane, Yuzuru,* by Junji Kinoshita. It had a tremendous success and can truthfully be called the first modern play that awoke a response among all levels of Japanese society. Kinoshita, the playwright, was born in 1914 and has been deeply concerned with social problems and the creation of a theatre alive to the integrity of its national origins yet in keeping with a new age. Like others of his colleagues, Kinoshita considers that a new drama must mirror the many problems caused by the social transition in Japan. Commenting on the kabuki, of which he has a deep and affectionate knowledge, he has this to say:

The kabuki was born and developed in the feudal Edo era, which was an era of seclusion. Consequently the classical kabuki plays performed today reflect the typical thoughts and feelings of a feudal era. The themes of most of these dramas are the acceptance and glorification of the absolute loyalty to one's lords and parents and the unconditional submission to the bondage of the 'family'. At the same time, however, the best of the kabuki plays, perhaps accidentally, reveal the agonizing sorrows of the human soul that must resist the unconditional surrender of itself while on one hand they decidedly do accept and glorify the feudal virtues. The kabuki actors have mastered through long years of training the remarkable technique of artistic exaggeration by which they convey all such emotions . . . by sifting the various elements of the kabuki we may arrive at some suggestion as to what kind of new play should be written by contemporary playwrights. However, a new play which is merely well suited to kabuki actors cannot answer the question as to what should be done about the kabuki drama. It should be a new play that would contain some idea that would appeal strongly to the people of today and at the same time it should be suitable not for realistic presentation of the modern drama, but should be most effective when presented with the traditional kabuki technique of exaggeration and expression. No such plays have yet been written but only when they are written can the kabuki live as contemporary drama.[15]

In his own search for a new means of expression Kinoshita first turned to folk legend. In his student days he had become interested in J. M. Synge, whose work helped him to direct his own thinking towards the rich Japanese folk tradition. *Twilight Crane* was first conceived during the playwright's war time seclusion in the country and modestly produced in Osaka for the first time in 1949 with the veteran shingeki actress Yamamoto Yasue in the leading role. The play was an instant success and was awarded the Mainichi Press Drama prize in 1950. In 1952 a major production was staged at the Shimbashi Embujo theatre in Tokyo with Miss Yamomoto again in the leading role. Public acclaim was greater than ever. Today *Twilight Crane* has been performed more times than any other Japanese play in the modern repertoire and it has been translated into several languages. The plot of the play has a simple, almost fairy-tale quality, which to the western reader might be deceptive at a first introduction. It is a dramatic parable about human greed. A peasant saves the life of a wounded crane brought down by a hunter's arrow. In gratitude the bird transforms itself into the spirit of a woman who offers herself as the peasant's wife. She weaves a magic cloth from her feathers which she presents to the peasant as a token of her love. Two of his companions discover his secret and finally corrupt him by persuading him to extort more and more cloth from his wife to sell in the capital. Saddened by his change of heart the spirit of the crane flies away for ever. The significant feature of the play in performance was the way in which the hallowed realistic tradition of the modern theatre movement had been rejected without imitating traditional conventions or impairing the high standards of contemporary production. Yet the inner depth and spirit of Japanese tradition were fastidiously realized. As a comment on the plight of the individual within a mass society and the ruthlessness of capitalistic power *Twilight Crane* made telling theatre, universal in its touching and uncomplicated statement of the human dilemma. In his play Kinoshita possibly came as near as any Asian dramatist has done to solving the problem voiced in his own comments on the kabuki.

The title shingeki, or new drama, is a misnomer today, for the movement has a history, somewhat chequered it is true, of some sixty years behind it. Though on the whole it still faces its perennial problem of a lack of permanent stages and organized financial support it remains an established element of the extraordinarily diverse theatrical scene characteristic of urban Japan. Among a score or so of modern theatre companies active in present-day Tokyo there are four which can be considered representative and which maintain certain standards and approaches. Two of them, The Actors' Theatre and The Literary Theatre, were active before the war; The People's Theatre and The Four Seasons Theatre are postwar. Though they are divided both in political and aesthetic viewpoints, ranging between social consciousness and social comedy, all of them share a consistent fidelity to the literary classics. Shakespeare, Molière, Ibsen and Chekov are regularly performed and usually assured of modest success. The Actors' Theatre has had its own stage for more than ten years, the Four Seasons Group has its headquarters

in a smart modern auditorium seating two thousand five
hundred people. It is situated in a tall commercial block belonging to a life insurance company who also run the theatre. This
troupe has specialized in modern French pieces and has staged
dramatists like Anouilh and Giraudoux. Tokyo's most lavish
theatre of all is the new Imperial Theatre built on the old site
of its namesake facing the palace. Seating an audience of just
under two thousand, it is a nine-storey building of stainless steel,
black marble and glass. It has a large revolving centre stage,
four elevator stages, a sound system for simultaneous translation
and, when required, sound effects can be produced from under
the seats! This showy theatre, which is owned by one of the
big theatrical-film combines, opened with a grand revue and went
on to stage a six months' run of a Japanese adaptation of
Margaret Mitchell's *Gone With The Wind*, an indication of the
rising trend for light and slick entertainment for which the
Imperial Theatre has now become the focus. The prestigious
new National Theatre opened in 1966 is state-owned and
devoted to the production and preservation of the classical forms.
It has no standing company but kabuki performances are
regularly given by the troupes controlled by the Shochiku
Company. A separate auditorium, The Little National Theatre,
is used for staging noh and bunraku as well as classical music
and dance recitals. A great standby for the more or less homeless shingeki have been the small theatres which are situated on
the top floors of most of the big department stores and rented
out to various organizations. It is an admirable system for
which many a struggling group has been thankful.

The growth of the Japanese film industry and the advent of
television have greatly affected theatre relationships of all kinds
during the last fifteen years. Until the arrival of television Japan
had a greater attendance at films per head of population than
any other developed nation, and the quality of her productions
long ago placed her in the first rank of international producers.
The film and television have in many ways brought about a
greater flexibility and mobility of acting talent. Television has
now overshadowed the film in terms of public entertainment and
Japan today is probably the most television-conscious nation in
the world not excepting America. More than ninety-five per cent
of all families, whether in town or country, possess a television

set. The government network is matched by forty-six private television or radio television companies controlling one hundred and
sixty-seven stations. An astonishingly diverse programme is put
out and theatre of every kind receives generous sponsorship.
Actors are increasingly drawn towards the new medium. The
pay is immeasurably superior and dramatists are in constant
demand for new scripts.

Japan was a pioneer country in the use of mass media for
education and today eight hours of nation-wide educational
television programmes are screened daily in what has been
described as one of the best developed school broadcasting
systems in the world. All of this is indicative in its way of the
manner in which the entire cultural tradition is adapting itself
to the demands of modernization and at the same time extending the cultural perspective of the average Japanese to an extent
unequalled anywhere. The tremendous eclecticism that has
marked the Japanese search for knowledge has reached the stage
where a great deal of externally derived cultural influence has
now become part of the contemporary Japanese tradition. This
in turn has released a further process of original creativity,
particularly noticeable in the case of the film, though less so
in the case of the theatre which by nature remains much more
compartmentalized.

In contrast to this picture of cultural stability and progress,
Japanese, like western society, has been violently affected by the
disillusionment and anarchy of youth, the growth of mass movements and the appearance of raw new cultural standards. A
product of 'winds blowing from the west' was the staging of
Hair, the American love-rock musical, a phenomenon of the
contemporary entertainment world. It was put on by the
Shochiku Company, the doyen of kabuki entrepreneurs, at their
thousand-seat Toyoko Theatre in Tokyo during December 1969.
As elsewhere, it drew the audiences in and the headlines in the
leading Tokyo daily, the *asahi,* were blazoned: 'Overflowing
enthusiasm of Youth.' Most of the performers were amateurs,
and in spite of the raggedness of the show on the opening night
the paper conceded that 'the original music and the overwhelming energy of youth put the performance across at one blow'. A
group of high school students armed with leaflets picketed the

theatre on the opening day for charging high prices and 'serving big capitalists'. They got their free seats.

The brother of the emperor, Prince Mikasa, who saw the show described it as 'very philosophical', adding 'I understand one-third very well, I feel I will be able to understand another third if I sleep on it overnight. But the last third probably will forever remain a closed book to me'.[16] His words unconsciously reflect one aspect of the cultural dilemma confronting contemporary society in Japan.

Disquiet of a different kind was suddenly revealed in November 1970 with the grisly suicide of Yukio Mishima, playwright and novelist, whose manner of dying profoundly shocked both Japanese and western society, while posing many unanswerable questions.[17] Mishima, born in 1925, was internationally acclaimed as a writer, and was also the idol of a new younger generation in Japan. He first received the adulation of western critics for his novels, but attracted attention as a dramatist when his *Five Modern Noh Plays* were published in an English translation in 1957. In these pieces Mishima took the themes of five traditional noh plays and rewrote them in an idiom whose imagery sprang from an obsession with pure Japanese tradition married to an extreme style of contemporary literary-psychological negativism.

The greater part of his prolific literary output, which included more than a score of plays, revealed the black depths of a mind haunted by death as an aesthetic ideal and justified through violence and sadism. In his last years he attempted to practise his credo by creating a private army and espousing the cause of extreme right-wing militarism. After an unsuccessful attempt to provoke a mutiny in Tokyo military headquarters, Mishima, assisted by one of his young followers, performed *seppuku*, that is to say ritual disembowelling followed by decapitation, in the office of the military commandant who had been made captive.

Seppuku, better known as hara-kiri in the west, is now only thought of as melodramatic stage ritual belonging to kabuki plays, an emotional evocation of a feudal past having nothing to do with the realities of contemporary life and psychology. That it could suddenly become actuality was a numbing intrusion in the lives of people who today consider themselves among the most advanced of consumer societies.

NOTES

1: THE FRAMEWORK OF ASIAN THEATRE

[1] Two Chinese examples illustrate this point well. In the traditional Peking play, *The Butterfly Dream, Hu Tieh Meng*, the flirtatious heroine at one point performs a highly conventionalized dance involving a good deal of seductive movement of hips and shoulders which finally takes her off-stage with a delicate but provocative kick. Her servant boy, played by a comic actor, then appears and proceeds to parody the whole performance with great exaggeration of effect. He finishes by wrenching his back and hobbles round the stage, usually to the great delight of the audience who are always ready to enjoy poking fun at the conventions of high art.

A gramophone record released in Peking in the early 1950s of a live performance of two famous cross-talk comedians provides a second example. The two comics, Hou Pao-lin and Kuo Ch'i-ju, whose art is really an extension of story-telling methods, discuss the art of theatre and in so doing introduce some brilliant parodies of the formalized role techniques of the traditional stage. Methods of weeping and laughing in both male and female roles are imitated as well as the vocal styles of the new-style actors and film stars. The audience are reduced to hilarious laughter by the clowning and at the same time moved to unstinted applause by the sheer technical skill of the caricature. (M242 Chung-kuo ch'ang p'ien 1961 Hsi-chü shen t'an.)

[2] Herrigel, *Zen in the Art of Archery*.

[3] *The Natyasastra* . . . (translated Ghosh), p. 33; Thapar, *Asoka and the decline of the Mauryas*, p. 86.

[4] Four classes of society (*ssu min*), scholar, farmer, artisan, merchant.

[5] The origins of the shadow puppet have always been a matter for dispute and it is impossible to be dogmatic on the subject. Claims advanced by many that India was the original home of the Asian shadow theatre have never been satisfactorily proved but the rich variety of shadow puppets found in India certainly suggest a very ancient tradition which would repay more detailed research.

In Andhra Pradesh state there are leather puppets called *tholu bommalata* which Indian authorities claim existed as early as the third century BC. The Andhra puppets are made of tanned hide and the limbs are articulated with knotted string and operated by means of a central grip made from thin bamboo. Sizes range from one to seven feet in height. The gigantic size of some of these puppets seems to point to very early attempts to reproduce the human form life size. They are painted with vegetable dyes and throw a coloured image on the screen. The screen is made from two white cotton sheets tightly stretched one above the other between two posts. The themes are taken from the great epics and mythological sources. No scripts are used, the performers working entirely from memory. A troupe usually consists of about half a dozen members and may include the wives of the puppeteers. All of them are skilled in singing and there are two instrumental musicians. The performance demands highly developed teamwork from the performers, who are trained from childhood and come from families which are related and carry on the profession as a hereditary occupation. The shows are given free in the villages and are usually sponsored by well-to-do families for the public's entertainment. A show lasts between six and eight hours, oil lamps being used. According to some Indian experts, the shadow show travelled into Islam and south-east Asia through migrations of the population from the Andhra coastal areas.

Another ancient form of shadow puppet is found in Orissa state. Here the puppets are made in a single piece from tanned goat hide and held erect with a bamboo grip. The performance is more like an animated illustration of a musically narrated theme, there is no dramatic gesticulation or dialogue. A long stretch of cloth is used for a screen and the lamps which are the source of light are in full view of the audience. Pieces representing houses, pavilions, thrones, trees, etc. are projected on the screen. A vertical jigging of puppets from side to side and towards or away from the screen characterizes the manipulation, while at times the puppets are made to revolve around their axis as they are faded in and out. The chief narrator sits in front of the screen and beats out the rhythm. His assistants work the puppets from behind the screen and sing in chorus certain sections of the narration which at times leads to the development of an argument between the chief narrator and the others. The art of the puppeteer lies in creating a symbolic pose by the puppet expressive of character and its relationship to similarly posed characters and the settings as they define the progression of the story.

Yet another ancient Indian shadow puppet form is the *parakuthu* of Kerala in southern India. The puppets in this are made from tanned deerskin and have articulated limbs. A thin bamboo framework gives rigidity to the puppets which are held in the hand by a stick. This form has very early ritualistic associations and suggests the religious origins of puppetry. It is usually staged in a covered enclosure about forty feet long placed at one end of a shrine compound or housed in a shed specially built. The front of the stage is completely draped with a white curtain and a black curtain covers the bottom half. The puppets are first arranged behind the white screen in a row immediately above the black lower half and small pottery basin lamps using coconut oil are arranged along the length of the screen. This installation rite is performed to the sound of drums. After this all but two of the puppets are removed and a recitative is given concerning the long line of departed pioneers of this art which ends with a blessing for the success of the show. A resumé of the previous night's entertainment is also introduced once the show is under way for the performance used to take as long as forty-one nights.

The play draws freely on the *Ramayana* composed for a Chola king by his court poet in the ninth century AD and the text remained a closely guarded secret. Different schools of puppeteers arose as they each developed their own interpretation. Heightened prose with poetic imagery and many figures of speech are used, the narrator developing a lively accompaniment of recitative, commentary and asides. The entire Rama, theme with its verses, commentaries and discourses, has been greatly shortened although it can still go on for between eleven to twenty-one nights even today. The play concludes with the coronation of Rama and the final evening on which this is staged is one of great ceremonial accompanied by special music and processions from the shrine as part of the play itself.

This shadow show is an example of how the early Hindu teachers used the form for propagating their religion and ethics. As the popularity of this kind of performance grew it became a stylized entertainment with a moral message but still retained its religious function.

The three forms of shadow play described here suggest that even if the form already existed in south-east Asia before the Hindu penetration, at least there are grounds for supposing that India was the source of some elemental approaches which influenced developments elsewhere.

[6] Jules Lemaître, drama critic of the *Journal des Débats,* in reference to the shadow theatre, *Le Chat Noir,* founded in 1881 by Rudolphe Salis at his historic *cabaret artistique* in Montmartre. The theatre became an elaborate affair whose repertoire was contributed by some of the most distinguished artists and writers of the period.

[7] Craig, *On the Art of Theatre,* p. 79-94.

[8] Borator, *Le Terkelème* which has a comprehensive description of the introductory phrases of Turkish storytellers. The Turkish name for storyteller is *meddah.*

[9] Awa Odori, Tokushima Prefecture.

[10] Beryle de Zoete, *Dance and Drama in Bali,* p. 16.

[11] Hanuman, the monkey deity, was sired by the Wind God. He has been greatly idealized in Hindu literature and in consequence throughout south-east Asian mythology. He was noted for his sagacity, incredible strength and ability to fly through the air at tremendous speed. He has been the subject of countless legends, but his real fame rests on the accounts of his exploits given in the

Ramayana epic in which he helps Rama rescue Sita from the clutches of Ravana, the demon ruler of Lanka. Hanuman has been portrayed in scores of dance dramas both in India and south-east Asia and naturally he has given great scope for skilled acrobatics and vigorous choreographic styles. He also appears on the shadow screens of Java, Bali, Cambodia, Thailand and Malaysia.

In China, Hanuman became Sun Wu-k'ung, a character in the famous classic, *Journey to the Western Regions, Hsi Yu Chi*, the source of a number of stage adaptations. In the Chinese legend Sun Wu-k'ung was credited with being able to travel 108,000 *li* in a single leap (a *li* was about a third of a mile) as well as performing incredible feats of strength with a rod of iron acquired from the Dragon King of the Eastern Sea There were actors in the Chinese theatre who made a speciality of the Sun Wu-k'ung role, which called for violent acrobatics, animal mime and virtuoso juggling with a chromium rod.

[12] *The Natyasastra* . . . (translated Ghosh) section 240, p. 195.

[13] Menon, 'Indian Music and its American Audience', *Saturday Review*, 27 January 1968, pp. 49, 50.

[14] The most famous of these is the Takarazuka Girls Opera. The original troupe consisted of sixteen girls who were recruited for training in stage performance, vocal and instrumental music, as well as both Japanese and western style dancing. After nine months hard work they gave their first performance in April 1914 at the Paradise Theatre which was part of an Amusement Centre at the new hot spring resort of Takarazuka ten miles west of Osaka. The creation of the troupe was the idea of Ichizo Kobyashi, manager of a new electric railway which served the resort. The idea caught on and in 1918 the company was invited to perform at the Imperial Theatre in Tokyo and in the same year the Ministry of Education accorded recognition to the Takarazuka Girls Opera Training School. By 1924 the now enlarged and very popular troupe moved into a new 4,000 seat theatre at Takarazuka. In 1927 *Mon Paris*, a western style revue, was staged and had the longest run on record in the Japanese show world. After this the troupe made great progress and in 1934 a big new theatre was also opened in Tokyo. The girls now numbered four hundred and were given one year of training in the preparatory course of the school before being allowed on stage. Once on stage they were called Research Course Students and divided into four divisions named Flower, Moon, Star and Snow, and they rotated between the main theatres and provincial tours. The training school was divided into four main sections, teaching Japanese traditional dancing, western dancing, vocal techniques and theatrical performance. Musical composition, design and lighting were all carried out by members of the teaching staff who were periodically sent to Europe and the United States to keep abreast of developments. In 1938 the Takarazuka Girls Opera, consisting of fifty-four members, made their first tour of Europe and in 1939 a troupe of sixty members made a first tour of the United States. The company was closed

down in 1944 and its members conscripted for propaganda performances. In 1946 they returned to the stage once again with a performance of Bizet's *Carmen*. The company regained a new popularity and performances became classified under three styles; Scheherezade, in which western opera and ballets were turned into typical Takarazuka spectacles; Tales of Genji and Flowers and their Tales, in which old classical pieces were given a modern revue presentation; and leg shows which yielded nothing to the celebrated Rockettes of New York.

From its inception no girl accepted for training by the Takarazuka School was allowed to marry and the rule was strictly enforced. Until the war the greater proportion of Takarazuka audiences were made up from girls, and the fan worship that went on, particularly with some of the stars who played male roles, has only been equalled by present day 'pop' followers. According to one Japanese sociologist, Mamory Mochizuki, the prewar Takarazuka Girls Opera was essentially a product of the social system and the restriction of women. Following the Girls Opera was the only outlet for young girls, who were permitted no social contact whatsoever with men so that parents and teachers considered the lesbian undertones of the fan-star relationships harmless in the light of accepted social taboos. The Takarazuka girls themselves were segregated in dormitories and forbidden any mixing with boys. The emphasis always was that they were 'students of singing and dancing' and the high school fans were urged to follow their example and study hard too.

Since the war new social attitudes and co-education have altered things a great deal, although the same strict training rules apply for the troupe, who continue to supply what Mochizuki defines as 'escapist entertainment with fantastic, exotic and romantic content', providing an outlet for the individual to escape into daydreams still, though the situation is in part changing and the old style fan fever is abating to some extent.

The Takarazuka has a rival in the Shochiku Revue Troupe which was founded in 1958 when twenty girls were selected for training. The troupe has been run on more or less identical lines to the Takarazuka group, its headquarters being the Kokusai Theatre, Tokyo, first opened in 1937 as the largest theatre in Asia. Bombed in 1945 it was re-opened in 1947 and in the 1950s attracted large audiences to see its forty-two Atomic Girls.

2: INDIA

[1] The themes and characters of the *Ramayana* have featured constantly in the repertoires of the storytellers, the puppet show, the theatre and the dance. Authorship of the *Ramayana* is usually attributed to the sage Valmiki, but the complete text as it exists was not written at one time and many additions were made to it through the cen-

turies. In its present form the work consists of seven books containing approximately 24,000 verses. Three revised versions exist, each from a different part of India and each version containing material which does not exist in the other two. The one from the Bombay area by virtue of its archaic expressions is considered the oldest. In the narrative itself there are indications that it was recited by minstrels and much of it seems to have been inspired by folklore themes and ballads.

There are many digressions in the main story and the whole contains a code of conduct and morals as exemplified through Hindu teachings. The *Ramayana* was in fact a mythic agent for propagating the Brahmanic or Sanskrit culture, but it eventually came to be retold and sung in the regional languages such as Tamil, through the poet Kamban's version, *c.* 1180–1223, and in Hindu through the version of Tulasidas, 1532–1623.

No story has been more venerated than the tale of Rama and Sita, the two principal characters of the epic. In Indian eyes this pair were the embodiment of male and female virtue and represented the ideal symbols of love and conjugal felicity. Sita symbolized purity and chastity while Rama was the hero devoted to the sacred law even though this compelled him to behave unfeelingly.

The seven books of the *Ramayana* are divided in the following way:

Book 1 The boyhood of Rama.
Book 2 The incidents at Ayodhya, Rama's marriage to Sita and their banishment.
Book 3 Rama's life in the forest with Sita and his brother Lakshmana; the abduction of Sita by Ravana.
Book 4 Rama's stay at Kishkindhya, the Monkey King's residence.
Book 5 The passage of Rama to Lanka across the bridge created by the monkey armies.
Book 6 The war with Ravana, the recovery of Sita and return to Ayodhya; the coronation of Rama.
Book 7 Banishment of Sita, birth of her twin sons, Rama's recognition, reunion with Sita, Sita's passage to heaven.

The dance and theatre themes which have been based on these incidents centre on the following principal characters:

KING DASARATHA OF AYODHYA
KAIKEYI   his consort and Rama's stepmother
RAMA   their son
LAKSHMANA ⎫
SHATRUGHNA ⎬ the three brothers of Rama
BHARATA   ⎭
SITA   Rama's wife, daughter of King Janaka
RAVANA   demon ruler of Lanka (Ceylon)
SHURPANAKHA sister of Ravana
MARICHA   warrior of Ravana

JATAYU   King of the Birds
SAMPATI   son of Garuda
SUGRIVA   King of the Monkeys
HANUMAN   commander-in-chief of the monkeys
AGNI   God of Fire

The incidents in which they figure are briefly as follows. When the time comes for Rama to succeed to the throne of Ayodhya he is driven out by the machinations of the queen, his stepmother. He goes into exile in the forest, accompanied by his faithful wife Sita and his brother Lakshmana. While Rama is hunting, Ravana, the demon ruler, lures Lakshmana away by a ruse and abducts Sita. During his flight with his victim he is attacked by Jatayu, the King of the Birds, who is mortally wounded by Ravana and discovered by Rama as he lies dying on the ground. Rama makes an alliance with the monkey kingdom, whose commander-in-chief, Hanuman, crosses the ocean with a single mighty leap to encourage Sita in her captivity. Rama then attacks Ravana's capital across a bridge of rocks and tree trunks built by the monkey armies. The demon forces are routed and Rama kills Ravana. Sita is released and taken in triumph to Ayodhya where Rama is crowned king.

Painful scenes follow. Doubtful of Sita's chastity during her captivity, Rama repudiates her. Sita voluntarily undergoes an ordeal by fire to prove her innocence. Rama's doubts return under the criticism of his subjects and he finally sends Sita into permanent exile at a hermitage. There she gives birth to twin sons. When the two sons reach adolescence they stray by chance one day to Ayodhya and are recognised by Rama. He recalls Sita to the capital to attest her innocence in a public assembly, calling upon the earth to verify her words. The ground thereupon opens up to receive Sita and she passes to the immortals.

See also under *the Ramayana* in the Bibliography.

[2] The *Mahabharata* is older than the *Ramayana* with which it shares the claim of a lasting influence on Indian thought and literature. Fictitiously attributed to the sage Vyasa, the *Mahabharata* is a vast wandering miscellany now divided into eighteen books totalling 100,000 couplets. The metre, style and structure of this unwieldy epic indicate that it has been subject to constant revision and additions from many sources. Within the narrative various stories are placed in the mouths of different characters. The main theme occupies about a quarter of the whole text, which includes the *Bhagavad Gita* with its discourses on the code of the warrior. A mass of other material is to be found within the whole, dealing with moral law, philosophy and other matters as well as numerous fables and stories which have no connection with the principal theme. Scholars have traced several chronological layers in the *Mahabharata*, some of which relate to very early periods and some to much later times. It is almost impossible to give it any kind of definitive chronology.

The great battle of Kurukshetra, on which the main story is based, is supposed to have taken place sometime between 850 and 650 BC.

The contents of the eighteen books of the *Mahabharata* are divided in the following way.

Book 1 The background and upbringing of the Kaurava and Pandava princes and their training. The growing enmity of the two houses. The great tournament and the quarrel between Arjuna and the Kaurava. First exile of the Pandavas. Slaying of the ogres by Bhima. Sojourn in Drupada's capital and the winning of Draupadi. Pandavas return from exile. Division of the kingdom. Exile and return of Arjuna. Slaying of Sisupala by Krishna.

Book 2 The assembly of the princes at Hastinapura. Yudishthira's game of dice with Sakuni. Loss of the kingdom, second exile of the Pandavas.

Book 3 The Pandavas in the forest. Adventures of Arjuna. Capture of Duryodhana and rescue by the Pandavas. Abduction of Draupadi by Jayadratha, and his defeat.

Book 4 The thirteenth year of the Pandava exile as disguised servitors to the King Virata.

Book 5 Preparation of the Kauravas and the Pandavas for war. Krishna and Balarama decide not to fight. Mustering of the armies at Kurukshetra.

Book 6 Description of the battlefield. The doubts of Arjuna. The teaching of the *Bhagavad Gita*. The battles with Kaurava armies. Bhishma, their commander, slain by Arjuna.

Book 7 The war during the command of the Kaurava forces by Drona. His death at the hands of the son of the King of Drupada.

Book 8 Karna's command of the Kauravas, his death at the hands of Arjuna.

Book 9 Salya's command of the Kauravas. Wounding of Duryodhana; only three Kauravas remain alive.

Book 10 Night attack by the remaining three Kauravas on the Pandava camp. Death of Duryodhana.

Book 11 Lament of the Queen Gandhari and the other women over the dead heroes.

Book 12 Coronation of Yudhishthira at Hastinapura followed by Bhisma's long discourse on politics and kingship to assuage Yudhishthira's grief.

Book 13 Bhisma's discourses on the duties of kings, liberality and fasting. His death.

Book 14 Yudhishthira's sacrifice. Further adventures of Arjuna.

Book 15 Retirement of Dhritarashtra, Gandhari and Kunti, mother of the Pandavas to a forest hermitage. The great forest fire which burns them all to death.

Book 16 The death of Krishna and Balarama. Submersion of Dvaraka under the ocean. Mutual extermination of the Yadavas fighting with clubs.

Book 17 Yudhishthira's renunciation of the throne. His departure with his brothers to the Himalayas and Indra's heaven.

Book 18 Admission to heaven of Yudhishthira and his brothers with their wife Draupadi.

The dance and theatre themes which have been based on these incidents centre round the following principal characters:

ARJUNA	Pandava brother, peerless warrior, skilled archer and great lover, son of Kunti by the God, Indra.
BALARAMA	Elder brother of Krishna. Fond of wine.
BHIMA	Pandava brother, a mighty warrior who fought with clubs, son of Kunti by the God of the Wind.
BHISMA	Elder statesman respected by both the Kauravas and the Pandavas.
BHISHMA	Most noble of the Mahabharata heroes. Son of King Satanu and Ganga, goddess of the sacred River Ganges. Adviser to both the Pandavas and the Kauravas, he finally fought on the side of the latter.
DHRITARASHTRA	Blind king of the Kurus.
DRAUPADI	Wife of the Pandava brothers, daughter of King Drupada, ravishing beauty.
DRONA	Priest warrior and tutor of the Pandavas who were brought up in the Kaurava family.
DUHSALA	The Kaurava daughter.
DUHSASANA	A Kaurava brother.
DURMUKHA	A Kaurava brother.
DURYODHANA	Eldest son of Gandhari, leader of the Kauravas, a great fighter with clubs.
GANDHARI	Queen of Dhritarashtra, mother of the ninety nine Kaurava brothers and of one daughter.
INDRA	First among the Vedic gods.
JAYADRATHA	Husband of Duhsala, daughter of Dhritarashtra and ally of the Kauravas. King of Sindhu.
KARNA	Handsome warrior of the Kauravas, the equal of Arjuna at whose hand he dies because the Gods have willed it. He was the abandoned infant son of Kunti.
KAURAVA BROTHERS	Four of the ninety-nine Kaurava brothers important in the dramas are Duhsasana, Duryodhana, the eldest and the leader, Durmukha and Subahu. The one daughter is Duhsala.
KRISHNA	First cousin of the Pandavas, part god and incarnation of the mighty Vishnu. Brilliant politician, strategist and master-mind, who makes victory for the Pandavas possible.

KUNTI	Wife of Pandu and mother of three of the Pandava brothers through illicit union with the gods.
MADRI	Wife of Pandu, mother of the other two Pandava brothers.
NAKULA	Pandava brother, son of Madri, skilled fencer.
PANDAVA BROTHERS	The five Pandava brothers, sons of Pandu, are Arjuna, son of Kunti by the God Indra, Bhima, son of Kunti by the God of the Wind, Nakula, son of Madri, Sahadeva, son of Madri, Yudhishthira, son of Kunti by the God of Justice.
PANDU	Brother of Dhritarashtra and father of the Pandava brothers.
SAHADEVA	Pandava brother, son of Madri, skilled fencer.
SAKUNI	Evil genius of the Kauravas.
SALYA	Handsome young warrior of the Kauravas.
SUBAHU	A Kaurava brother.
YUDHISHTHIRA	Eldest Pandava brother, son of Kunti by the God of Justice, skilled in chariot fighting.
YUYUTSU	Son of Duhsala by Jayadratha, King of Sindhu.

The events to which the contents of these books refer may be summarized as follows.

There is bitter rivalry between the princely houses of the Kauravas and the Pandavas, who are cousins. The five Pandava brothers have a common wife, Draupadi, and they are forced into exile with her twice by the jealous Duryodhana, leader of the Kauravas. The second banishment is the result of a game of dice arranged by Duryodhana between the eldest Pandava brother and Sakuni, the evil genius of the Kauravas, who has loaded the dice. During their long period of exile which lasts twelve years the five brothers have many adventures and confrontations. At the end of their period of banishment they return to prepare for the inevitable war in which both sides enlist the aid of tribes from all over India. The battle rages for eighteen days, favouring now this side, now that with the dead ever thicker on the ground. After the clash of troops comes a series of single-handed combats between heroes, who one by one are killed until the Kauravas are annihilated and the Pandavas left victors. The queen and the women of the Kauravas mourn the cruel slaughter of their men and with the old king retire to a forest hermitage. Here they all perish in a great fire. The Pandavas finally renounce the throne they have won by conquest and set off through the eternal snows to reach the abode of Indra. One by one they perish on the way and pass to heaven.

See also under *The Mahabharata* in the Bibliography.

[3] *The Artha Sastra*, or *Doctrine of Prosperity*, is the most important single source in Indian secular literature. Its author is said to be Kautilya, who was minister to the Emperor Chandragupta of the Maurya state in the fourth century BC. The text in the form that it exists is a later compilation. It was edited and commented upon by different writers and finally worked over by Visnagupta around the third or fourth centuries AD, to include whatever interpolations had occurred by then. It is written in difficult but economic prose interspersed with stanzas of verse.

[4] Majumdar, *Indian Dance Theory and Practice*. Munshi and Diwakar, *Indian Inheritance*, vol. 2, pp. 29–41.

[5] Ghurye, *Caste, Class and Occupation*, pp. 42–6.

[6] The names of the four castes were first given as *Brahmana, Rajanya, Vaisya* and *Sudra*, and were said to have come respectively from the mouth, the arms, the thighs and the feet of the creator. Eventually the four castes were stratified under the names *Brahmin, Kshatriya, Vaisya* and *Sudra*. Only the first three castes were eligible to take part in religious initiation rites. The fourth caste, the Sudra, and the huge class of outcastes known as *panchama* were forbidden the rites. The panchama included many people of different stock and occupations but all of them were regarded as completely beyond the pale of orthodox Hindu society.

  The four castes are commonly distinguished as Brahmins, priests, teachers and the guardians of sacred knowledge; Kshatriya, warriors and administrators; Vaisya, traders and farmers; Sudra, ordinary workers, a term which covers a multitude of occupations. The panchama were the untouchables. There are many more fine distinctions than these but for further information see under Ghurye in the Bibliography.

[7] Coomaraswamy, *Dance of Shiva*, pp. 66–78.

[8] Shekar, *Sanskrit Drama*, p. 20.

[9] Bhavnani, *Dance in India*, p. 18; Weber, *Religion of India*, p. 354; Shekar, *Sanskrit Drama*, pp. 102–6; Singer, 'The great tradition of Hinduism in the City of Madras', Leslie, *Anthropology of folk religion*, pp. 137–41; Munshi and Diwakar, *Indian Inheritances*, vol. 2, pp. 29–31; Iyer, *Bharata Natyam*, p. 17.

[10] Chatterjee, *Art of Hindu Dance*, p. 99; Bhavnani, *The Dance in India*, p. 29.

[11] Singer, 'The great tradition of Hinduism in the City of Madras', Leslie, *Anthropology of Folk Religion*, pp. 143–8.

[12] The *Natya Sastra of Bharata*. Natya is a generic term for theatrical presentation, sastra is the name given to a treatise of scriptural laws. Bharata is the name of the supposed author of this work. The name Bharata is an ancient Vedic one and a tribal designation, it is also a synonym for an actor. The name is little more than a cipher and there is no historical evidence to support the existence of a sage bearing this name (see Kale).

  Summary of contents of the *Natya Sastra* (after Kale):

1 Origin of the drama.
2 Construction of theatres.
3 Rites of offering worship to the various stage deities.
4 Characteristics of Tandava dance.
5 Preliminaries to a performance.
6 An account or *rasa*.
7 Modalities and their indication.
8 The minor use of bodily forms of theatrical presentation, eyes. eyebrows, nose, lips, cheeks, chin.
9 The major uses of bodily forms, hands, chest, buttocks, abdomen, waist, thighs and legs.
10 The basic foot movements and stance in dance.
11 Choreographic sequences.
12 Characterization through gait and posture.
13 The conventions and modes of the stage.
14 Elements of speech and prosody.
15 Poetic metres.
16 Figures of speech and qualities of style.
17 Elements of speech in Prakrit style.
18 The ten types of drama.
19 The structural points of drama.
20 An account of styles of interpretation.
21 Exterior and material form of theatrical presentation.
22 The normal form of theatrical presentation.
23 A manual for gallants.
24 Dramatic characters and their interpretation.
25 Pictorial form of theatrical presentation (use of the body to describe or represent pictorially).
26 Types of dramatic expression.
27 The assessment of the success of a performance.
28 Elements of music.
29 Aspects of instrumental music.
30 Aspects of reed instruments.
31 Cymbals, beat and rhythm, time measurement.
32 Songs in a play.
33 A discourse on musical qualities.
34 Drums and other skin percussion instruments.
35 Distribution of roles.
36 The story of the actor's curse. Bharata tells the story of how his sons were cursed for mimicking certain sages and lost their high caste to become sudra.

Theory of rasa
Chapter 7 of the *Natya Sastra* expounds a psychological theory of dramatic communication which has generated some of the more obscure jargon of its kind in scholarly explanations. The more involved they become the more puzzled the theatre student is likely to be. It will be enough to say here that the theory sets out to explain

what happens when a play is seen performed, and what is the transient process which results from the interaction of a performance by trained artists watched by an equally knowledgeable audience. The theory assumes that certain responsive mental states are created in the onlooker's mind and the drama as a medium determines these reactions by the means and suggestion used. A state of aesthetic awareness is produced through this fusion so that the spectator is drawn from the material action of the play into consciousness of an enduring reality. The process takes place both on the stage and in the mind of the individual; it is rather like the western psychologist's definition of empathy except that it has a transcendental implication. To those brought up to western logic, the rasa theory is difficult to accept. On the other hand the Indians have never claimed that this aesthetic experience is for everybody. It is regarded as a highly select occurrence demanding a trained mind both in the performance and in the appreciation of art. In short, the theory of rasa as defined in the *Natya Sastra* is an attempt to describe, within the very severe limitations of a printed text, the nature of theatrical experience according to the classical canons.

See also under *Natya Sastra* in the Bibliography.

[13] Coomaraswamy, *Mirror of Gesture*, pp. 16–7; *Natya Sastra Sangraha*, vol. 1, pp. 12–3.

[14] The *kathakali*, literally story-play, of Kerala in southern India, has a history of approximately three hundred years. It has well defined connections with the ancient classical forms but its graphic mimetic character marks it apart from any other style. A remarkable feature of the technique is the extensive use of hand gestures—the actors remain mute and mime the narration through their hands. The bizarre and elaborate make-up of the actors is another striking aspect of this dance-drama, whose powerful acting style is marked by emotional bombast.

Kathakali is essentially an open-air performance. Though it is often staged indoors today, traditionally it takes place at night in a sixteen foot square clearing lit by a single large oil flare in a metal container standing in front of the performing area. There is a stool or two for the actors to sit on and the musicians stand in the stage area behind the actors. The orchestra consists of two or three singer-narrators, two drummers, and cymbal and gong players. The play is announced by a blast on a conch shell followed by a sustained period of tempestuous drumming which calls the audience from far and near.

One of the drummers plays a *maddala* which is fastened to the waist by a cotton belt and held in a horizontal position, being played on both heads simultaneously with the palm and fingers. The second drummer plays a *cenda*, a cylindrical drum peculiar to Kerala. It is held in position by a cotton strap suspended over the shoulder and is played in an upright position with two sticks on the singlehead. It is characterized by its wild and penetrating rhythms. Drumming

...nsifies the high drama of a kathakali performance as well as controlling tempo and rhythm in the acting.

The singing style of the narrators is extremely forceful and it is they who lead the other musicians. The songs are structured around hieratic style modes and the modal patterns are determined by the mood being expressed. The singer is the intermediary upon whom the actor depends. Every line of a song is repeated until it is translated word by word in the movement and gesture of the actor. Kathakali rhythms are based on five basic timing systems and the dance movements are accommodated to the combinations formed by these.

A hypnotic technique used by the actors is called peering over the curtains, *thiranottam*, usually performed by demons and fierce characters. There may be as many as five or six of these incidents in the course of a performance and they create a tremendous tension. The drumming suddenly grows intense, heightening the suspense of the onlookers, and two stage hands stand holding a rectangular curtain between them in front of the oil flare. Behind the curtain the actor begins a vigorous dance, stamping and strutting, occasionally showing a hand for a brief moment over the top of the curtain or a glimpse of his head dress. Each time the curtain is dragged down a little further, the titillation going on for ten minutes or so. Suddenly the curtain is ripped aside and the actor rushes forth among the tense audience, his grotesque make-up illuminated by the flickering light of the oil flare.

Kathakali make-up is distinguished by five main conventionalized styles green, knife, beard, black and polished, each one symbolizing a specific character and qualities. The colour schemes and desings vary for each role and a peculiar feature are the *chutti*, stiff protuberances of rice paste which are built up around the line of the cheeks, mouth and nose. Most male characters wear long silver nails on the fingers of the left hand and these add to the effect of the mudra patterns. It is a custom for kathakali actors to redden the pupil of the eyes with a special little seed pod. It has no ill effect but provides vivid accentuation to the power of expression, especially in the case of the demons, whose eyes roll left and right with the movements of their fluttering hands. The use of such devices adds a particular dramatic emphasis to the charged silence of the actors, who are no longer human beings but dream characters from another world, the gods descended to earth.

Kathakali dance movements are characterized by great strength and majesty and often punctuated with mighty leaps. In the actor's basic stance the knees are splayed, with the legs forming a kind of rhomboid, the arms bent at the elbows, and the palms placed on the hips, re-emphasizing the angular posture of the legs. The actor's soles are never flat against the stage, for in maintaining balance the weight is thrown on the outer edge of the feet which remain slightly bent and curved.

The plays consist of excerpts from the *Ramayana* and *Mahabharata* and the repertoire ranges through about fifty pieces, of which around twenty are still regularly performed. Traditionally the kathakali has always been played by men. Training is long and arduous and demands great physical control from the pupils who begin their studies around the age of ten.

At one time seen only in its native province, the kathakali has now been nationally recognized and is seen played in many parts of India, although the Kelamandalan in Kerala remains the classical centre of training. Kathakali dance is today listed as one of the four major styles of traditional dance, the other three being bharata natyam, kathak, manipuri.

[15] *The Natya Sastra . . .*, (trans. Ghosh), section 99, p. 227.
[16] *Ibid.*, section 37, p. 218.
[17] *Ibid.*, sections 31–2, p. 217.
[18] India has been a major source for many of the dance and theatrical traditions of south-east Asia. Although countries in this area developed their strongly individualistic styles, to which indigenous elements contributed their own character, it is nevertheless impossible to separate them from the Indian sources which gave them form in the beginning. In Java, Bali, Cambodia, Burma, Thailand and Ceylon, the presence of India is always there as a reminder of forces which lie deep beneath the cultural currents of these countries.

As in India itself, the *Ramayana* and the *Mahabharata* have had a lasting influence in south-east Asia. The shadow puppet theatres of Java, Bali, Cambodia and Malaysia drew upon both these epics as a major source of material, even though eventually they preserved only the plots and the principal deeds of the Indian models, moulding them to their own cultures. The dance dramas of Burma, Ceylon, Java, Bali, Thailand and Cambodia again owe a large debt to the two great epics.

Java was profoundly subjected to the influence of Indian culture although many questions remain unanswered as to how and when Indian influences first came to the fore. It will suffice to say here that Javanese culture was deeply affected by both Hindu and Buddhist influences in turn, from around the second century AD until the fourteenth century, when the Islamic religion first began to infiltrate the country. By the end of the fifteenth century Islam had superseded all other faiths and remained dominant from then on. As a theatrical influence Islam was negative and calls for no comment here.

Java's unique contribution to theatrical expression has been the *wayang purwa* or shadow play, known more often by the general term *wayang kulit* today. *Wayang* means a dramatic play in general, *kulit* means leather or hide, a reference to the heavy buffalo parchment from which the shadow figures are made. *Purwa* means plays based on the Indian epics only. For centuries the shadow play has been a national recreation and ritual in Java and its influence on

Javanese thought has been enormous. The shadow figures bear the names of the characters from the Indian epics and follow the main themes although there are sometimes marked differences in both their characters and their adventures. The clowns in the Javanese shadow play, who always make their appearance around midnight, are considered to be quite indigenous, with possible origins in the earliest Javanese folklore. The code of ethics, the moral values, the outlook on life as represented on the shadow screen have had an influence on Javanese thinking that cannot be overestimated. Dramatic opposition between the forces of good and evil is portrayed through the self-restraint as well as the unrestrained passions of the two parties from the *Mahabharata* as they appear on the screen. Both forces are indispensable and essential to the universal harmony of which they are equally a part. This opposition and unity is found in all areas of thought and action and it is characteristic of a good deal of dance, choreography for example. Although this philosophy here takes on its special Javanese flavour, it is after all one that underlies much Asian intellectual and artistic expression and has its roots in the elemental conclusions of Indian philosophical speculation.

A shadow play performance goes on all night and is usually divided into three distinct phases. The first period extends usually from 9 in the evening to midnight and is related to the youthful period of life as portrayed through the characters. It is from this portion that children learned the Javanese ethical values and correct modes of behaviour. The second period begins around midnight and lasts until 3 in the morning. It is prefaced by what is called *gara-gara*, or the turmoil of the elements. The clowns make their entry at this point and there is fierce fighting and much complication of the plot. The young adult's confrontation with society is expressed in this phase. The last phase runs from 3 until dawn. Action intensifies, good triumphs over evil, and a philosophical ending represents the sagacity and wisdom of age. The final battle in this phase always concludes with a victory dance.

Each phase is dominated by particular musical modes, music and percussion effects being an integral part of the action on the screen. Every shadow character has his own musical-sound accompaniment for entering the stage, specific scenes have specific melodies, and so on. The puppeteer creates a very characteristic percussive effect by beating a bundle of metal plates fixed to the chest in which the puppets are stored. The audience watches the show from both sides of the screen, the *dalang*, or puppeteer's side, and the shadow side. There have been many theories as to the origins of this double viewing point but it seems to be generally accepted that the true connoisseurs today stay on the dalang's side. The dalang himself sits before the centre of the screen, the light suspended behind him as he works the shadow figures from shoulder height. A complete cast of figures, allowing for a number of duplicates of characters to portray different ages and emotions, may number anything up to three hundred and fifty figures. There is an indivisible relationship between the *gamelan* orchestra and its singers and the action on the screen. Moods, types of action and characterization are all reinforced and developed through the musical accompaniment. The audience is thoroughly familiar with this close interrelationship which though intimately Javanese is none the less the debtor of principles first set down in the *Natya Sastra*.

Java has been a land of many courts, and the four which formerly graced the two capitals of Solo and Jogjakarta in central Java were regarded as the centre of the classical dance tradition. The court dances were carried to a pitch of ultra-refinement and were forbidden to the vulgar gaze, being associated with the most intimate rituals of the *keraton* or palace. The beauty of these dances lies in the harmony and counterpoint created between the choreography and the music of the gamelan orchestra. They are distinguished by controlled, almost languid, movements punctuated by subtle flicks of a long sash worn by the dancers and gentle kicks and turns with long flowing trains. They are essentially displays of the most delicately realized form whose airy quality and static postures almost appear to be a negation of dancing as the term is understood in the west. The *serimpi*, a group dance performed by four women, is typical and was formerly the prerogative of women of noble birth. Raffles, in his *History of Java*, has given a vivid description of this dance on pp. 340–4. He describes the dancers as concubines of the ruling princes.

In 1918 the son of the ruling sultan of Jogjakarta obtained permission to open his own school to teach commoners the court dances which have today become the basic classical dance style for girls. The prince teacher, Gusti Pangeran Haria Tedjakusuma, is today an old man in his nineties whose school, although it is going through a period of financial stringency, is still carried on by his family. In 1970 the aged prince, who is as straight as a ramrod and a martinet as a dance teacher, allowed the writer to make a short film of him instructing his great grand-daughter.

The court drama is required study for the students of the New National Academy of Dance founded in 1963 in Jogjakarta. It is directed by Soedarsono, an accomplished dancer, who is descended from the Palace family. A brother of the last reigning sultan is the secretary of the school. Although Palace society has disappeared in the new republic of Indonesia, its heirs continue to be the guardians of the great tradition in classical dance and music. The Palace in Jogjakarta is also responsible for maintaining a school for dalang, shadow puppeteers, and conducts a three year course of training. Every year in April examinations are held and the new dalangs are put through their paces. The school was founded in 1925 with the idea of preserving the best in the art of shadow theatre. The director is K. R. T. Madukusumo, who is the head of the Department of Culture in the Palace, an old man in his seventies who is a talented musician as well as a shadow play specialist. The former sultan is now a member of the national government and it is perhaps thanks to his emergence as a personality in the era of independence that the Palace still continues to function as a centre of the traditional arts.

The island of Bali has been described as the last outpost of ancient Indian culture in south-east Asia, and this is true to some extent. The elaborate code of religious ethics which governs the life of the people springs directly from Hinduism although the Balinese have imposed their own qualities of interpretation and this applies to their arts as well.

When Islam finally subdued Java at the end of the fifteenth century, great numbers of the Javanese nobility, as well as priests and scholars, fled to Bali. The Balinese assimilation of the refined Hindu-inspired culture at this time had considerable implications for the dance and dance-drama. It has been said of the Balinese that for them watching dancing is almost a state of being, a feeling rather than an action. Certainly there has never been a people for whom dancing has become such an integrated element of the community as the Balinese.

Bali has been and to a great extent still remains a land of self-contained village communities. Each village is a tightly knit organism in which harmony and cooperation are the operating factors. There is a tremendous sense of mutual responsibility which is reflected in the arts. Each community is ruled by its own council, everyone has his equal rights and obligations. Dance and music are group activities with no place for individual expression or self-aggrandizement. The music club, entirely male, is the pride of most villages, who meet regularly to show off their progress and practise new compositions. They prepare for the next village festival or rehearse with the dancers who are equally a part of the communal artistic life.

The rhythm of village life in Bali is marked by a recurrent pattern of religious festivals, none of which would be complete without dance or music. No villager would ever think of getting married or taking part in any domestic occasion or village event without these indispensable accompaniments to an occasion. Of all the kinds of performance which go on, none is more representative of the depth and quality of village culture than the *legong* dance. In this form the ordinary villager demonstrates a skill which is typical of the way the Balinese dance simply for the prestige of the community and to entertain their neighbours.

The dancers in the legong are young village girls chosen for their physical suitability and usually from families who have dance traditions; the mother of a selected new pupil has more often than not been a legong dancer in her time also. The girls begin training at the age of seven or eight and dance until they are fourteen or fifteen, after which their career in legong is over unless they become teachers themselves, which also happens. The girls of the Balinese village watch dancers and dancing continuously from the day they can walk, and grow up with the rhythms, music and movements in their blood. Certain villages have a continuing tradition in legong and it is difficult for a village to start a troupe from scratch.

Training today takes six months of daily routines which start with intense physical training until the young dancers' bodies are conditioned to the necessary degree of suppleness. After this they begin to learn short sequences of movements, spending about six weeks on basic forms. The girls have their own professional pride and practise constantly at home in addition to the long rehearsals they go through daily with their teachers and companions. There is no special ceremony to mark the completion of their training. The costumes of the dancers are the property of the village, as are the instruments of the orchestra.

There are usually three dancers in a legong performance. The dancing is characterized by vigorous passages of choreography punctuated by abrupt but precise pauses and timing of climaxes to the music. A sudden tremulous shuddering of the shoulders and torso is also very characteristic and accompanied by swift eye movements. The dancers perform in the area between the files of musicians who, seated before their instruments, define the periphery of the stage area on either side. The dancers make their appearance through a temple door reached by a flight of steps and dance their way down the steps into the stage area. A solo dance can last for as long as an hour and the small performers show no signs of exhaustion or disruption of pace and timing. The dance seems to flow through their agile and graceful figures, their arms and hands become part of the dance itself, delicate arabesques of gesture. A much loved item is the Lasem theme, based on an old legend. The dance depicts Princess Rangkesvari, who was stolen by the arrogant King Lasem but rejected his suit. She would not submit to him even when he offered to call off the battle he was waging against her father whom he finally threatened to kill. The enraged monarch went off to carry out his threat but a black bird flew down through the battle in front of him. It was an unlucky omen and Lasem himself was killed.

Three small dancers portray the arrogant king, the princess and the black bird, but the action is so stylized and so interwoven with the choreographic pattern that it becomes more a demonstration of exquisitely rendered movement for its own sake than the miming of a story. The climax comes when the dancer playing the bird takes up a pair of small leather gold-painted wings placed on the ground beforehand. Crouching on her bended knees she advances and retreats in a crescendo of movement, fluttering the wings and at times beating the earth with them. She darts at the king, impeding his progress. The dance and music quicken to a furious pace. Then suddenly it is over. The dancers have reached the foot of the temple steps and relax as they trip up the flight. One minute they are the epitome of an unbelievable sophistication of grace and movement and the next simple village girls scurrying from view as the audience disperses to the daily round.

The theatres of Thailand and Burma have an artistic interrelationship that owes a great deal to early Indian influences although
these have become diffused through a cross fusion of styles. The
basis for it all nonetheless was the *Ramayana*. The people known today
as the Thais, formerly called the Siamese, did not obtain political
control of their present territory until the thirteenth century. Their
original home was Nan-chao, a powerful kingdom which was situated
in the area that is now Yunnan in south-west China. When the
Mongol invaders under Kublai Khan annexed this area the Thais
were driven out. In fact they consummated a slow infiltration
towards the south which had been going on for some time. Such
movements of population over what used to be called the Indo-
Chinese peninsula were very characteristic of south-east Asia in
this formative period.

Long before the Thai people settled in their new home it had
come under Buddhist influences from lower Burma, and Buddhism
was finally established there in the eleventh century by a conquering
Burmese monarch. Previous to this there had been considerable
Hindu penetration, as in most of this geographical area. When the
Thai people settled in their new home they found a region already
converted to Buddhism, albeit this overlay earlier Brahmanical
influences.

The earlier text of the *Ramayana* had already been brought to
these regions in its Sanskrit and Pali forms. Pali was an early literary
language used for preserving the Buddhist canons. In the Indo-
Chinese peninsula the *Ramayana* again became translated into local
languages. Each translation involved adaptation, additions or cuts
according to local needs, and the monks who made the translations
were versed in the scriptures, local customs and superstitions, so
that they were able to preserve the greatest ritualistic appeal with
the maximum popular attraction. It is possible also that the
Ramayana adaptations were not only inspired by the original version
but also by other tales which dealt with the love of Rama and Sita.
The Thais, who were the last arrivals in the peninsula, found local
variations of the *Ramayana* in existence, but adapted these to suit
their own outlook and so created a different version of the epic which
in Thai became known as *Ramakien*.

Three different kinds of performance contributed to the growth
of the traditional Thai theatrical style, a masked dance-drama. First
of these was the *khon*, based on the *Ramayana* and consisting of the
scenes in which the demon forces of evil were conquered by the
virtuous. The actors were masked, and performed in mime to sung
recitation with instrumental accompaniment. The second was the
rabam, in which only women took part, dancing out certain passages
from the *Ramayana*. The performance was highly ritualistic, one of
the dances being given to propitiate the gods for rain. In both these
forms the performers were members of the court or high-born
families. The third form was the *nang*, a shadow play, the word nang

Notes

243

meaning leather or hide. The figures used were quite large and the human and animal forms are cut within a frame and supported on two sticks held by the manipulator who sways and bends behind the screen as he keeps time to the music. In maintaining balance between the movements of the figures which are held against the surface of the screen, and the movements of his own body, the manipulator in fact performs a ritual dance. The nang was given out of doors, often in a temple courtyard and especially during festivals, so that it tended to be seen by a far greater audience than the previous two forms described. It was also given in the court, often in sequence, with the other two forms so providing a ritualistic unity through the triple performance. Many of the themes of the nang were taken from the *Ramayana* and this style of performance is thought to have originated in Hindu-ruled Java. Although the Thai form is obsolete today, it is interesting to note that a similar performance, *robam nang sbek thom*, is still found in Cambodia. *Ream Ker*, the Cambodian version of the *Ramayana*, is presented. Again the plot and the principal events of the Indian epic remain but have been adapted to produce a version that is essentially Cambodian. The episodes take seven nights to perform.

A fourth style of Thai theatrical performance was called *lakon*. This word, which means play or dramatic story, is also common to Java and Malaysia. In Thailand it was associated with a more popular kind of presentation given by three actors who played both male and female roles. Their parts were in verse, recited, sung and danced to musical accompaniment and a chorus. The company travelled around performing in public places at festival times. There was nothing solemn about this performance, which had a repertoire based on a limited number of stories of Hindu origins.

The establishment of a unified theatrical style from the four forms which have been described was a gradual process in which the rabam underwent the greatest change. From being only a ritual piece it was developed technically to become much more of an entertainment. During the sixteenth century fresh material was absorbed by the lakon, which had to meet a new public demand. There was an increase in the number of actors, improved acting techniques and new musical forms. In the period between the seventeenth and nineteenth centuries there was a fusion between lakon on the one side and khon and rabam on the other, although this was at first exclusive to palace entertainment and became known as *lakon nai*, inner lakon. The palace entertainment was greatly enlarged as a result of these borrowings, whose effect were later felt outside the privileged circles of the court.

In the first half of the eighteenth century there were new advances made in the Palace entertainments with Javanese material added and many technical improvements in music and dance. The court poets were kept busy and visual attraction on the stage was emphasized. Frequent changes of actresses and court favourites meant a constant change of material for their use. The writer responsible for the first full version of the *Ramakien* as a court drama was King Rama I (1736–1809), a respected monarch, a patron of the theatre and a moving spirit behind the literary developments of the age. Under his ministrations the court poets worked at preparing a new repertoire for performance. His *Ramakien* was composed in committee with the help of his entourage and family, the king revising the final version with his own hand. His son Rama II (1767–1824) was an even better playwright than his father and produced his own version of the *Ramakien*. It was regarded as a masterpiece of poetic style and is still staged today.

The traditional Thai theatre of present times is descended more or less directly from the old court theatre, although a whole new repertoire has been created in addition to old favourites like the *Ramakien*. The Thai drama is a dance drama in which masks are used and the actors perform and mime to the accompaniment of wind and percussion instruments and chanted verse. The percussion consists of drums, gongs and xylophones of different kinds, and one instrument which consists of small chimes suspended in a rattan frame. The poetic devices used in stage narration are marked by elaborate linguistic devices with stanzas linked by rhyme and with emphasis on alliteration and tonal patterns. Such devices also provide cues for the actors.

The Thai dance drama is today state supported through a School of Dramatic Art maintained under the Ministry of Education. First established in 1934, in the following year it took charge of the dancers, teachers and musicians attached to the Palace. It was renamed the School of Sangkhit. This is the Thai version of *sangita*, the old Sanskrit word which signified dance, dramatic expression and music, and it is indicative of primary influences. In 1945 the school was completely reorganized as an institution whose stated aims were to be a central institution for teaching traditional dance and music, preserving and propagating these arts, and stabilizing the status of the actor and musician.

Students must not be older than thirteen when accepted for training and must have passed the fourth class of primary school. They are enrolled for a preliminary course of six years, during which time they study two branches of their art, i.e. dance and music, and are given a general education which demands progress at the rate of one class a year. At the end of this period they receive a certificate of efficiency. This admits them to an intermediate course of three years, at the end of which they take an examination and if successful receive their certificate of proficiency. Finally comes an advanced course, to enter which they must have a 60 per cent pass in every field of both professional and general education. At the end of this training they qualify for the diploma of advanced dramatic art. Only the most talented students survive the course.

Four categories of role are required in the Thai dance drama, human male, human female, demon and monkey. The last two roles are taken by men only. Students are selected for their physical suitability for a role and once embarked on training they do not change. Instruction commences with basic physical exercises as well as vigorous acrobatics in the case of the monkey and demon roles. A vital preliminary is moving to set musical rhythms which the students themselves learn to chant out onomatopoeically. This kind of practice goes on for weeks until the students have learned to coordinate specific hand and foot movements with the vocally enunciated rhythms in fast and slow tempos. Once these are mastered students begin on the 'alphabet of dancing'; this consists of sixty-eight sequences of movement for the male and female roles, both played by women, and begins with Salutation to the Celestials, and goes on to phrases like the Peacock Dances, Stag Walking in the Forest, and so on. Movements have become so stylized over the centuries that most of them are now choreographic abstractions whose names identify a particular sequence of footwork and gesture rather than serve any descriptive purpose. Specific meaning has virtually disappeared from Thai hand gestures although many of them suggest their distant ancestry in the *Natya Sastra*. Thai dance is characterized by slow undulations in which the movements flow into one another with the torso inclined to the rhythmic progression.

A walk round the school in Bangkok reveals the boys and girls at work in separate classes under male and female teachers respectively. Here a group of small boys beginning training in the monkey role are lined up wearing scarlet breeches and white tops, the uniform of the school, as one after the other they learn to turn flying somersaults under the guiding hand of an instructor. In another room a group are practising the basic footwork for the demon roles. An instructor stands beating out the time with a small bamboo baton as their legs are raised up and down, up and down in a continuous beat. They turn, sidestep, retreat, advance and perform a mighty somersault in unison; hour after hour of unrelenting practice until their responsive bodies move as though without effort. In yet another part of the school, girl students are learning to dance in formation, a continuous gentle flow of undulating movement, feet, hands, head and torso, in precise coordination to the limpid rhythms of a xylophone. The patterns are continuous and repetitious as the instructor goes round straightening an arm here, correcting a foot movement there. Day in day out an ancient tradition is handed on from teacher to pupil through unremitting effort aimed at nothing less than total mastery by every participant.

In 1767 Thailand was conquered by Burma and her capital destroyed. The members of the Thai court were taken back as captives to the Burmese capital of Ava and with them went the court dancers of the Rama play, the high artistry of which fascinated the Burmese. They were not unfamiliar with the Rama story, which long before the Christian era had been taken to Burma, where the Vishnu cult

I

from India, in which Rama is an important figure, had taken root. Later, when Buddhism reached Burma it did not affect the public's affection for the story of Rama, who in Buddhist literature became portrayed as an aspirant for Buddhahood.

Intrigued by the masks, charming dances and spectacular costumes of the Thai court play, the Burmese began to stage it in their own palace, where the courtiers particularly studied the music, which was new in melody and form. The play in those times required two or three days for presentation in entirety, but leisure was not lacking and the Burmese nobility set to work to produce a more or less faithful version of the original, whose style was jealously guarded by the purists.

Eventually the play no longer remained the prerogative of the court. The original language was changed to Burmese and the play gained a new kind of popularity. Poets began to write new plays in their own language, borrowing themes from other sources but basing them on the Rama style of presentation. As a result of the play's popularity at court it became the fashion for officials and others all over the country to stage their own performances. The status of the actor went up. In Burma there was a saying which ran 'Actors and beggars, eaters of food thrown away as waste'. Travelling companies now began to call themselves 'the king's actors'; there was a new prestige in the profession and an actor would describe himself as having performed before such and such a high personage as proof of his artistic standing.

As the Rama play penetrated every area of the country in this way the story became shortened, new scenes were inserted and the whole piece acquired a Burmese flavour. Once again the same process was repeated with this ever-popular theme. Then a famous Burmese poet wrote his own version of the Rama story, treating it as pure romance rather than an epic and this had lasting repercussions.

The Rama play has continued into present times, though it long ago lost all pretensions to being a refined court entertainment. Formerly it took as many as twenty-one nights to stage the complete episodes, but today the show lasts for ten or twelve nights and is staged out of doors. It begins about ten in the evening and goes on all night, although until midnight the audience are entertained with various dances which have nothing to do with the play. In the past there was no stage or lighting but today there is a formal proscenium and the floor of the audtiorium is spread with mats, on which the audience sit, recline or sleep. The orchestra, consisting of percussion and strings, sits just below the front of the stage. The crowd is noisy and good humoured and the scene is redolent of a fair. Foodstalls and pedlars of every kind surround the approaches.

All the characters in the play wear masks except Sita and Queen Kaikeyi. The masks themselves are objects of veneration placed in two separate sheds which serve as a form of shrine near the entrance to the theatre. The demon masks are separated from the others. The

costumes glitter with gold and silver thread and are reminiscent of
their Thai prototypes. Each actor dances as well as sings and the
characters enter the stage dancing and wearing their masks. At the
climax of each dance the actor raises his mask to reveal his normal
countenance and from being a figure from a supernatural world
with highly formalized deportment and control, he is suddenly seen
as a human being again. The dialogue is marked by highly conventionalized poetic speech but the actors often depart from the original,
relapsing into everyday usage. They address the audience and
instruct the musicians. Then the clowns take over, reducing the most
solemn moments to absurdity. They have absolute freedom to *ad lib*
and once they are on the stage the serious business of the drama is
forgotten. As soon as they vanish formality takes over again and the
stylized dance is resumed, and dignity restored in the conventional
gesture and postures which reveal their Indian-Thai sources.

The present-day treatment of the Burmese Rama play is designed
in every sense to cater to the popular taste. It is the culmination of
a long process of assimilation and adaptation which to the connoisseur seems nothing less than a lapse from grace. Both in Thailand
and Burma the Rama story has been embellished to accommodate
the temperamental differences and native genius of each, but while
in Thailand it has been retained at the level of a highly polished
national art, in Burma it has become the entertainment of the crowd.
What is perhaps the most significant thing throughout south-east
Asia, nevertheless, is the fertile source of invention the *Ramayana* has
been without ever really shedding the stamp of its true origins.

[19]   Achwal, 'Ancient Indian Theatre', *Natya*, Winter, 1959–60, pp. 22–3.
[20]   *The Natya sastra* . . . (trans. Ghosh), section 28, pp. 2, 3.
[21]   Ghurye, *Caste, Class and Occupation*, p. 225; Tandon, *Punjabi Century*,
       pp. 79–81.
[22]   Saletore *Sangeet Natak Akademi Bulletin. Centenary number. Rabindranath
       Tagore, 1861–1961* (*jatra* is often spelled *yatra*.)
[23]   Das Gupta, *Indian Stage*, vol. 1, pp. 130–1.
[24]   *Ibid.*, p. 187.
[25]   *Ibid.*, pp. 234, 235.
[26]   Guha-Thakurta, *The Bengal Drama, Its Origin and Development*, pp.
       57–63.
[27]   *Ibid.*, pp. 83–5.
[28]   Das Gupta, *Indian Stage*, vol. 2, p. 255.
[29]   *Ibid.*, p. 221.
[30]   *Ibid.*, pp. 267–9.
[31]   Ward, *India and the West*, pp. 119-21.
[32]   Saletore, *Sangeet Natak Akademi Bulletin. Centenary number. Rabindranath
       Tagore, 1861–1961.*
[33]   Sarris, *Interviews with Film Directors*, p. 414.
[34]   Barnouw and Krishnaswamy, *Indian Film*, p. 148.
[35]   Subramanyan, 'Traditional Tamil Drama and the Present Impasse'
       Sangeet Natak Journal, vol. 4, 1967, p. 32.

[36] Sarris, *Interviews with Film Directors,* p. 416.
[37] Shankar, *My Music, My Life,* pp. 76, 77.
[38] Singer, 'The Great Tradition of Hinduism in the City of Madras', in Leslie, *Anthropology of Folk Religion,* pp. 148, 149.
[39] Mrinalini Sarabhai to the author in 1964.
[40] *Bharata natyam.* The classical south Indian temple dance is performed solo by women dancers. It is considered to be derived from the oldest traditions and in this sense it is not a mere regional product but a comprehensive system of classical performance as laid down in the ancient texts. The word natyam in fact signifies both acting and dancing in combination. According to Singer, the words bharata natyam mean dance based on the technique originally laid down by Bharata, the supposed author of the *Natyasastra,* and was first used regularly by the Madras Sanskrit scholar, V. Raghavan, who played a significant part on the learned side in the renaissance of the art. According to Bhavnani the name bharata was based on the first syllables of the terms *bhava, raga* and *tala,* meaning mood, mode and rhythm. In the past the great temples had their own distinctive versions of the dance and the present form is really a distillation of these styles which was devised by famous teachers.

A performance of bharata natyam today is usually arranged in six different sequences. First comes what is called the opening of the bud into blossom, *alarippu,* an invocation danced without music but to the accompaniment of rhythmic syllables chanted by a singer. The dancer starts with the feet a short distance apart, knees bent outwards and the hands folded above the head. She then passes into slow movements in time to the recitative with a deliberate sway of the head from left to right and a great deal of eye glancing and raising of the eyebrows. This passage is repeated with the dancer squatting poised on the toes, knees outspread. The tempo then quickens, with more complex footwork and choreographic embellishment, ending in a swift finale and what is called *thirmana* in which the dancer makes a final graceful circular movement of the arm across the head bringing the arm sharply downwards so that the hand is pointing before the feet. This movement is used as a climactic finish to phrases all the way through the dance and also to separate long and short sequences. The movement is usually completed three times at three different speeds which increase in tempo.

As the dance unfolds from this point it is seen to combine pure dancing with mime, representative gesture and facial expression in sequences which carry the spectator through a series of moods leading the dance on to its splendid climax. The second phase of the dance, called *jatisvaram,* is pure dance, emphasizing elaborate time-rhythm patterns and a brilliant display of movement and gesture in which every part of the dancer's body adds to an effect of vibrant grace.

Next follows the *sabdam,* a purely interpretative passage in which the dancer uses gesture and emotional acting to interpret some theme, sacred or heroic; great play is made of hand movement, facial expression and neck movements. As the singer translates the words of the singer into dance form she walks gracefully in time to simple rhythms.

After this comes the *varnam*, to which everything else has been leading up; it is a *tour de force* which may continue for as long as an hour. The term varnam is one used in classical south Indian music and it is a kind of love lyric in which the songs are marked by passages of highly emotional interpretation through the movements and facial expression of the dancer. Sequence after sequence is accompanied by the most intricate rhythmic motifs and themes. Each sequence is repeated three times, and each time with a different interpretation, finishing with an elaborate finale. In this piece every possibility of the dance is explored and developed to the utmost pitch of expression.

In contrast to this brilliant cascade of movement and rhythm the dancer glides into a softer sequence in which seven-line lyrics, dealing with mother love and romantic themes, are interpreted largely through the hands and facial expression of the dancer. The main theme of each song is repeated over and over again and interpreted each time with variations of gesture and with the dancer sometimes playing the role of two different persons. After this two lines of each song are similarly interpreted, giving the effect of unfolding every aspect of the motif until it is fully displayed in all its beauty.

Finally comes *tillana*, a grand climax of brilliant virtuoso interpretation in fast tempo in which the feminine qualities of the dancer are emphasizedwith swift moving arms, great play on facial expression and the thrusting movement of the neck that is so characteristic of this form of dancing. The haunting melody of the music recurs again and again above the accelerating rhythms and dazzling footwork which round off the programme.

Traditionally the performance ends with a *sloka*, a short Sanskrit verse dedicated to God. There may be some variations in this arrangement but this is the general pattern of a full-scale performance.

[41] Sangeet Natak Akademi, Academy of Dance, Drama and Music. Lalit Kala Akademi, National Academy of Art and Architecture. Sahitya Akademi, National Academy of Letters.

3: THE ISLAMIC WORLD

[1] The principal spoken language of Islam is Arabic but countries like Turkey and Iran, which are also a part of the Islamic world, have their own languages. Moreover Arabic itself differs in its classical and dialect usage. The language of the Koran is regarded by Islam as the purest classical form and apart from some changes in grammar and vocabulary introduced to meet contemporary needs it is the basis of style for all cultural and educational purposes. People with

a classical Arabic education can understand each other even though they are from different countries; Arab dialects on the other hand can vary to the extent where North African forms cannot readily be understood by countries as far east as Syria or Iraq.

India, Malaysia, Indonesia and China all became important areas of Islamic infiltration at different periods in the past. The first three countries have significant Islamic populations in proportion to their other religious communities. The Islamic conquest of northern India and establishment of an empire whose heyday spanned the sixteenth and seventeenth centuries aided the spread of Islam to south-east Asia. In India it was by the successful adaptation to Hindu culture rather than overt opposition to it that Islamic identity was maintained. Its glory was perpetuated in a spate of architectural monuments as well as literary and musical creativity.

During the fourteenth century the Islamic faith was first introduced into Sumatra by Indian and Arab merchants. The establishment of the kingdom of Malacca in the early fifteenth century and the conversion of its Indian ruler provided impetus for the penetration of Islam in Java and from there it spread to surrounding regions. In south-east Asia, as in India, the success of Muslim penetration was often helped by its accommodation to established local cultural patterns rather than to total domination.

In China few historical facts are available concerning the introduction of the Islamic faith. However, there is a long established Muhammadan population particularly in the western and north-western regions. The general opinion seems to be that China's Muslim population was greatly expanded as a result of the Mongol wars of conquest in the thirteenth century. Chinese Muhammadans have in general retained a separate identity through marriage customs although they are often of mixed blood with the Chinese strain predominating. Politically, Muhammadans have today been classed as one of the many national minority groups in China.

[2]	Muhammad is a controversial figure regarded by his followers as the Prophet of God but attributed with many faults and weaknesses by his numerous biographers. It is difficult at this distance of time to separate criticism from the pious legend which inevitably surrounds his memory as the founder of a religion. He was born in Mecca, *c.* AD 570, and through his great grandparents had blood ties with Medina, a town important in his future. His family were poor, his father died and he was brought up by an uncle and his grandfather. As a young man he became an agent for the caravan trade working for a widow, Khadijah, whom he eventually married and who bore him two sons and four daughters. At the age of forty he began to have visions which after great torment convinced him that he had been selected through the voice of the Angel Gabriel to carry the word of God to his own people. Only a minority accepted him at first and the men of Mecca scorned his preaching on the existence of one God demanding men's obedience to his will. Then Muhammad's

wife died and the Prophet went into retreat. He was invited to Medina to settle a dispute between tribesmen, who became impressed by his authority. In 622 he left for Medina and there he became recognized and the picture changed. The flight to Medina, Hijra, now marks the beginning of the Muhammadan calendar. At Medina Muhammad formulated the principles of his creed and increased his band of followers. At first he sought alliance with the Jewish community but when they refused their support he ordered his followers to drive them out and confiscate their lands. Though harbouring bitterness against Mecca he recognized the importance of the town to his religious aims, and unable to use peaceful means he resorted to aggression. His forces attacked a Meccan caravan and then in 624 defeated a superior force in a pitched battle now celebrated as the Day of Deliverance. A year later the Prophet suffered a defeat, and finally, in 628, he concluded a truce with the men of Mecca; then, with the sacred city firmly under his control, he quickly drew the rest of Arabia to his cause. He himself made a pilgrimage to Mecca; entering the area of the sacred shrine, the Kaaba, he smashed its many idols, declaring the territory around sacred and forbidden to infidels. In 632 Muhammad made the pilgrimage to Mecca for the last time. Three months after his return to Medina he was seized with a fever and taken to the quarters of Aishah, the last of his wives, where he died.

[3] The death of Muhammad resulted in a severe crisis of succession and eventually caused a split which divided Islam into two major factions, the Sh'ia and the Sunni. The Sh'ia began as a legitimist movement advocating the claims of Ali the Prophet's son-in-law as the only true successor. This movement eventually became divided into subsects, one of which became dominant in Persia. The Sunnites, who represent the other faction and the majority of the Islamic community, accepted the principle of electing the caliph as temporal leader, although he had no jurisdiction over the formulation of the sacred law which was the practical aspect of the religion itself. The spiritual prerogative of the Prophet, therefore, was inherited by the community as a whole. There are four orthodox schools of Sunnites. The quarrel in Islam, therefore, has been based on the final interpretation of the sacred law on earth rather than any change of the law itself.

Mecca, the sacred city of Islam, was situated at the crossways of the main commercial routes in pre-Muhammadan times. Its religious significance centred on a shrine called the Kaaba, for which there are no historical records although it is thought that an older structure was destroyed and replaced by a new one in the second half of the sixth century. Long before Muhammad's day, worship at the shrine had become a cult that entailed marching round the shrine with processional rites between two great stones called Safa and Marwa. The Arabs are believed to have worshipped a god called Allah, *the* God, before Muhammad, and even earlier a god called Hubal, whose idol was placed in the shrine. Before Muhammad it was also customary to worship Allah's three daughters, al-Lat, al-Uzza and Manat, as female deities. Subordinate gods were also worshipped and the people of Mecca believed there was a relationship between Allah and the spirits or *djinn* to whom they made offerings (Kitagawa, *Religions of the East*, p. 222–77).

One consequence of the sectarian split in Islam was the development of what has been called the 'Persian Passion Play', the Persian word is *ta'ziya* or *tazieh*, as it is also romanized. The Persians are Shia Muslims belonging to the sect which holds that the caliphate descended directly from the Prophet through his heirs. Ever since Ali, the son-in-law of the Prophet, was assassinated and the son of Ali killed, in 680, the events have been commemorated in recitative which by the time of the Shah Abbas in 1587 had become elaborate exhortations. These were the prototypes for emotional dramatic representations performed during Muhuwan, the first month of the Muslim calendar which based its reckonings from Hijra, July 622, the date of Muhammad's migration from Mecca to Medina. The performances take place from the 10th of the month.

The ta'ziyas consist of thirty or forty episodes, each of which requires two or three hours to perform. The majority of these portray the misfortune of the leaders of Islam and their betrayal according to the Shia belief. The incident dealing with the death of Ali's son is a particularly emotional one which raised the audiences to a pitch bordering on frenzy.

E. G. Browne, the British Persian scholar, described the theatre specially constructed for a performance as being a large, roofless circular building, but covered with an awning. Boxes were placed all round with a specially large one reserved for the shah. The ordinary spectators crowded round the arena with the women and children in front. A circular stone platform in the centre was the stage, there was no curtain or exit, and the performers simply stood aside when not in action. The acting was described as crude but powerful and providing a sense of communication between actors and audience.

The American minister to Persia in 1884 also described the scene as a circular theatre, 200 feet in diameter and 80 feet high, seating thousands of men and women who attended ten days of performances, which were given in the afternoon and at night when the theatre was illuminated by a huge chandelier and bracket lamps supported by the tiers.

The ta'ziya was both a state and a religious festival which was finally abolished by the father of the present shah of Persia as a measure to weaken the powers of the religious teachers.

[4] Nutting, *The Arabs*, p. 23.
[5] Nicholson, *A Literary History of the Arabs*, pp. 87–9.
[6] *Ibid.*, p. 71.
[7] *Ibid.*, p. 135.

The Koran (or Qur'an), the sacred book of Islam, represents the principal record of the life and teaching of the Prophet Muhammad, although it cannot be considered an authentic record of his revelations. He did not write it down himself and according to some authorities he could not even read. It is therefore assumed that followers first set down the gist of some of his revelations. These scattered materials were not collected together until after the Prophet's death and it is thought that the first caliph, Abu Bakr, was responsible for the compilation. An authorized version of the Koran was not established until the time of the Caliph Uthman, 644–656. It is said that there were four other versions in use before that. Western scholars have never been able to understand the seemingly irrational arrangement of the contents of the orthodox version. Once codified, the Koran was implicitly accepted by the Islamic community as the undisputed word of God transmitted by the Angel Gabriel through the Prophet.

Besides the Koran an important source of guidance for the faithful is the Hadith, or Traditions. As it exists this deals with the whole duty of man through precept and example and is the basis for all social and legal usage in the Islamic community. Its authenticity rests, in the words of Guillaume, 'on a long line of witnesses going back in the following manner: A told me, saying that B had said that C had informed him, saying D mentioned that he had heard E relate, "I heard F ask the Apostle of God so and so".' In this way the Hadith has provided criteria for belief and practice in Islam (Alfred Guillaume, *Islam*, p. 23).

[9] Constantinople was captured by the Turkish Sultan Mehmed II (1451–1481), a powerful and complex personality, ruthless yet cultivated. His court patronized a Greek chronicler and he invited the Italian Giovanni Bellini to do his portrait. Mehmed, who was ambitious to capture the Byzantine capital, made thorough military preparations. Early on the day of 29 May 1453 his great armies mounted an attack which countered all resistance; the Byzantine Emperor Constantine XI died fighting sword in hand. The fall of the historic capital of Christendom, later renamed Istanbul by the Turks, ushered in a new and splendid era of Islamic power.

[10] Lewis, *Istanbul and the Civilization of the Ottoman Empire*, p. 100.

[11] *Ibid.*, pp. 137–44.

[12] Ullah, *Islamic Literature*, pp. 370–428; Kritzeck, *Anthology of Islamic Literature*, pp. 141–3; Levonian, *The Turkish Press*, pp. 86–92; Lewis, *Emergence of Modern Turkey*, pp. 419–24.

[13] And, *History of Theatre and Popular Entertainment in Turkey*, pp. 39–42.

[14] Karagoz is the principal character of the Turkish shadow puppet play which reached a high point between the seventeenth and nineteenth centuries in the Ottoman empire. He became popular in other Islamic countries and was introduced into the Piraeus from Constantinople in the mid-nineteenth century. His Greek name is Kharaghiozes. The Turkish prototype has a round face, large eyes,

pug nose, a shaven poll and a round black beard. His costume represents the traditional Turkish dress of the Ottoman period. Karagoz had no trade or profession of his own but masqueraded under various guises. He was frequently out of work, always being duped, and quick to fool others. Impulsive in behaviour and speech, which was that of the common man, he was shrewd, obscene, good natured and stupid in turn. He always had an eye for the main chance and seldom failed to direct his rude irony against authority. He was partnered by a foil, Hacivat, who was cultured, learned and respected where his companion was crass. The pair of them were constantly engaged in extricating themselves from situations into which their respective virtues and failings had plunged them. Karagoz was supposed by many Turkish authorities to be a gypsy. He is still active in Greece, where he has assumed a somewhat different character. There, according to Whitman, he is 'an utter tatterdemalion, dwelling in sordid poverty in a hovel with his wife and three children, strongly disinclined towards honest labour but superbly gifted at stealing and living by his wits. This quality, *poneria*, is his chief characteristic but to it is added a kind of half-innocent madness, an antic humour as difficult as Hamlet's to assign wholly either to irony or sincerity. This combination makes him inevitably appealing despite his repulsive appearance.'

Sir Richard Burton has the following reference to Karagoz (in volume 4, p. 193, of his translation of *The Thousand and One Nights Entertainment*): 'Arab Khya afterwards called Kara Gyuz "blacke eyes" from the celebrated Turkish Wazir. The *mise-en-scène* was like that of Punch but of transparent cloth, lamp lit inside and showing silhouettes worked by hand. Nothing could be more Fescennine than Kara Gyuz who appeared with a phallus longer than himself and made all the Consul-Generals periodically complain of its abuses while the dialogue, mostly in Turkish, was even more obscene. Most ingenious were Kara Gyuz's little ways of driving an obstinate donkey and of tackling a huge Anatolian pilgrim. He mounted Neddy's back face to tail and, inserting his thumb like a clyster, hammered it with his right, when the donkey started at speed. For the huge pilgrim he used a ladder. These shows, now obsolete, used to enliven the Ezbekiyah Gardens every evening and explained Ovid's words: Delicias videam Nile jocose, tuas!'

Sir Thomas Arnold writes of Karagoz: 'Another concession was made to popular usage by the theologians in respect of the shadow plays which have for several centuries been connected in Turkey with the name of Karagoz and are popular in Egypt and Tunis also. The puppets of this shadow play are quite frankly imitations of human figures, made of strips of camel hide, scraped so as to be transparent, and variously coloured. The theologians gravely discussed the legitimacy of such puppets and came to the conclusion that since a hole had to be made in each figure in order that it might be suspended from a string, and since the hole went right through it in a manner that would have been quite impossible in the case of a living human being, there was therefore clearly no irreverent or presumptious attempt made to rival the creative activity of God'. Arnold, *Painting in Islam*, pp. 13–5.

One of the best sources of information for the English reader is *Karagoz* by Siyavusgil. And's *History of Theatre and Popular Entertainment in Turkey*, Landau's *Studies in the Arab Theatre and Cinema*, and Martinovitch's *Turkish Theatre* all contain valuable information on the famous shadow screen character and the plays in which he was featured. Georg Jacob, the German scholar, is probably the most erudite authority on the subject in the western world and has published extensively on the shadow theatre in his own language.

[15] Siyavusgil, *Karagoz*, pp. 4–5; Landau, *Studies in the Arab Theatre and Cinema*, pp. 12–46.

[16] The Koran makes explicit the Islamic attitude towards the sexes: 'Men have authority over women because Allah has made the one superior to the other and because they spend their wealth to master them. Good women are obedient. They guard their unseen parts because Allah had guarded them. As for those from whom you fear disobedience, admonish them and send to beds apart and beat them. Then if they obey you take no further action against them. Allah is high, supreme.'

Although the apologists for Islamic tenets affirm that their doctrine does not in fact impose a degraded status, the subjugation of women and their seclusion from the active world was a major barrier to theatre development. The words of a contemporary Arab writer define the situation: 'Instead of the home there was the harem, instead of a balanced and complete social life in which women played a healthy active part (as indeed had been the case with the Arabs before Islam) there was the segregation of the sexes and the keeping of women in a degraded position from which they did not begin to rise again until the present century. In defence of the Prophet and Islam it must be said that Muhammad never ordained the veiling or segregation of all women. He segregated his wives but made it quite plain that this was on account of their special status as belonging to the Apostle of God and was not to be taken as a precedent for other Muslims. His practice, nevertheless, came to be copied, particularly in conjunction with the growth of concubinage and conquest-swollen harems. It is only just, however, to add that in some respects the position of a married Muslim woman has always been superior to what the position of her English sister was before the recent legal emancipation of the latter.' Atiyah, *The Arabs*, pp. 27–8.

[17] De Planhol, *The World of Islam*, pp. 2–28.

[18] Arab music, like Indian music, is modal and the classical style is characterized by a single melodic line played either on one instrument or several in unison with percussive accompaniment. A technical feature is the quarter tone, which may be used as the smallest

interval, in contrast to the western semi-tone. Each scale of seven steps, called *maqam*, may be divided into as many as twenty-four quarter tones as against the western thirteen Not every maqam uses these quarter tones. Quarter tones occur most in grace notes and embellishment. Arab music has an elaborate pattern of modes, each of which is identified by a particular name as in other forms of Asian music. These modes are regarded as expressive of the human spirit in all its moods, for Arab music is highly emotional. Fine appreciation and awareness of the musician's powers of interpretation and mastery of all the permutations and combinations within the prescribed technical range distinguish the Arab connoisseur of musical form,

[19]   Farmer, *Minstrelsy of the Arabian Nights*, pp. 18–22. Bulos, Arab music. p. 16.

[20]   Bulos, *Arab Music*, p. 17.

[21]   Caliph is an Arabic word meaning deputy and it was used by the followers of the Prophet to denote his successors as spiritual heads of the Islamic community. With the rise of the Islamic empire, and especially with the accession to power of the Abbasid caliphate at Baghdad, 720–1528, the title became that of the supreme sovereign who combined both temporal and religious powers under his jurisdiction. Eventually all real power passed to the sultans and princes at a secular level and the caliphs, though retaining some authority, became titular heads only. Their era of great power ended with the extinction of the Abbasid caliphate when Baghdad was captured by the Mongols in 1258.

[22]   Bulos, *Arabic Music*, p. 17.

[23]   Chase, *The Music of Spain*, p. 25.

[24]   Levy, *The Social Structure of Islam*, pp. 79–80.

[25]   Farmer, *The Minstrelsy of the Arabian Nights*, p. 6.

[26]   Yates, *The Modern History and Condition of Egypt*, pp. 216, 217.

[27]   Dickson, *The Arab of the Desert*, pp. 244–6.

[28]   *Ibid.*, pp. 219–25.

[29]   Diqs, *A Bedouin boyhood*, p. 114.

Charles M. Doughty describes a similar scene: 'A little later will come hither of the young herdsmen returning boisterous from the field; they draw to the merry noise of the muzayyin that feels a lightness in their knees to dance. A-row, every one his arms upon the next one's shoulder, these laughing weleds stand, full of good humour; and with a shout they foot it forth, reeling and wavering, advancing, recoiling in their chorus together; the while they hoarsely chant the ballad of a single verse. The housewives of the booth clap their palms and one rising with a rod in her hand, as the dancing men advance; she dances out to meet them; it is the mother by likelihood, and joyously she answers them in her song; whilst they come on bending and tottering in a row together, with their perpetual refrain. They advance upon her, she dances backward, feinting defence with the rod; her face is turned towards them who maintain themselves, with that chanted verse of their manly throats, as it were pursuing and pressing upon her . . .' (Doughty, *Arabia Deserta*, p. 109).

[30] Penzer, *The Harem*, p. 184.
[31] Lewis, *Istanbul and the Civilization of the Ottoman Empire*, pp. 132, 133.
[32] Among the desert Arabs coffee brewing was a ritual defining the strict obligations of host and guest. Arab coffee is made from freshly ground beans and is unsweetened. It is served in minute cups without handles and custom decreed that it should be offered three times by the host unless the guest declined the second cup. Dire consequences could arise from a guest refusing to drink coffee or the neglect of a host in not serving it. Turkish coffee on the other hand is brewed with sugar and frothed into a thick liquid served in small-handled cups with saucers. No ritual of numbers is involved, although drinking coffee in Turkey is no less a mark of hospitality and social grace Turkish coffee is drunk a great deal in Egypt and northern Arabia. where it is universally served in the coffee houses. Whatever the, way of serving it, coffee has remained vital to the conduct of human affairs throughout the Islamic world. Tea is another favourite drink, brewed as a clear liquid in glasses or made from different plants rather like the French *tisane*. The chewing of dried melon seeds invariably accompanied tea drinking in Turkey as it did in China. No theatre patron in either country would have felt complete without dried sunflower or melon seeds to crack.
[33] Martinovitch, *The Turkish Theatre*, pp. 10–6.
[34] Baer, *Egyptian Guilds in Modern Times*, p. 26.
[35] Siyavusgil, *Karagoz*, pp. 11–2.
[36] *Ibid.*, pp. 10, 11.
[37] Miller, *The Palace School of Muhammud the Conqueror*.
[38] Vucinich, *The Ottoman Empire, Its Record and Legacy*, p. 70.
[39] And, *A History of Theatre and Popular Entertainment in Turkey*, pp. 44–8.
[40] Vucinich, *The Ottoman Empire, Its Record and Legacy*, pp. 44–66.
[41] Landau, *Studies in Arab Theatre and Cinema*, pp. 17–47.
[42] A Turkish friend of the writer on being questioned recalled that the youngsters of his generation, in the forties, always flocked to see the Karagoz show. 'I remember drawing pictures of many different characters in a Karagoz cast; in fact among the very limited number of toys we could get in the streets we could always find a wooden Karagoz with movable knees and elbow joints. Two long sticks with strings attached enabled Karagoz to perform strange acrobatics with a little manipulation. I remember also with a friend setting up a stage in our basement with a bed sheet and a candle to perform a Karagoz show. We charged five piastres admission and attracted not only our friends but our elders as well, including my grandmother.' Extract from a letter from Mr Sev Oktai, New York, April 1969.
[43] And, *A History of Theatre and Popular Entertainment in Turkey*, p. 39.
[44] Barque, *The Arabs, Their History and Future*, pp. 201–10.
[45] *Ibid.*, p. 197; Landau, *Studies in Arab Theatre and Cinema*, pp. 57–63.
[46] *Ibid.*, pp. 57–9.

[47] *Ibid.* p. 63.
[48] *Ibid.*, p. 58.
[49] *Ibid.*, pp. 64, 65.
[50] *Ibid.*, p. 65.
[51] *Ibid.*, pp. 57, 74.
[52] *Ibid.*, pp. 71, 72.
[53] *Ibid.*, p. 71.
[54] *Ibid.*, p. 76.
[55] *Ibid.*, pp. 76–8.
[56] *Ibid.*, p. 92.
[57] Barque, *The Arabs, Their History and Future*, pp. 201–3.
[58] *Ibid.*
[59] Sayyid Darwish, quoted by Barque.
[60] Barque, *The Arabs, their History and Future*, pp. 227, 228, 235; Tanner, *New York Times*, 17 November 1967.
[61] And *A History of Theatre and Popular Entertainment in Turkey*, p. 67.
[62] *Ibid.*, p. 66.
[63] During Ramadan (Turkish Ramazan) Muhammadans must fast from sunrise to sunset during the ninth month of the Islamic year. In consequence there was a good deal of social activity in the evening periods and Ramazan was one of the busiest times of the year for showmen and theatre people in Turkey.
[64] And, *A History of Theatre and Popular Entertainment in Turkey*, p. 68.
[65] *Ibid.*, pp. 78, 79.
[66] *Ibid.*, p. 68.
[67] *Ibid.*, pp. 69, 70.
[68] Ibrahim Sinasi (1826–1871). The Turkish title of the play was *Sair Evlenmesi*, a one-act comedy. The hero is a young poet in love with a girl whose family schemes to make him marry her eldest and ugly sister. Friends and a bribed priest help him to escape his dilemma.
[69] And, *A History of the Theatre and Popular Entertainment in Turkey*, p. 76.
[70] The official name of the group was the Committee of Union and Progress and it was inaugurated in 1889 by a group of students at the Imperial Military Medical School. They gave themselves the name Young Turks and their avowed purpose was the overthrow of the sultanate. Their existence was discovered by the authorities in 1892 and several of the members fled abroad to escape arrest by the police. Most of them concentrated in Paris where they published subversive newspapers. In 1896 an abortive attempt to seize the government in Istanbul provided a serious setback to the cause but activities continued and other secret societies which came into being carried the work of the revolution forward.
[71] Macgowan, 'Notes on the Turkish Theatre', *Drama Survey*, vol. 1, no. 1, Winter 1962, pp. 321, 322.
[72] *Ibid.*, pp. 324, 325.
[73] The Ankara State Theatre in 1967 controlled six theatres: Buyuk Tiyatro, seating 762; Kucuk Tiyatro, 605; Oda Tiyatrosu, 65; Ucuncu Tiyatro, 590; Yeni Sahne, 205; Altindag Tiyatrosu, 400.

The State Theatre also controls theatres in the towns of Izmir and Bursa.

The State Opera and Ballet Company gives its performances in the Buyuk Tiyatro.

The Municipal Theatre of Istanbul, until 1966 under the direction of Muhsin Ertugrul, controls four playhouses: Dram Tiyatrosu, seating 450; Yeni Tiyatro, 765; Fatih Tiyatrosu, 362; Uskudor Tiyatrosu, 362. The Municipal Opera performs at the Dram Tiyatrosu three times weekly.

In addition there are four private playhouses in Ankara, the smallest of which seats 180 and the largest 320.

In Istanbul there are twelve private theatres with maximum seating for 673 and a minimum for 165.

See *Theatre in Turkey*, No. 3, Turkish Centre I.T.I. Istanbul.

[74] Graham, 'Turkey Trains its Own Classical Ballet Company', *Christian Science Monitor, c.* 1962.

[75] 'Un Profond Malaise Social', *Le Monde*, 18 Juin 1970.

4: CHINA

[1] Confucianism is acknowledged by the Chinese as one of their three religions, *san chiao*, and therefore one facet of the same truth. Its doctrines, in fact, represented a supreme expression of the moral and cultural forces which moulded Chinese society and ensured its stability throughout many dynastic changes. The traditional dates given for Confucius are 551–479 BC. Like other teachers and prophets, he has been attributed with pronouncements and theories which make it difficult to distinguish legend from fact. His sayings, supposedly handed down by disciples, underwent revision and editing. The *Analects* are regarded as the most reliable expression of his teachings. The ideas attributed to him provided a lasting framework for the institutional and intellectual structure of Chinese civilization. His teachings were propagated by followers after his death and in the reign of the Han Emperor Wu, 140–87 BC, Confucianism was promoted as a state doctrine. His followers were entrusted with official posts, so laying the foundation of a civil service which controlled Chinese affairs until the early twentieth century.

The teachings of Confucius are summed up in the word *tao*, an elusive term which the sage himself never explained except by implication. Very briefly it can be said to indicate practice of the virtues which define the whole man. The Confucian gentleman conformed to the will of heaven by honouring these virtues scrupulously and with decorum. According to Confucianism, true nobility of character was the result of education and personal conduct, and any man with aptitude and training could attain the ideal as it did not depend on birth. Wisdom, goodness and courage had to be cultivated through moderation of outward behaviour and inner feelings. A knowledge of traditional rites and ceremonies helped to develop deportment. Integrity of word and loyalty to superiors were the true marks of a gentleman who renounced violence and by gracefully giving way to others perfected himself.

Filial piety was the supreme virtue and the basis of morality. Respect for one's parents implied respect for all elders and superiors and through them the spirits of the ancestors. A filial son was a good citizen because, if his family status was regularized, it followed that his status in society was in equal harmony. The family was the basis of social unity, family authority reinforced state authority. The true way to achieve tao was not by speculation on heaven's meaning but in knowing one's position in relation to others and living according to this knowledge.

The family relationship which dominated the Confucian moral code also provided the motive for creating a vast bureaucracy with rigid discrimination in social status. In spite of its humanitarian and democratic basis, rationalization of the patriarchal system finally sanctioned authoritarianism.

[2] Edicts published at intervals in 1313, 1369, 1625 and 1770 forbade actors or their families to sit for the imperial examinations. This ban remained in force until 1905 when the examinations were abolished. See Wang Hsiao-ch'uan, *Yuan Ming Ch'ing san tai chin hui hsiao-shuo hsi-chu liao*, pp. 6, 11.

[3] The four main role classifications of the Peking style were 1 *sheng*, 2 *tan*, 3 *ching*, 4 *chou*, male, female, painted face and comic. Each of these main divisions had its further subdivisions. Under sheng, for example were *lao-sheng, wu-sheng* and *hsiao-sheng*. Lao-sheng were bearded characters and represented patriarchs or virtuous middle-aged scholars and officials. Wu-sheng were fighting characters skilled in sword play and weapons. Hsiao-sheng were the youthful males, handsome heroes or pining lovers, unbearded and skilful with their fans or in manipulating the long pheasant plumes worn on the head-dress of the hero types. Under the tan division came the *ch'ing-i*, the virtuous wife or filial daughter, the *hua-tan*, the coquette or flighty maidservant, *ts'ai-tan*, the shrew (often played by the comic actors), *lao-tan*, the matriarch, and *wu-tan*, an Amazonian type combining feminine charms with martial prowess and skill in weapons. The ching were the painted-face characters who played generals, brigands, gods and supernatural beings and were characterized by their bizarre painted make-ups whose colours and patterns were symbolical in purpose. Ch'ou were divided into *wen-ch'ou* and *wu-ch'ou*; the first played a variety of roles, from woodcutter to petty official, but the second category played military characters and were skilled in sword-play and tumbling. All these roles were distinguished by their own prescribed speech, song and movement techniques as well as costume and make-up.

[4] *Lao-tan* role.

[5] Hucker, *Index to Terms and Titles in Government Organizations of the Ming Dynasty*, p. 10.

[6] Goodrich, *Short History of the Chinese People*, p. 144; Hsu, 'Chin san-pai nien lai Chung-kuo ti nu-chuang', *Ta Kung Pao*, 6 November 1939; Pruitt, *Daughter of Han*, p. 22.

[7] Goodrich, *Short History of the Chinese People*, p. 218.

[8] *Ts'ai-ch'iao.* In order to simulate the gait of women with bound feet on the stage acting apprentices were trained to use ts'ai-ch'iao. This was a contraption that resembled a kind of small stilt to which the actor's foot was firmly bound. It entailed walking *au point* the whole time, the wooden base of the ts'ai-ch'iao being shaped to resemble the hoof-like form of a bound foot. It was a difficult technique that required long years of practice and the actors who played Amazon roles were noted for their fencing skill and acrobatics while wearing ts'ai-ch'iao.

Mei Lan-fang, in his memoirs (vol. 1, pp. 37, 38), has described learning this technique in his youth. 'I remember in my younger years I practised *wu-kung* [acrobatic and fighter exercises] by using a long bench on which was placed a square brick. I had to stand on this brick while wearing ch'iao and remain there for the period it required to burn a stick of incense. At first it was very painful and I trembled when I first stood up there, I could not bear it and had to jump down. After a time, however, one's waist and legs became hardened and it was possible to stay in position. In winter we had to practise fighting movements and running round the stage on the icy ground. A careless slip and down you went. After wearing ts'ai-ch'iao on the ice one felt as light as a feather when it came to running on the real stage. Everything had to begin with the hard and difficult way and so lead up to the easier methods. When I practised there were always blisters on my feet and I felt miserable. I thought that my teacher should not inflict such severe training on a ten-year-old boy. Everything was done under compulsion in those conditions and at heart I rebelled against it. But today I am nearly sixty years old and I can still perform plays like *Tsui Chiu, Mu K'o Chai* and *Hung Ni Kuan*, all *tao-ma tan* plays. I cannot help but think that the severity of the fundamental training given by my teachers was good.'

The plays mentioned by Mei all have leading female character roles requiring the most vigorous type of fighting and acrobatic techniques. When actresses began to supersede actors on the Chinese stage, the ts'ai ch'aio were replaced by small high platform-soled slippers which gave the impression of bound feet and were bound to the actresses' legs in rather the same way as the ts'ai-ch'iao, but were much simpler to manipulate in every respect. These techniques have now been banished from the communist stage where representation of bound feet by any method has disappeared entirely.

[9] Pruitt, *Daughter of Han*, pp. 72, 73.

[10] Fortune, *A Residence Among the Chinese*, pp. 255–8.

K

[11] Davis, *The Chinese, General Description of the Empire of China and its Inhabitants*, pp. 177, 178.

[12] Hsiao, 'Past and Present', *Chinese Literature*, no. 11, 1959, pp. 132–9.

[13] Liu, *Introduction to Chinese Literature*, p. 160; Fitzgerald, *China, A Short Cultural History*, pp. 490, 491.

[14] Liu, *Introduction to Chinese Literature*, pp. 161–8.

[15] Hummel, *Eminent Chinese of the Ch'ing Dynasty*, vol. 1, pp. 495, 496.

[16] *Ibid.*, pp. 53, 54.

[17] Yao, 'Rise and Fall of the K'un Ch'u', *T'ien Hsia*, January 1936, pp. 63–84.

[18] Li, *Yang-chou hua-fang lu* (A guide-book to Yangchow published in the late eighteenth century and reprinted in Peking, 1960). It has a great deal to say about actors and actresses and the brothel quarters of the city in its heyday as a centre of merchant culture.

[19] Hummel, *Eminent Chinese of the Ch'ing Dynasty*, p. 103.

[20] Mei, *Wu-t'ai sheng-huo ssu-shih nien*, vol. 1, pp. 62–77.

[21] Two hazards faced by Chinese actors were the voice breaking in adolescence (*tao ts'ang*) or losing the voice completely (*t'a chung*). The first happened to every actor at one of the most crucial points of his training and it was always an anxious time for both students and their teachers. It sometimes happened that a boy who started out with great promise never recovered the singing quality of his voice after it had broken. His future as an actor was then impaired.

    To lose the voice completely, either through illness or overstrain, was a disaster that sometimes befell an actor and meant retirement from an active life on the stage. Chinese theatrical singing makes a tremendous demand on the vocal chords and once an actor's voice was damaged there was little that could be done about it.

[22] Mei, *Wu-t'ai sheng-huo ssu-shih nien*, vol. 1, pp. 26, 27.

[23] Brecht, *Brecht on Theatre*, p. 94.

[24] Gamble, *Peking, a Social Survey*, p. 439. (The information on the south China guilds was given the author by Mr Kwok On.)

[25] Leung, 'Lin Shu-shen in the Dramatic Role of Kuang Kung', *China Journal of Arts and Sciences*, vol. 5, 1926, pp. 4–88.

[26] Mei, *Wu-t'ai sheng huo ssu-shih nien*, vol. 1, pp. 215–7.

[27] *Ibid.*, pp. 60–1.

[28] Gamble, *Peking, a Social Survey*, p. 230.

[29] Fortune, *Three Years Wandering in the Northern Provinces of China*, pp. 136–7.

[30] Mei, *Wu-t'ai sheng-huo ssu-shih nien*, vol. 2, pp. 132, 133.

[31] Cash was a copper coin and formerly the only one made in China. One thousand cash equalled one tael, the unit of account by which all payments to the imperial government were reckoned. A tael was a silver ounce (*liang*) made in the form of an ingot, but the weight varied according to the degree of fineness of the silver and different standards applied to different areas. The old East India Company reckoned the tael at 6s. 8d. or 80 U.S. cents.

[32] Hsiao, 'Past and Present', *Chinese Literature*, no. 11, 1959, pp. 132–9.

[33] Mei, *Wu-t'ai sheng-huo ssu-shih nien*, vol. 1, pp. 52, 53.

[34] Ibid, vol. 1, pp. 147, 148.

[35] The Kuang Ho Lou Theatre in Jou-shih, Peking.

[36] Mei, *Wu-t'ai sheng-huo ssu-shih nien*, vol. 1, pp. 50–4.

[37] Hummel, *Eminent Chinese of the Ch'ing Dynasty*, vol. 1, p. 21.

[38] The *Shen-p'ing shu*.

[39] Hummel, *Eminent Chinese of the Ch'ing Dynasty*, vol. 1, p. 573.

[40] Hsiao, 'Past and Present', *Chinese Literature*, no. 11, 1959, pp. 133, 134.

[41] Ou-yang Yu-chien, in the *Peking Evening News, Beijing Wanbao*, June 1961. At that time he was head of the Central Drama Institute, Peking.

[42] Gamble, *Peking, a Social Survey*, p. 226.

[43] The Chung Hua Company (Chung-hua kung-ssu).

[44] The Central Drama Institute (Chung-ying hsi-chü hsüeh-yüan), for training actors, directors, stage designers in modern western style drama. The China Theatrical Research Institute (Chung-kuo hsi-chü yen-chiu yüan), for carrying out research in the history, methods and styles of Chinese theatre. The China Drama Headquarters (Chung-kuo ching-chü yüan), for administration of Peking troupes and a rehearsal centre. The Chinese Drama Training School (Chung-kuo hsi-chü hsüeh-hsiao), co-educational training centre for the Peking-style theatre and also the *p'ing-chü*, a local drama which was given new importance after 1949. The China Dramatists' Union (Chung-kuo hsi-chü chia-hsieh hui-pien). These were the principal institutions in Peking in 1956 when the author visited that city.

[45] Chung and Miller, *Madame Mao*, pp. 20–3.

[46] *Wen-hui Pao*, 10 November 1965.

[47] On 1 July 1968 Hsinhua, the official Chinese press agency, announced the performance of a new opera, *The Red Lantern*, using piano accompaniment instead of the traditional string, percussion and wind instruments. *The Red Lantern, Hung Teng Chi*, was first staged in 1964. The hero is Li Yu-ho, a railwayman working in a Japanese-occupied town in north-west China and a loyal party member. His lantern is the signal for clandestine contact with communist guerrillas operating in the mountains. He gives his life for the cause, as most Maoist heroes do.

The use of the piano was hailed as an artistic triumph for Mao's wife, Chiang Ch'ing, who had advocated its replacing traditional instruments as early as 1964 but had been opposed by 'counter revolutionary revisionists'. The Hsinhua agency justified the new musical accompaniment in these words: 'This successful trial in making foreign things serve China brings forth a new creation in the proletarian revolutionary literature and art. It has opened up a new way for western musical instruments and symphonies and for musical accompaniment to traditional Chinese operas. . . . It is another flower of proletarian revolutionary art shining with the brilliance of Mao Tse-tung's thought.'

5: JAPAN

[1] *Yari Odori* is a dance based on the movements of a *yakko*, the burly, bearded spearman who used to clear the way for a daimyo's procession, performing a kind of processional dance in the process. It became very fashionable in the Genroku period (1688–1720) when it was the custom for the *onnagata*, female impersonators, to play this very masculine role as a kind of novelty. There were many later dances based on the *yakko*; one, first staged in the Tempo period (1830–1843), *Tomo Yakko*, depicts a retainer coming to escort his lord from the gay quarters. It is still performed today and is characterized by the vigorous footwork and stamping of the dancer, based to some extent on the original yakko style.

[2] The four classes were *shi min*, *shi–samurai*, *no* or *hyakusho* (farmers), *ko* or *takumi* (craftsmen), *sho* or *akindo* (merchants). The last three were classed as common folk.

[3] Sadler, *The Beginners' Book of Bushido*, pp 8, 9.

[4] Koda and Wigmore 'The Rice Trade', *Transactions of the Asiatic Society of Japan*, vol. XIV, June 1937, pp 123–37.

[5] O'Neill, *Early No Drama*, pp. 17–9.

[6] *Ibid.*, pp. 31, 32, 41–52.

[7] Toyotaka, *Japanese Music and Drama in the Meiji Era*, pp. 13–25, 83–95.

[8] Dunn and Torigoe, *The Actor's Analects*, pp. 49–57.

[9] Brecht, *Brecht on Theatre*, p. 94.

[10] Toyotaka, *Japanese Music and Drama in the Meiji Era*, p. 204.

[11] *Ibid.*, p. 194.

[12] *Ibid.*, pp. 291, 292.

[13] *Ibid.*, pp. 291–6.

[14] Kurahashi, 'Western Drama in Japan', *Japan Quarterly*, vol. 5, no. 2, 1958, pp. 178–85.

[15] Hamamura, *Kabuki*, pp. 129–157.

[16] Oka, 'Japan Hails Dawning Age of *Hair*', *New York Times*, 10 December 1969, p. 64.

[17] Etiemble, 'Le Patriotisme de Mishima', *Le Monde (des Livres)*, 4 December 1970, pp. 15–7; 'A gesture from the past in Japan', *The Times* (London), 27 November 1970, p. 11; 'Samurai '70: the death of Mishima', *Newsweek*, 7 December 1970, pp. 9–11.

BIBLIOGRAPHY

The following is a select list of background material relevant to the study of the theatre in Asia and includes works directly referred to in the text. The only non-English works included are essential references used by the author and not available in translation.

GENERAL

Bedouin, Jean-Louis, *Les Masques*, Paris, Presses universitaires de France, 1961. 'Que sais-je?' Le point des connaissances actuelles, no. 905.

Brecht, Bertolt, *Brecht on Theatre, the Development of an Aesthetic* (edited and translated by John Willett), New York, Hill and Wang, 1966.

Craig, Edward Gordon, *On the Art of the Theatre*, London, Heinemann, 1962.

Jacquot, Jean (ed.), *Les Théâtres d'Asie* (études de Jeanine Auboyer *et al.*), Paris, Editions du Centre National de la Recherche Scientifique, 1961.

Kitagawa, Joseph M., *Religions of the East*, Philadelphia, Westminster Press, 1968.

McNeill, William H., *The Rise of the West, a History of the Human Community*, New York, New American Library, 1965.

Metraux, Guy S. and Crouzet, François, *The New Asia, Readings In the History of Mankind*, New York, New American Library, 1965.

Mukerjee, Radhakamal, *The Social Function of Art*, (2nd ed.), Bombay, Hind Kitabs, 1951.

Myrdal, Gunnar, *Asian Drama, An Enquiry into the Poverty of Nations*, New York, Pantheon, 1968. (In spite of its great length and some contentious judgements on non-economic matters, the reader concerned with the social background of contemporary Asia cannot afford to ignore this study.)

Sinai, I. Robert, *The Challenge of Modernization, the West's Impact on the Non-Western World*, New York, Norton, 1964.

Sjoberg, Gideon, *The Pre-Industrial City, Past and Present*, New York, Free Press, 1960.

Tylor, Edward B., *Researches into the Early History of Mankind and the Development of Civilization* (edited and abridged by Paul Bohannan), University of Chicago Press, 1964.

INDIA

BOOKS

Barnouw, Erik and Krishnaswamy, S., *Indian Film*, New York, Columbia University Press, 1963.

Basham, A. L., *The Wonder that was India*, London, Sidgwick and Jackson, 1954.

Behanan, Kovoor T., *Yoga, a Scientific Evaluation*, New York, Dover Publications, 1937.

Benegal, Som, *A Panorama of Theatre in India*, Bombay, Indian Council for Cultural Relations, 1968.

Bharatiya Natya Sangh (Theatre Centre) Bombay, *Theatre for the People in India, a Report and Review of Today's Problems*, Bombay, 1955.

Bhavnani, Emakshi. *The Dance in India. The Origin and History, Foundations. The Art and Science of the Dance in India, Classical, Folk, Tribal*. Bombay, Taraporevala, 1965.

Chatterjee, Manjulika Bhadhury Santosh, *The Art of Hindu Dance*, Calcutta Bankim Chandra Chatterjee, 1945.

Conze, Edward, *Buddhism, Its Essence and Development*, New York, Harper and Row, 1959.

Coomaraswamy, Ananda K., *The Dance of Shiva*, New York, Noonday Press, 1951.

Das Gupta, Henendranath, *Indian Stage*. Calcutta, 1934.

De Bary, Theodore, *Sources of Indian Tradition*, New York, Columbia University Press, 1960.

Gargi, Balwant. *Folk Theatre of India*, Seattle, University of Washington Press, 1966.

Ghurye, G. S., *Bharatanatya and its Costume*, Bombay, Popular Book Depot, 1958.

Ghurye, G. S., *Caste, Class and Occupation*, Bombay, Popular Book Depot, 1961.

Guha-Thakurta, P., *The Bengal Drama, Its Origin and Development*, London, Kegan Paul, 1930.

Gupta, Chandra Bhan, *The Indian Theatre*, Banaras, Motilal Banarsidass.

Haas, George Christian Otto, *The Dasarupa, a treatise on Hindu Dramaturgy*, by Dhanamjaya, (translated from the Sanskrit), New York, Columbia University Press, 1912.

Humphreys, Christmas, *A Popular Dictionary of Buddhism*, New York, Citadel Press, 1963.

Iyer, E. Krishna, *Bharata Natyam and other dances of Tamil Nad*, Baroda, The Maharaja Sayajirao University of Baroda, College of Indian Music, Dance and Dramatics, 1957.

Iyer, Bharata, *Kathakali, Sacred Dance Drama of Malabar*, London, Luzac, 1953.

Jairazbhoy, R. A., *Foreign Influence on Ancient India*, New Delhi, Asia Publishing House, 1963.

Kalakshetra, *Prospectus 1964–1965* (in English), Tiruvanmiyur, Madras, 1964.

Kalidasa, *The Dramas of Kalidasa* (translated by Bela Bose), Allahabad, Kitabistan, 1945.

Kama Sutra of Vatsyayana (translated by Sir Richard Burton and F. E. Arbuthnot, edited by W. G. Archer), London, Allen and Unwin, 1963.

Keith, Arthur Berriedale, *History of Sanskrit Literature*, London, Oxford University Press, 1928; *The Sanskrit Drama in its Origin, Development and Practice*, Oxford, Clarendon Press, 1924.

Kleen, Tyva de, *Mudras, the Ritual Hand-poses of the Buddhist Priests and the Shiva Priests of Bali*, London, Dent, 1924.

Lal, P., *Great Sanskrit Plays in Modern Translation*, New York, New Directions, 1957.

Leslie, Ch., (ed.), *Anthropology of Folk Religion*, New York, Vintage Books, 1960.

Levi, Sylvain, *Le théâtre indien*, Paris, Bibliothèque de l'Ecole des Hautes Etudes, 1890.

The Mahabharata, by Jnaneshvari, incorporating the text of the Bhagavad-Gita (S. Radhakrishnan translation; translated from the Marathi by V. G. Pradhan; edited and with an introduction by H. W. Lambert), London, Allen and Unwin, 1967.

The Mahabharata of Krishna Dwaipayana Vyasa (translated from the original Sanskrit by P. C. Roy), Calcutta, Oriental Publishing Co., 1956.

The Mahabharata (an English abridgment compiled by John Murdoch), Oxford, Clarendon Press, 1898.

The Mahabharata, The Bhagavad-Gita (translated from the Sanskrit with an introduction by Juan Mascaro) London, Penguin Books, 1962.

The Mahabharata (an English version based on selected verses by Chakravarthi V. Narishiman), New York, Columbia University Press, 1964.

The Mahabharata (analysis and index by Edward P. Rice), London, Oxford University Press, 1934. See also *The Ramayana*, and under Indonesia and Thailand Bibliographies.

Majumdar, R. C., *Ancient Indian Colonization in S.E. Asia*, Baroda, University of Baroda Press, 1935.

Mathur, J. C., *Drama in Rural India*, New Delhi, Asia Publishing House, 1964.

Mena, Rekha, *Cultural Profiles, Calcutta, Santineketan, Madras, Trivandrum, Cochin*, New Delhi, International Cultural Centre.

Menon, Narayana, *Balasaraswati*, New Delhi, International Cultural Centre, 1964.

Munshi, K. M. and Diwakar, R. R., *Indian Inheritance;* vol. 1, *Literature, Philosophy and Religion;* vol. 2, *Arts, History and Culture*, Bombay, Bharatiya Vidya Bhavan, 1959.

Nandikesvara, *Abhinayadarpanam* (2nd ed.) (English translation and notes and text critically edited by Manomohan Ghosh), Calcutta, Mukhopadhay, 1957; *The Mirror of Gesture, being the Abhinaya Darpana of Nandikesvara* (translated by A. K. Coomaraswamy and Duggirala Gopalkrishnayya), New York, Weyhe, 1936.

Natya Institute of Choreography, *Prospectus* (in English), New Delhi, Natya Institute of Choreography, 1964.

The Natyasastra, ascribed to Bharata Muni (translated with notes by Manomohan Ghosh), Calcutta, Asiatic Society, 1961.

The Natyasastra of Bharata. A Selective Critical Exposition for the Western Theatre Scholar by Pramod Kale, Madison, University of Wisconsin, 1967 (unpublished Ph.D. thesis).

The Natyasastra Sangraha (translated by R. Vasudeva Sastri, A. Krishnaswami Mahadick and G. Nagaraja Rao), Tanjore, Saraswati Mahal Library, 1953.

Raghavan, M. D., *Folk Plays and Dances of Kerala,* Trichur, Rama Varma Archaeological Society, 1947.

The Ramayana. The Ayodhya Canto of the Ramayana as told by Kamban (translated from the Tamil by C. Rajagopalachari), London, Allen and Unwin, 1961.

The Ramayana and the Mahabharata (condensed into English verse by Romesh C. Dutt), London, Dent, 1966. See also under Indonesia and Thailand Bibliographies.

Rawlinson, H. G., *India, a Short Cultural History,* New York, Praeger, 1952.

Renou, Louis, *Les Littératures de l'Inde,* Paris, Presses Universitaires de France, 1951; *The Nature of Hinduism* (translated by Patrick Evans), New York, Walker, 1962.

Rexroth, Kenneth, *The Classics Revisited,* New York, Avon, 1969.

Saletore, R. N., *Life in the Gupta Age,* Bombay, Popular Book Depot, 1943.

The Samskrita Ranga Annual, vol. II, Madras, 1961 (with a bibliography of English translations of Sanskrit dramas).

Sangeet Natak Akademi Bulletin. Centenary number. Rabindranath Tagore, 1861–1961, New Delhi, Sangeet Natak Akademi, 1961.

Sarabhai, Mrinalini, *Understanding Bharata natyam,* Baroda, University of Baroda Press, 1965.

Sarris, Andrew (ed.), *Interviews with Film Directors,* New York, Avon, 1967.

Schuyler, Montgomery, jr, *A Bibliography of the Sanskrit Drama,* New York, AMS Press, 1965.

Sengupta, Padmini, *Everyday Life in Ancient India,* London, Oxford University Press, 1950.

Shankar, Ravi, *My Music, My Life,* New York, Simon and Schuster, 1968.

Shekar, Indu, *Sanskrit Drama, its Origin and Decline,* Leiden, Brill, 1960.

Smith, Donald Eugene, *India as a Secular State,* Princeton University Press, 1963.

Tandon, Prakash, *Punjabi Century, 1857–1947,* Berkeley, University of California Press, 1968.

Thapar, Romilar, *Asoka and the Decline of the Mauryas,* London, Oxford University Press, 1961.

Tulasidas, *Kavitvali* (translated by Raymond Allchin), London, Allen and Unwin, 1964.

Ward, Barbara, *India and the West,* (rev. ed.), New York, Norton, 1964.

Weber, Max, *The Religion of India, the Sociology of Hinduism and Buddhism* (translated by Hans H. Gerth and Don Martindale), New York, Free Press, 1958.

Wells, H. W., *Sanskrit Plays,* Bombay, Asia Publishing House, 1963.

Wheeler, Mortimer, *The Indus Civilization*, London, Cambridge University Press, 1953.

Yajnik, R. K., *The Indian Theatre, its Origins and Later Developments under European Influence*, London, Allen and Unwin, 1933.

Zoete, Beryl de, *The Other Mind, a Study of Dance in Southern India*, London, Gollancz, 1953.

ARTICLES

Achwal, M. B., 'Ancient Indian theatre', *Natya*, Winter 1959–60.

Coomaraswamy, Ananda K., 'The Theory of Art in Asia', in A. K. Coomaraswamy, (ed.), *The Transformation of Nature in Art*, Cambridge, Harvard University Press, 1934.

Ingalls, Daniel H. H., 'Sanskrit Poetry and Sanskrit Poetics', in Horst Frenz (ed.), *Asia and the Humanities, Papers*, Bloomington, Indiana University Press, 1962.

Khokar, Mohan, 'Thullal Karan, Dancer-Raconteur of Kerala', *Natya*, vol. 9, no. 3, 1966. 'The Mahabharata', in K. Rexroth (ed.), *The Classics Revisited*, New York, Avon, 1969.

Majumdar, A. K., 'Indian Dance Theory and Practice', in K. M. Munshi and R. R. Diwakar (eds.), *Indian Inheritance*, Bombay, Bharatiya Vidya Bhavan, 1959.

Marg (Bombay), Bharata natyam number, vol. xi, no. 1, December 1957.

Marg (Bombay), Kathak number, vol. xiii, no. 1, December 1959.

Marg (Bombay), Kathakali number, vol. xii, no. 1, September 1959.

Marg (Bombay), Puppet number, vol. xxi, no. iv, 1968.

Mather, J. C., 'Theatre and Theatre Architecture in India Today', *Natya*, vol. 4, 1960.

Menon, R. R., 'Indian Music and its American Audience', *Saturday Review*, 27 January 1968.

Panchal, Goverdhan, 'Koottampalam, Sanskrit Stage of Kerala', *Sangeet Natak Journal*, vol. 8, April-June 1968.

Raghavan, V., 'A Bibliography of English Translations of Sanskrit Dramas', *Indian Literature*, October 1959–March 1960; 'Music in Ancient Indian Drama', *Journal of Madras Music Academy*, vol. 25, pts. 1–4, and *Sangeet Natak Akademi Bulletin*, no. 4, March, 1956; 'Theatre Architecture in Ancient India', *Treveni* (Madras), vol. iv, no. 6, November 1931.

Raja, K. Kunjunni, 'Kutiyattam, the Staging of Sanskrit Plays in the Traditional Kerala Theatre', *The Samskrita Ranga Annual*, vol. 2, 1959–60.

Rao, Banda Kanakalingeswara, 'Kushipudi Dance Drama', *Illustrated Weekly of India*, 4 November 1962.

Singer, Milton, 'The Great Tradition of Hinduism in the City of Madras', in Leslie, *Anthropology of Folk Religion*, 1960.

Subramanyan, Ka Naa, 'Traditional Tamil Drama and the Present Impasse', *Sangeet Natak Journal*, vol. 4, March–April 1967.

Thalpalyal, Kiran Kamar, 'Sitabenga Cave: Theatre or Pleasure House', *Natya*, vol. vi, no. 1, March 1962.

SOUTH-EAST ASIA

General

Bowers, Faubion, *Theatre in the East, a Survey of Asian Dance and Drama,*
Edinburgh, Nelson, 1956
Brandon, James R., *Theatre in Southeast Asia,* Cambridge, Harvard University Press, 1967.
Coedes, Georges, *The Indianized States of Southeast Asia* (translated by
Susan Brown Cowing), Honolulu, East West Center Press, 1967.
Hall, D. G. E., *A History of South-East Asia,* New York, St Martin's Press,
1955.
Le May, Reginald, *Culture of South-East Asia,* London, Allen and Unwin,
1964.
McGee, T. G., *The South-East Asian City,* New York, Praeger, 1969.

Burma

Aung Htin, *A History of Burma,* New York, Columbia University Press,
1968.
Maung Htin Aung, *Burmese Drama, a Study, with Translations of Burmese
Plays,* London, Oxford University Press, 1955.
Mi Mi Khaing, *Burmese Family,* London, Orient Longmans, 1946.
Shway Yoe (Sir James George Scott), *The Burman, His Life and Notions,*
New York, Norton, 1963 (originally published, 1882).

Cambodia

BOOKS

Chaufen Throunn, *Danses cambodgiennes,* Hanoi, Institut Buddhique, 1950.
Pym, Christopher, *The Ancient Civilization of Angkor,* New York, New
American Library, 1968.

ARTICLES

Brunet, Jacques, 'Nang Sbek, Danced Shadow Theatre of Camboda',
*International Institute for Comparative Music Studies and Documentation,
Publication,* Berlin, n.d.
Cuisinier, Jeanne, 'The Gestures in Cambodian Ballet', *Indian Arts and
Letters,* vol. 1, no. 2, 1927.
Gangoly, O. C., 'Shadow Play in Cambodia', *India Antiqua Suparna. Commemorative Volume in Honour of J. Ph. Vogel,* Leiden, Kern Institute, 1947.
Ly Singko, 'Lakhon and the Chinese Theatre', *Eastern Horizon* (Hong
Kong), vol. iv, no. 6, June 1965.

Ceylon

Sarathchandra, E. R., *The Sinhalese Folk Play and the Modern State,* Colombo,
Ceylon University Press, 1953.

Zoete, Beryl de, *Dance and Magic Drama in Ceylon*, London, Faber and Faber, 1957.

Indonesia

BOOKS

Anderson, Benedict R. O' G., *Mythology and the Tolerance of the Javanese*, Ithaca, N.Y., Cornell University Press, 1965.

Belo, Jane, *Bali, Rangda and Barong*, New York, American Ethnological Society, 1949.

Brandon, James R., *On Thrones of Gold, Three Javanese Shadow Plays*, Cambridge, Harvard University Press, 1970.

Covarrubias, Miguel, *Island of Bali*, New York, Knopf, 1937.

Cuisinier, Jeanne, *La Danse sacrée en Indochine et en Indonésie*, Paris, Presses Universitaires de France, 1921.

Geertz, Clifford, *The Religion of Java*, New York, Free Press, 1961.

Hardjowirogo, *Sedjarah wajang purwa*, Djakarta, P. N. Balai Pustaka, 1968.

Holt Claire, *Art in Indonesia*, Ithaca, N.Y., Cornell University Press, 1967.

Krida Beksa Wirama, Jogjakarta, *Pitedah pepatokaning piwoelang djoged bedaja-srimpi*, Jogjakarta, Krida Beksa Wirama, 1940.

Kunst, Jaap, *Music in Java* (translated by Emile van Loo), The Hague, Nijhoff, 1949.

McPhee, Colin, *Music in Bali*, New Haven, Yale University Press, 1966.

Mangkunagara VII of Surakarta, *K.G.P.A.A. On the Wayang Kulit (Purwa) and its Symbolic and Mystical Elements* (translated by Claire Holt), Ithaca, N.Y., Dept. of Far Eastern Studies, S.E. Asia Program, Data Paper no. 27, 1957.

Mellema, R. L., *Wayang Puppets, Carving, Colouring and Symbolism Including the Translation of a Javanese Article on the Construction of Wayang Puppets by Sukir* (translated by Mantle Hood), Amsterdam, Koninklijk Instituut voor de Tropen, 1954.

Moebirman, *Wayang Purwa, Shadow Play of Indonesia*,

Peacock, James L., *Rites of Modernization, Symbolic and Social Aspects of Indonesian Proletarian Drama*, University of Chicago Press, 1968.

Raffles, Sir Stamford, *History of Java*, London, Oxford University Press, 1965.

The Ramayana; Rama stories in Indonesia (ed. by Sutjipto Wirjosuparto), Djakarta, Bhratara, 1969.

Rassers, W. H., *Panji, the Culture Hero, A Structural Study of Religion in Java*, The Hague, Nijhoff, 1959.

Wagner, Fritz, *The Art of an Island Group*, New York, McGraw Hill, 1959.

Wertheim, W. F., *Indonesian Society in Transition*, The Hague, Van Hoeve, 1956.

Zoete, Beryl de, *Dance and Drama in Bali*, London, Faber and Faber, 1938.

ARTICLES

Cuisinier, Jeanne, 'Le Théâtre en Indonésie', in J. Jacquot (ed.), *Les Théâtres d'Asie*, 1961.

Heins, E. L., 'Cueing the Gamelan in Javanese Wayang Performance', *Indonesia*, no. 9, April 1970.

The Mahabharata, 'A Javanese Version According to the Lakon', and *The Ramayana*, 'A Javanese Version According to the Lakon', appendices to B. R. O' G. Anderson, *Mythology and the tolerance of the Javanese*, 1965.

Tirtaamidjaja, Nusjirwan, 'A Bedaja Ketawang Dance Performance at the Court of Surakarta', Ithaca, N.Y., Cornell University, Modern Indonesia Project, vol. 1, April 1967, pp. 31–62.

Malaya

BOOKS

Osman, Mohd. Taib, *An Introduction to the Development of Modern Malay Language and Literature*, Singapore, Eastern Universities Press (Donald Moore), 1961.

Skeat, Walter William, *Malay Magic*, New York, Dover Publications, 1967 (originally published 1900).

Winstedt, Richard, *The Malays, a Cultural History*, London, Routledge and Kegan Paul, 1961.

ARTICLES

Rentse, Anker, 'Origin of Wayang Theatre', *Journal of the Royal Asiatic Society, Malaya Branch*, vol. xx, pt. 1, 1947; 'Shadow play', *Journal of the Royal Asiatic Society Malaya Branch*, vol. xiv, pt. iii, 1936.

Thailand

BOOKS

Cuisinier, Jeanne, *Le Théâtre d'ombres à Kelantan*, Paris, Gallimard, 1927.

Dhanit Yupho, *Khon Masks* (2nd ed.), Bangkok, Thailand Government, Fine Arts Dept., 1962.

Dhanit Yupho, *The Preliminary Course of Training in Thai Theatrical Art* (rev. ed.), Bangkok, 1954.

Dhaninivat Kromamun Bidyalabh Bridhyakorn, Prince, and Dhanit Yupho, *The Khon* (4th ed.), Bangkok, Thailand Government, Fine Arts Dept, 1963.

Dhaninivat Kromamun Bidyalabh Bridhyakorn, Prince, and Dhanit Yupho, *The Nang*, Bangkok, National Culture Institute, 1954.

The Ramayana. The Ramakirti (Ramakian) or the Thai version of the Ramayana by Swami Satyananda Puri and Charoen Sarahiran from the original version written by King Rama I of Thailand, Bangkok, Chalermit Bookshop, 1965.

Schweisguth, P., *Etude sur la littérature siamoise*, Paris, Maisonneuve, 1951.

Thailand Government, Fine Arts Dept, *The Dresses and Ornaments of the Important Characters in Siamese Dance Dramas and Masked Plays*, Bangkok, 1958.

Thailand Government, Fine Arts Dept, *Education and the Ceremony of Paying Respect to the Teachers at the School of Dramatic Art*, 1962.

Vella, Walter F., *Siam Under Rama III*, Locust Valley, N.Y., Augustin, 1957.

ARTICLES

Scott-Kemball, J., 'The Kelantan "Wayang Siam" Shadow Puppets, "Rama" and "Hanuman" ', *Man*, vol. lix, May 1959.

Vietnam

BOOKS

Cuisinier, Jeanne, *La Danse sacrée en Indochine et en Indonésie*, Paris, Presses universitaires françaises, 1951.
Song Ban, *The Vietnamese Theatre*, Hanoi, Foreign languages Publishing House, 1960.

ARTICLES

Gaspardone, Emile, 'Le théâtre des Yuan en Annam', *Sinologica*, vol. vi, no. 1, 1959.
Tran Van Khe, 'Le théâtre vietnamien', J. Jacquot, *Les théâtres d'Asie*, 1961.

ISLAM

BOOKS

Abdel-Malek, Anouar, *Egypt: Military Society. The Army Regime, the Left and Social Change under Nasser* (translated by Charles Lam Markman), New York, Vintage Books, 1968.
Ammar, Hamed, *Growing Up in an Egyptian Village*, London, Routledge and Kegan Paul, 1954.
And, Metin, *A History of Theatre and Popular Entertainment in Turkey*, Ankara, Forum Yayinlari, 1963–4.
Arnold, Sir Thomas W., *Painting in Islam*, New York, Dover Publications, 1965.
Atiyah, Edward, *The Arabs*, London, Penguin Books, 1955.
Baer, Gabriel, *Egyptian Guilds in Modern Times*, Jerusalem, The Israel Oriental Society, 1964.
Barque, Jacques, *The Arabs, Their History and Future* (translated by Jean Stewart), New York, Praeger, 1964.
Berger, Monroe, *The Arab World Today*, New York, Doubleday, 1964.
Borator, Perter Naili, *Le Terkerlème*, Paris, Cahiers de la Société Asiatique, 1963.
Browne, Edward Granville, *Literary History of Persia*, London, Macmillan, 1929–30.
Browne, Edward Granville, *A Year Amongst the Persians*, London, Black, 1959.

Bulos, Afifa A., *Arabic Music*, Beirut, Catholic Press, 1955.

Burton, Sir Richard, *A Plain and Literal Translation of the Arabian Nights Entertainment Now Entitled The Book of the Thousand Nights and a Night* (London), printed by the Burton Club for private circulation only, 1885. Aden edition.

Chase, Gilber, *The Music of Spain*, New York, Dover Publications, 1941.

Dickson, H. R. P., *The Arab of the Desert*, London, Allen and Unwin, 1949.

Diqs, Isaak, *A Bedouin Boyhood*, London, Allen and Unwin, 1967.

Doughty, Charles M., *Arabia Deserta. Selections by Edward Garnett*, London, Cape, 1949.

Farmer, Henry George, *Historical Facts for the Arabian Musical Influence*, London, Reeves, 1930.

Farmer, Henry George, *The Minstrelsy of the Arabian Nights*, Bearsden, Scotland, privately printed by the author, 1945.

Grünebaum, Gustave E. von, *Medieval Islam*, University of Chicago Press, 1946.

Guillaume, Alfred, *The Tradition of Islam*, Oxford, Clarendon Press, 1924.

Hitti, Philip K., *A History of the Arabs* (5th ed.), London, Macmillan, 1953.

Kinross, John Patrick Douglas Balfour, *Ataturk, a Biography of Mustafa Kemal, Father of Modern Turkey*, London, Weidenfeld and Nicolson, 1964.

The Koran (translated by N. V. Dawood), London, Penguin Books, 1966.

Kritzeck, James, *Anthology of Islamic Literature*, New York, New American Library, 1964.

Landau, Jacob M., *Studies in Arab Theatre and Cinema*, Philadelphia, University of Pennsylvania Press, 1958.

Lane, Edward W., *An Account of the Manners and Customs of the Modern Egyptians* (5th ed.), New York, Dutton, 1923.

Lerner, Daniel and Pevsner, Lucille, *The Passing of Traditional Society, Modernizing the Middle East*, New York, Free Press, 1964.

Levonian, Lutfy (translator, editor), *The Turkish Press, Selections from Turkish Press Showing Events and Opinions, 1925–1932*, Athens, School of Religion, 1932.

Levy, Reuben, *The Social Structure of Islam*, Cambridge University Press, 1967.

Lewis, Bernard, *The Emergence of Modern Turkey*, Oxford University Press, 1961; *Istanbul and the Civilization of the Ottoman Empire*, University of Oklahoma Press, 1963.

Longrigg, Stephen H., *The Middle East, a Social Geography*, London, Duckworth, 1963.

Makal, Mahmut, *A Village in Anatolia*, London, Valentine, Mitchell, 1954.

Martinovitch, Nicholas N., *The Turkish Theatre*, New York, Theatre Art Books, 1933.

Miller, Barnett, *Palace School of Muhammad the Conqueror*, Cambridge, Harvard University Press, 1941.

Nicholson, Reynold A., *A Literary History of the Arabs*, Cambridge University Press, 1969.

Nutting, Anthony, *The Arabs, A Narrative History from Mohammed to the Present*, New York, New American Library, 1965.

O'Leary, De Lacy, *How Greek Science Passed to the Arabs*, London, Routledge and Kegan Paul, 1964.

Orga, Irfan, *Portrait of a Turkish Family*, New York, Macmillan, 1950.

Penzer, Norman Mosley, *The Harem*, An account of the institution as it existed in the palace of the Turkish sultans with a history of the grand seraglio from its foundations to the present time. London, Harrap, 1936.

Pierce, Joe E., *Life in a Turkish Village*, New York, Holt, Rinehart and Winston, 1967.

Planhol, Xavier de, *The World of Islam*, Ithaca, N.Y., Cornell University Press, 1959.

Rahman, Fazlur, *Islam*, New York, Doubleday, 1968.

Ramsaur, Ernest E., *The Young Turks*, Princeton University Press, 1957.

Rezvani, M., *Le Théâtre et la danse en Iran*, Paris, Maisonneuve et Larosc, 1962.

Siyavusgil, Sabri Esat, *Karagoz, Its History, its Character, its Mystic and Satiric Spirit*, Ankara, Saim Toraman Basimevi, Turkish Press, Broadcasting and Tourist Dept, 1955.

Turkish Information Office, New York, *Turkish Music*, n.d.

Turkish National Center of the International Theatre Institute. *Theatre in Turkey*, no. 3. Ankara, 1967.

Ullah, Najib, *Islamic Literature, Introductory History With Selections*, New York, Washington Square Press, 1963.

Vucinich, Wayne S., *The Ottoman Empire, Its Record and Legacy*, Princeton, N.J., Van Nostrand, 1965.

Walker, W. X. and Ahmet E. Uysal, *Tales Alive in Turkey*, Cambridge, Harvard University Press, 1966.

Yates, William Holt, *The Modern History and Condition of Egypt*, London, 1848.

Young, T. Cuyler (ed), *Near Eastern Culture and Society*, Princeton University Press, 1951.

ARTICLES

Goitein, S. D., 'The Rise of the Near-Eastern Bourgeoisie in Early Islamic Times', *Journal of World History*, vol. 3, 1957.

Grünebaum, Gustave E. von, 'Arabic Poetics', *Asia and the Humanities* (Papers edited by Horst Frenz), Bloomington, University of Indiana Press, 1962.

Lewis, Bernard, 'The Islamic Guilds', *Economic History Review*, vol. 8 (1st series), 1937.

Macgowan, Kenneth, 'Notes on the Turkish theatre', *Drama Survey*, vol. 1, no. 1, Winter 1962.

Marcais, William, 'L'Islam et la vie urbaine', *Comptes Rendues des Séances de l'année 1928*, Paris, Académie des Inscriptions et Belles-Lettres, 1928,

Quinby, G. H., 'Iran', George Freedley and J. A. Reeves (ed.), *A History of Theatre*, New York, Crown, 1968.

Spatharis, Eugene, 'Karaghiozis', *World Theatre*, vol. viii, no 4, 1959–60.

Tanner, Henry, 'An Arab Singer Stirs Pandemonium in Paris Hall', *New York Times*, 17 November 1967.

Virolleaud, Charles, 'Le théâtre persan ou le drame de Kerbela', Jacquot, J. (ed.), *Les Théâtres d'Asie*, 1961.

Whitman, Cedric Hubbell, 'Karaghiozes and Aristophanic comedy', Appendix to Whitman, *Aristophanes and the Comic Hero*, Cambridge, Harvard University Press, 1964.

Yalman, Tunc, 'Turkey', George Freedley and J. A. Reeves (ed.), *A History of Theatre*, New York, Crown, 1968.

CHINA

BOOKS

All-China Conference of Artists and Writers, *The People's New Literature: Four Reports* (by) Chou En-lai, Kuo Mo-jo, Mao Tun, Chou Yang. Peking, Cultural Press, 1950.

Bishop, John Lyman, *The Colloquial Short Story in China, a Study of the San-Yen Collections*, Cambridge, Harvard University Press, 1965.

Boorman, Howard L. (ed.), *Biographical dictionary of Republican China*, New York, Columbia University Press, 1967.

Burgess, J. S., *The Guilds of Peking* (5th ed.), New York, Dutton, 1923.

Ch'i Ju-shan, *Ch'üan-chi* (*complete works*), Taipei (Taiwan), 1964.

Chiang Ch'ing, *On the Revolution of Peking Opera*, Peking, Foreign Language Press, 1968.

Chiang, Moulin, *Tides from the West*, New Haven, Yale University Press, 1947.

Chou I-pai, *Chung-kuo hsi-chü shih* (*A History of the Chinese drama*), Shanghai, 1953.

Chow Tse-tsung, *The May Fourth Movement*, Cambridge, Harvard University Press, 1960.

Chung Hua-min and Miller, Arthur C., *Madame Mao, a Profile of Chiang Ch'ing*, Hong Kong, Union Research Institute, 1968.

Croft, Michael, *Red Carpet to China*, London, Longmans, 1958.

Davis, John Francis, *The Chinese, a General Description of the Empire of China and its Inhabitants*, London, 1836.

Eberhard, Wofram, *Chinese Festivals*, London, Abelard-Schuman, 1958.

Fitzgerald, Charles Patrick, *China, a Short Cultural History* (3rd ed.), New York, Praeger, 1961.

Fortune, Robert, *A Residence Among the Chinese, Inland, on the West and at the Sea*, London, John Murray, 1857.

Fortune, Robert, *Three Years Wandering in the Northern Provinces of China*, London, John Murray, 1847.

Gamble, Sidney D., *Peking, A Social Survey*, New York, Doran, 1921.

Gernet, Jacques, *Daily Life in China on the Eve of the Mongol invasions, 1250–1276* (translated by H. M. Wright), New York, Macmillan, 1962.

Goodrich, L. Carrington, *A Short History of the Chinese People* (3rd ed.,) New York, Harper and Row, 1963.

Granet, Marcel, *Danses et légendes de la Chine ancienne*, Paris, Presses universitaires de France, 1959.

A Great Revolution on the Cultural Front (Talks at the Festival of Peking Opera on Contemporary Themes, June, 1964, etc.) Peking, Foreign Language Press, 1965.

Hu, William, *Yüan tsa-chu* (*A bibliography for Yüan opera*), University of Michigan, Center for Chinese Studies, Occasional Papers, no. 1, Ann Arbor, 1962.

Hucker, Charles O., *An Index to Terms and Titles in Government Organizations of the Ming Dynasty*, Cambridge, Harvard University Press, 1969.

Hummel, Arthur W. (ed.), *Eminent Chinese of the Ch'ing Period (1644–1912)*, Washington, D.C., Library of Congress, U.S. Government Printing Office, 1944.

Isaacs, Harold, *The Tragedy of the Chinese Revolution* (rev. ed.), Stanford University Press, 1951.

Koningsberger, Hans, *Love and Hate in China*, New York, New American Library, 1967.

Lang, Olga, *Chinese Family and Society*, New Haven, Yale University Press, 1946.

Li Tou, *Yang-chou hua-fang lu* (*Yangchow guide book*), Peking, Chung-hua shu-pao ch'u-pan, 1960.

Liu, James J. Y., *The Art of Chinese Poetry*, University of Chicago Press, 1966.

Liu Wu-chi, *An Introduction to Chinese Literature*, Bloomington, Indiana University Press, 1966.

Mao Tse-tung, *Talks at the Yenan Forum on Art and Literature*, Peking, Foreign Language Press, 1956.

Mei Lan-fang, *Wu-t'ai sheng-huo ssu-shih nien* (*Forty years of stage life*), Peking, Jen-min wen-hsüeh ch'u-pan she, 1952–4.

Menzel, Johanna M. (ed.), *The Chinese Civil Service; Career Open to Talent?*, Boston, Heath, 1966.

P'an Kuang-tan, *Chung-kuo ling-jen hsüeh yüan chih yen-chiu* (*Research on family relations of Chinese actors*), Ch'ang-sha, China, 1941.

Panikkar, K. M., *In Two Chinas*, London, Allen and Unwin, 1955.

Peng Chen *et al.*, *A Great Revolution on the Cultural Front*, Peking, Foreign Language Press, 1965.

Pruitt, Ida, *A Daughter of Han; the Autobiography of a Chinese Working Woman* (by Ida Pruitt, from the story told her by Ning Lao T'ai-t'ai), Stanford University Press, 1967.

Scott, A. C., *The Classical Theatre of China*, London, Allen and Unwin, 1957; *Literature and the Arts in Twentieth Century China*, New York, Doubleday, 1963; *Traditional Chinese Plays* (translated, described, annotated and illustrated by A. C. Scott), Madison, University of Wisconsin Press, 1967, 1969, vol. 1, *Ssu Lang Visits His Mother; The Butterfly dream*, vol. 2, *Longing for Worldly Pleasures; Fifteen Strings of Cash*.

Silcock, Arnold, *Introduction to Chinese Art and History*, London, Faber and Faber, 1935.

Snow, Edgar, *Red Star over China*, New York, Grove Press, 1961.

Tchiao Tch'eng-tchih, *Le théâtre chinois d'aujourd'hui*, Paris, Librairie E. Droz, 1938.

Wales, Nym (Mrs Helen Foster Snow), *My Yenan Notebooks*, Madison, Conn., privately printed, 1961.

Wang Hsiao-ch'uan, *Yüan Ming Ch'ing san tai chin hui hsiao-shuo hsi-chu liao.* (*Records of novels and dramas from three dynasties, Yüan, Ming and Ch'ing*), Peking, Tso-chia ch'u-pan she, 1958.

Weber, Max, *The Religion of China, Confucianism and Taoism* (translated and edited by Hans H. Gerth), New York, Macmillan, 1964.

Wimsatt, Genevieve, *Chinese Shadow Show*, Cambridge, Harvard University Press, 1936.

Yang, Daniel Shih-p'eng, *An Annotated Bibliography of Materials for the Study of the Peking Theatre*, Madison, University of Wisconsin Press, 1967.

Yang, Martin C., *A Chinese Village, Taitou, Shantung Province*, New York, Columbia University Press, 1965.

Zung, Cecilia, *Secrets of the Chinese Drama*, London, Harrap, 1937, New York, Blom, 1969 (reprinted).

ARTICLES

Chen, David Y., 'The Trilogy of Ts'ao Yü and Western Drama', *Asia and the Humanities* (edited by Horst Frenz), Bloomington, Indiana University Press, 1959.

Chen Lin-jui, 'China's Shadow Plays', *China Pictorial*, July-Aug. 1954.

'Chinese ballet goes abroad', *Peking Review*, 26 January 1962.

'Chinese shadow theatre, first visit to Europe', *The Times* (London), 17 June 1957.

Eisenstein, Sergei, 'The Entertainer from the Pear Garden', *Theatre Arts*, vol. xix, no. 10, p. 761–770, 1935.

Fei Chu and Sha Hsi, 'Fukien Puppet Show', *People's China*, 16 December 1957.

Giles, Herbert, 'Dance in Ancient China', in *Adversaria Sinica*, Shanghai, Kelly and Walsh, 1906.

Ho P'ing-ti, 'The Salt Merchants of Yang-chou, a Study of Commercial Capitalism in 18th Century China', *Harvard Journal of Asiatic Studies*, xvii, June 1954.

Hsiao Chang-hua, 'Past and Present', *Chinese Literature*, no. 11, November 1959.

Kalvodová, Dana, 'Clowns in the Szechuan Theatre', *Bulletin of the School of Oriental and African Studies*, University of London, vol. 28, pt. 2, 1965; 'The Origin and Character of the Szechwan theatre', *Archiv Orientālrī*, 34, 1966 (Prague, Czechoslovak Academy of Sciences).

Leung, 'Lin Shu-shen in the dramatic role of Kuang Kung', *China Journal of Science and Arts*, vol. 5, 1926.

'A Sino-Soviet Swan Lake', *Peking Review*, 1 December 1961.

Trewartha, Glenn T, 'Chinese Cities, Origins and Functions', *Annals of the Association of American Geographers*, xlii, March 1952.

Waley, Arthur, 'Chinese Stories about Actors', *The Listener,* London, 7 February 1957.

Wong Ou-hung and Ah Chia, 'The Red Lantern, a Peking Opera Adapted . . . from the Shanghai Opera Version', *Chinese Literature,* no. 5, 1965.

Wu Han, 'On Hai Jui', *Chinese Studies in History and Philosophy,* vol. 1, no. 2, 1968.

Wu Wei-yun, 'The Chinese Puppet Theatre', *Chinese Literature,* no. 2, March-April 1958.

Yang, Daniel Shih-P'eng, 'Chinese Plays in English Translation, 1741–1967', *Theatre News,* vol. 1, no. 2, November 1968.

Yang, Daniel Shih-P'eng, 'Peking Drama With Contemporary Themes', *The Drama Review,* vol. 13, no. 4, Summer 1969; 'The Peking Theatre Under Communism', *Theatre Annual,* vol. xiv, December 1968.

Yao Hsin-nung, 'Rise and Fall of the K'un ch'ü', *Tien Hsia Monthly,* January 1936; 'When Sing-Song Girls Were Muses', *Tien Hsia Monthly,* April 1937.

TIBET

BOOKS

Ekvall, Robert B., *Religious Observances in Tibet, Patterns and Function,* University of Chicago Press, 1964.

Jerstad, Luther G., *Mani-Rimdu, Sherpa Dance Drama,* Seattle, University of Washington Press, 1969.

Snellgrove, David and Richardson, Hugh, *A cultural History of Tibet,* New York, Praeger, 1968.

ARTICLES

Fischer, Emil S., 'The Sacred Lamaist Dances As Seen At the Monlam or Lamaist Great Prayer Festival in Jehol's Lamaseries', *Journal North China Branch Royal Asiatic Society,* vol. lxxii, 1946.

Hsieh Kai, 'Tibet's First Modern Drama Troupe', *Peking Review,* 2 February 1962.

Stein, R. A., 'Le théâtre au Tibet', J. Jacquot, *Les théâtres d'Asie,* 1961.

Tanvir, Habib, 'The Buddhist Theatre of Tibet', *Natya,* vol. 9, no. 3, p. 22–26, 1966

'Tibet on the stage', *Peking Review,* 10 May, 1960.

JAPAN

BOOKS

Araki, James T., *The Ballad Drama of Medieval Japan,* Berkeley, University of California Press, 1964.

Ashihara Eiryo, *The Japanese Dance,* Tokyo, Japan Travel Bureau, 1964.

Atsumi Seitaro, *Hogaku buyo jiten* (*Dictionary of Japanese Dance and Music*), Tokyo, Fusanbo, 1956; *Kabuki buyo* (*Kabuki Dance*), Tokyo, Sogen-sha, 1956.

Beaujard, André, *Le théâtre comique des japonais, introduction à l'étude des Kyoghen*, Paris, Maisonneuve, 1957.

Bowers, Faubion, *Japanese Theatre*, New York, Hermitage Press, 1952.

Dore, Ronald P., *City Life in Japan*, Berkeley, University of California Press, 1958.

Dore, Ronald P., *Education in Tokugawa Japan*, London, Routledge and Kegan Paul, 1965.

Dumoulin, Heinrich, *A History of Zen Buddhism* (translated by Paul Peachey), Boston, Beacon Press, 1969.

Dunn, Charles J., *The Early Japanese Puppet Drama*, London, Luzac, 1966.

Dunn, Charles J. and Bunzo Torigoe (editors and translators), *The Actor's Analects* (*Yakusha rongo*), New York, Columbia University Press, 1969.

Ernst, Earle, *Kabuki Theatre*, New York, Grove Press, 1956.

Fane, R. A. B., *Kyoto*, Kyoto, Ponsonby Memorial Society, 1956.

Florenz, Karl (translator), *Scènes du théâtre japonais. L'Ecole de village, Terakoya. Drame historique en un acte*. Tokyo, Hasegawa, 1900.

Fujinami Yohei, *Kodogu* (*Small Properties*), Tokyo, Engeki Shuppanshu 1954.

Garfias, Robert, *Gagaku, the Music and Dance of the Japanese Imperial Household*, New York, Theatre Arts Books, 1959.

Halford, Aubrey S. and Giovanna M., *The Kabuki Handbook*, Tokyo, Tuttle, 1960.

Hamamura Yonezo et. al., *Kabuki* (edited by the Society of Traditional Arts under the auspices of Institute of the Pacific, translated by Fumi Takano), Tokyo, Kenkyusha, 1956.

Hasegawa Nyozekan, *The Japanese Character, a Cultural Profile* (translated by John Bester), Tokyo, Kodansha International (UNESCO), 1966.

Hearn, Lafcadio, *Japan, An Attempt At Interpretation*, Tokyo, Tuttle, 1955.

Herrigel, E., *Zen In the Art of Archery* (translated by R. F. C. Hull), London, Routledge and Kegan Paul, 1953.

Ishibashi Hiro, *Yeats and the Noh: Types of Japanese Beauty and their Reflection in Yeats' Plays*, Dublin, Dolman Press, 1966.

Japanese National Commission for UNESCO, *Theatre in Japan*, Tokyo, Ministry of Finance Printing Bureau, 1963.

Kato Hidetashi (editor and translator), *Japanese Popular Culture*, Tokyo, Institute of Science of thought in Japan, Tuttle, 1959.

Keene, Donald, *Bunraku*. Palo Alto, Calif., Kodansha International, 1965; *Major Plays of Chikamatsu*, New York, Columbia University Press, 1961; *No, the Classical Theatre of Japan*, Palo Alto, Calif., Kodansha International, 1966.

Kobayashi Ichizo, *The Story of Takarazuka, Japan's Modern Living Theatre*, Takarazuka, Japan, 1952 (pamphlet).

Kokusai Bunka Shinkokai, Tokyo (Society for International Cultural Relations), *K.B.S. Bibliography of Standard Reference Books for Japanese*

Studies With Descriptive Notes, vol. vii B. *Theatre, Dance and Music,* Tokyo, 1960.

Koyama Takashi, *The Changing Social Position of Women in Japan,* Paris, UNESCO, 1961.

Kunio Yanagida, *Japanese Manners and Customs in the Meiji Era* (translated and adapted by Charles S. Terry), Tokyo, Obunsha, 1957.

McKinnon, Richard, *Selected Plays of Kyogen,* Tokyo, Uniprint, 1968.

Malm, William P., *Japanese Music and Musical Instruments,* Tokyo, Tuttle, 1959.

Masakatsu Gunji, *Kabuki* (translated by John Bester), Palo Alto, Calif., Kodansha International, 1970.

Mishima Yukio, *Five Modern Noh Plays* (translated by Donald Keene), New York, Knopf, 1957.

Morris, Ivan, *The Life of an Amorous Woman,* London, Chapman and Hall, 1963.

Morse, Edward S., *Japanese Homes and Their Surroundings,* New York, Dover, 1961 (originally published 1886).

Nippon Gakujutsu Shinkoku, *Japanese No Drama; Ten Plays Selected and Translated from the Japanese,* edited and published by the Japanese Classics Translation Committee, Tokyo, 1955–60.

Norbeck, Edward, *Changing Japan,* New York, Holt, Rinehart and Winston, 1965.

Okazaki, Viglielmo, *Japanese Literature in the Meiji Era,* Tokyo, Obunsha, 1955.

O'Neill, P. G., *Early No Drama, Its Background, Character and Development, 1300–1450,* London, Lund Humphries, 1958.

O'Neill, P. G., *A Guide to No,* Tokyo, Hinoki Shoten, 1953.

Peri, Noel, *Etudes sur le no, drame lyrique japonais,* Tokyo, Maison Franco-Japonaise, 1944.

Plath, David W., *The After Hours; Modern Japan and the Search For Enjoyment,* Berkeley, University of California Press, 1964.

Reischauer, Edwin O., *Japan Past and Present* (3rd ed.), New York, Knopf, 1964.

Sadler, Arthur Lindsay, *The Beginner's Book of Bushido, Being a Translation of Daidoji Yuzan's Budo Shoshinshu,* Tokyo, Kokusai Bunka Shinkokai (Society for International Cultural Relations), 1941.

Sansom, Sir George, *Japan, a Short Cultural History,* (rev. ed.), London, Cresset Press, 1946.

Scott, A. C., *Kabuki Theatre of Japan,* London, Allen and Unwin, 1955, New York, Collier, 1967; *Puppet Theatre of Japan,* Tokyo, Tuttle, 1963.

Sheldon, Charles David, *The Rise of the Merchant Class in Tokugawa, Japan, 1600–1688,* Locust Valley, N.Y., Augustin, 1958.

Shioya Sakae, *Chushingura, An Exposition,* Tokyo, Hokuseido Press, 1940.

Suda Atsuo, *Nihon gekijo shi no kenkyu (Study on the History of Theatres in Japan),* Tokyo, Sangami Shobo, 1957.

Suzuki, Daisetsu Teitaro, *Zen and Japanese Culture,* London, Routledge and Kegan Paul, 1959.

Tanaka Ryo, *Kabuki Joshiki butai-zu shu* (*Designs for Kabuki Stage Sets*), Tokyo, Dai Nihon Yuben-kai Kodansha, 1958.

Toita Yasuji, *Shibai meisho hitomakumi* (*The Topographical Background of Japanese Plays*), Tokyo, Shiromizu, 1958.

Toyotaka Komiya (compiler and editor), *Japanese music and drama in the Meiji era* (translated and adapted by Donald Keene and Edward G. Seidensticker), Tokyo, Obunsha, 1956.

Tsubouchi Shoyo, *History and Characteristics of Kabuki, the Japanese Classical Drama* (edited and translated by Ryozo Matsumoto), Yokahama, Yamagata, 1960.

Vogel, Ezra F., *Japan's New Middle Class*, Berkeley, University of California Press, 1963.

Waley, Arthur, *The Nō Plays of Japan*, London, Allen and Unwin, 1951 (reprinted New York, Grove Press, 1957).

Wheeler, Post, *Tales from the Japanese Storytellers, As Collected in the Ho-Dan-Zo* (selected and edited by Harold G. Henderson), Tokyo, Weatherhill, 1964.

Zeami, *The Secret of Nō Plays, Zeami's Kadensho*, (translated by Sakori, Hayashi, Sato and Miyai), Tokyo, Sumiya Shinobe Scholarship Doshisha University, 1968.

ARTICLES

Akimoto Shunkichi, 'Kabuki Audiences, Past and Present', *Japan Quarterly*, vol. 3, no. 1, p. 99–104, January-March 1956.

Koda, S. and Wigmore, H., 'The Rice Trade of Japan', *Transactions of the Asiatic Society of Japan*, vol. xiv, June 1937.

Kurahashi Takeshi, 'Western Drama in Japan', *Japan Quarterly*, vol. 5, no. 2, April-June 1958.

McKinnon, Richard N., 'Zeami on the Art of Training', *Harvard Journal of Asiatic Studies*, vol. 16, 1953.

Mills, J. G., 'W. B. Yeats and Noh', *Japan Quarterly*, vol. 2, no. 4, October-December 1954.

(Mishima, Yukio) Etiemble, 'Le Patriotisme de Mishima', *Le Monde* (*des Livres*), 4 December 1970, pp. 15–7; 'A Gesture From the Past in Japan', *The Times* (London), 27 November 1970, p. 11; 'Samurai '70: the Death of Mishima', *Newsweek*, 7 December 1970, pp. 9–11.

Oka Takashi, 'Japan Hails Dawning Age of "Hair"', *New York Times*, 10 December 1969, p. 64.

Ortolani, Benito, S. J., 'Shingeki: the Maturing New Drama of Japan', *Monumenta Nipponica*, special no. 1964.

Scott, A. C., 'Kodogu no kirikubi. Death Masks in the Kabuki Theatre', *Journal of Oriental Studies*, vol. 2, no. 1, 1955.

Shively, Donald H., 'Bafuku versus Kabuki', *Harvard Journal of Asian Studies*, vol. 18, nos. 3 and 4, 1955.

Tanizaki Junichiro, 'A Prose Elegy; in Praise of Shadows', *Japan Quarterly*, vol. 1, no. 1, October-December 1954.

Teele, Roy E., 'Formal and Linguistic Problems in Translating a Noh Play', *Studies on Asia*, 1963.

Ueda Tatsunosuke, 'Some Business Women in Saikaku', *Japan Quarterly*, vol. 2, no. 4, October-December 1955.

Okinawa

Kerr, George H., *Okinawa, the History of an Island People*, Tokyo, Tuttle, 1958.

Korea

BOOKS

Choe Sang-su, *A Study of the Korean Puppet Play*, Seoul, Korean Book Pub. Co. 1961; *A Study of the Mask Play of Ha-hoe*, Seoul, Korean Book Pub. Co., 1959.

Osgood, Cornelius, *The Koreans and Their Culture*, New York, Ronald, 1951.

ARTICLES

Heyman, Alan C., *Dances of the Three-Thousand-League Land*, New York, Sheppard Black, 1964, Dance Perspectives no. 19.

INDEX